The Gospel
for the
New Millennium

The Gospel
for the
New Millennium

A Collection of Essays

J. Chris Schofield, General Editor

BROADMAN
&HOLMAN
PUBLISHERS

Nashville, Tennessee

0–8054–2199–8

Published by Broadman & Holman Publishers,
Nashville, Tennessee

Dewey Decimal Classification: 269
Subject Heading: EVANGELISM

Library of Congress Cataloging-in-Publication Data

The Gospel for the new millenniuim : a collection of essays /
Chris Schofield, general editor.
   p. cm.
   Includes bibliographical references.
   ISBN 0–8054–2199–8 (pbk.)
1. Evangelistic work. I. Schofield, Chris, 1959–

BV3790.G734 2001
269'.2—dc21
                            2001018076
    1 2 3 4 5 6 7 8 9 10 05 04 03 02 01

Contents

114959

Foreword

SELDOM, IF EVER, DOES A SEMINARY PROFESSOR HAVE THE privilege of inaugurating a department of evangelism in a theological seminary. Perhaps never in history has anyone done it twice, with the exception of Delos Miles. Evangelism, as an academic discipline, had its beginning at both Midwestern Baptist Theological Seminary in Kansas City and Southeastern Baptist Theological Seminary in Wake Forest, North Carolina, under his leadership.

No one was better qualified for this than Delos Miles. Having experienced an evangelical conversion as a boy of eleven, he later forsook his childhood faith while serving in military service. Out of a harrowing experience in the Korean war, he dedicated himself anew to the Lord and sensed the call of the Lord to vocational Christian ministry. His background in evangelism is rich and varied. He served as an evangelistic pastor in Virginia and South Carolina. He then served as state director of evangelism in both of these states. When Midwestern Seminary called its first professor of evangelism, no one was more qualified to fill this place than Delos Miles.

Few men in academic evangelism have been more prolific in writing than Dr. Miles. A number of books and many articles have come from his gifted pen. His book, *Introduction to Evangelism* is a classic, and one which I have used in my own classes at Southwestern Seminary.

Those of us who have known Delos have been aware that he stands tall among his peers. He is a devoted

Christian and every inch a gentleman. Uncounted numbers of students and friends have been greatly influenced by his life. I am privileged to have been among them. The privilege is heightened by being asked to write the foreword to this book.

Roy J. Fish
Distinguished Professor of Evangelism
Southwestern Baptist Theological Seminary
Fort Worth, Texas

Acknowledgments

THIS WORK IS WRITTEN IN HONOR OF DELOS MILES. In addition, many other thanks are due to a whole host of people who have contributed to the final completion of this project. To the many secretaries who have assisted in this work I say thanks, especially to my faithful secretary at the NAMB, Betsy Roland. Thanks is also due to Susan McDaniel, editing manager at the North American Mission Board, for her timely assistance.

A special thanks is in order for the many professors who have been a wonderful support since day one of my mentioning my desire to compile this work in honor of Delos Miles (e.g., George Braswell, Alvin Reid, and Paige Patterson). Dr. Patterson, thanks for having more confidence in me than I have in myself. Thanks to your encouragement and example to press on, this volume is finally completed.

I also need to say thank you to the many gifted and talented contributors. Your hard work in the writing of your chapters is truly a labor of love for Delos Miles. Thanks also for your patience with me, since this was my first experience at compiling and editing a work such as this.

Finally and most importantly, I say thanks to my wonderful family. What an honor to be the father of four precious daughters: Heidi, Hannah, Haley, and Hilary (my 4-H club), and the husband of such a wonderful and darling wife, Tamee. You have prayed for me and given time for me to pursue the completion of this project. Thanks for your support, encouragement, and love. I thank my Lord every day for each of you.

Introduction

DR. DELOS MILES HAS BEEN USED OF GOD IN THE LIVES of thousands of seminary students to inspire, challenge, and equip them in the area of evangelism. His gentlemanly Christian spirit coupled with his genuine concern for people made him a respected professor and practitioner of evangelism in Southern Baptist life.

Hopefully this collection of essays in his honor will accomplish four things. First, I pray that it will pay tribute to a man of God who has made an immeasurable contribution through service and the written word in the field of evangelism. Second, my desire is that this book will be an encouragement to pastors, students, lay witnesses, and evangelists in their daily practice of evangelism. Third, I hope this volume will be used in college and seminary classrooms to challenge students in the academic study of evangelism. Above all, in every way, I desire that Christ will be lifted up through this volume.

Contributing authors to this work are from various areas of ministry: seminary presidents, college and seminary professors, and denominational leaders. All are attuned to the major issues confronting the evangelical church in a new millennium. All are prolific writers in the field of evangelism or in related disciplines. Most are former students, colleagues, or colaborers who have been influenced by Dr. Miles's ministry of teaching, writing, or preaching. All share a mutual respect and admiration for Delos Miles.

The general theme of this volume is built around Delos Miles's belief that biblically based evangelism is three-dimensional. Thus, as is suggested by Delos Miles's classic definition of evangelism, evangelism is "being," "doing," and "telling" the gospel. This is evangelism that is modeled after Christ. As Christ walked upon this earth, he "was" (is) the gospel, he "did" the gospel, and he "preached" the gospel.

The essays in this book are broken down into three sections. Part I focuses on incarnational evangelism. This is also referred to by church growth experts as "presence evangelism." The essays in this section examine different elements of "being" the gospel to the world. Part II includes essays that relate to ministry-centered *(diakonia)* evangelism. They highlight the concept of "doing" the gospel. Part III concentrates on proclamation evangelism. This corresponds to the aspect of "telling" the gospel or the biblical idea of *kerygma.*

Finally, I trust that, in some way, this work will say thanks to a man of God, who after being saved and renewed in his faith at a young age, has sought to follow His Lord's example in being, doing, and telling the gospel to a lost and dying world.

J. Chris Schofield
Alpharetta, Georgia

A Tribute to Delos Miles

J. Chris Schofield

DR. DELOS MILES, RETIRED PROFESSOR OF EVANGELISM AT
Southeastern Baptist Theological Seminary, is an evangelist par excellence. More than that, he is a Christian
gentleman, a family man, a pastor, and gifted
preacher/teacher. He is one of the most prolific writers
on the discipline of evangelism in Southern Baptist Life.
If you have taken an evangelism course in college or
seminary over the past fifteen years, chances are you
have either used one of his books as a textbook or have
read from some of his writings. His impact on the evangelistic ministry of the church through his writing and
teaching ministries will long be felt beyond the span of
the life of Delos Miles.

Delos Miles—A Biographical Sketch[1]

Delos Miles was born in Florence County, South
Carolina, in 1933. His father was an uneducated farmer
and his mother's education only went through the third
grade. The family lived on a tobacco farm in an atmosphere of moral and economic poverty. Delos was the
second of four children and grew up very poor. Often,
he and his older sister would have to steal chickens to
help their parents feed the family. His early childhood
years were marked by hardship and despair.

When Delos Miles was seven years old his mother
left his father. She took the baby girl of the family with
her and never returned. A year later, his father was tragically killed in a drunken brawl, leaving the children with

nowhere to go. Subsequently, Delos Miles thought that he had lost the last adult person in the world who sincerely cared for him. Because of these two events he became very bitter toward his mother and toward the man who killed his father. This was a very low time in his life, and his future did not look promising.

After living with relatives for a few months, Delos Miles was blessed with a foster family that genuinely loved and cared for him. They sought to meet his spiritual, physical, and emotional needs. This family provided a stable environment for him. The most important event of this period in his life was his conversion experience. The foster family made sure he was in church each week. He learned about the Bible and about the Christ of which it bears witness. At age eleven Delos Miles confessed his sins to God and received Christ as his personal Lord and Savior. He soon followed Christ in baptism and joined the Baptist church.

At age fourteen Miles ran away from his foster home in search of his mother. He borrowed money from a friend and caught a bus to Charleston, South Carolina, where his mother was supposed to be living. It was at this point that Delos Miles's life began to take a drastic turn—one in which God's providential hand can be seen in a profound way.

God's Providential Hand

After arriving in Charleston, Miles began to search for his mother's home. After a day of searching through the large subdivision, he sat down on the street corner at its entrance. He was discouraged and all alone. Some time later, his mother and stepfather and their children came by in their car. His brother Dallas spotted Delos and began calling to him. It was truly a providential moment in Delos Miles's life.

This happy occasion was short-lived. Soon Miles discovered that his stepfather was a heavy drinker. He became very unhappy and decided to join the armed services. He finished the ninth grade, lied about his age, and persuaded his mother to sign for him to become a soldier in the U. S. Army. Within the next three years, this fourteen-year-old would become a moral reprobate, experience God's delivering hand more than once, and eventually, through a series of miraculous events, experience spiritual renewal and answer the call to the gospel ministry.

His account of these life-changing events is so moving that I have simply reproduced a portion of his spiritual autobiography which explains in detail the various changing events that transpired while he was a soldier and fighting in the Korean War.[2]

> I was a platoon sergeant of a rifle platoon in an infantry company. We had made our way deep into North Korea through the Changin Reservoir within five miles of the Yalu River, the boundary between Manchuria and North Korea. Snow was many inches deep on the ground. Sometimes at night the temperature would drop down to twenty or thirty degrees below zero.
>
> On the night of November 26, 1950, about midnight, we heard bugles blowing and rifles firing. My platoon was not under attack. But for the first time in the Korean War the Chinese Communists had entered the war in our section of the front.
>
> Soon we got an order on the telephone to move our platoon out of position and to try to plug one of the holes where the Chinese had broken through our lines. We moved as rapidly as possible across the snow, engaged the enemy until about mid-morning on November 27. Then they broke off the battle.
>
> We discovered that during the night the Chinese had completely encircled our position and cut us off

from the First Marine Division some twelve to fifteen miles behind us. There was no way to get our dead or wounded out, and no way to get food and ammuntion supplies in—both of which were running low. On that particular day the overcast was too heavy for an air-drop.

So we regrouped, placed our men two to the hole, and dug in a few feet apart on the forward slope of the mountain for the attack which we felt would certainly come when darkness fell. I was in the platoon command post with our lieutenant and our platoon medic and messenger. Our command post was a large bunker which the North Koreans had dug into the side of the mountain. It consisted of two parts. Each part was about six by six feet and was covered with poles and dirt; and the parts were connected with a trench about four feet deep.

About dusk the Chinese began to probe our lines. They shot flares into the air and charged our position in successive waves at the sound of a bugle. The lieutenant and I were in the trench which connected the two parts of our bunker, firing at the Chinese and giving orders to our men, trying to encourage them to hold fast. To our right in one part of the bunker were our medic and messenger passing ammunition to us and taking care of our telephone contact with the company command post.

Bullets were flying all around us. There were so many of the Chinese that we couldn't stop them. When I saw they were going to overrun us, I turned to the lieutenant and said: "Sir, what are we going to do?"

He said: "Sergeant, you know what the orders are." We had orders not to withdraw under any circumstances. In a matter of moments the lieutenant was shot. He fell over in the trench and groaned for a while before he died.

I didn't know what to do. But the thought came to me to throw down my M-1 rifle in the snow and to jump back into the vacant end of our bunker and to play dead. I lay down on my back, sort of on my right side, facing the entrance to the hole.

Almost immediately a Chinese soldier came into the bunker firing his rifle. He didn't see me at first because of the darkness. However, one of his bullets hit me in my right little finger, entering at the end joint and going out at the knuckle. It scared me. I thought I was going to die. I had not prayed for a long time. But I began to pray silently in my mind to God.

As the soldier came on into the hole and found me, he shook me with his hand and shouted something in Chinese. Then, I guess he wanted to make sure I was dead. So he placed his rifle on my forehead. When I felt that cold steel, I thought it was the end. I don't remember everything I said to God, but as best I recall, my thoughts went something like this: *Lord, if you are all powerful like I've always heard you are, you can bring me out of here alive. If you will save my life, I'll do anything you want me to do.* I was so desperate I was trying to bargain with God for my life. And, God is my witness, when the soldier pulled the trigger, instead of going through my head, the bullet went down past my right ear. It did not knock me out. In my memory, as I reflect back upon it, it seems like a red hot iron had been placed against my head and left there. There was that burning sensation.

He went on out. After an hour and a half or maybe two hours, the firing ceased. Two Chinese came into the hole with me. They slept and rested a couple of hours. Then two more would come in. All night long there were two in the hole with me. The next morning two of them came in and searched me. They removed my gloves from my hands, took everything from my pockets, ran their bayonets up my arm and took my military watch. They pushed several layers of clothing up on my stomach and felt around, and pulled my pants out of the top of my combat boots where I had them bloused. This was another difficult time for me.

To make a long story short, I lay there in that hole for more than eighteen hours slowly bleeding and freezing to death, without consciously moving a muscle in my body, reliving my past life in my memory and imagination. I confessed all of my sins to God and made the most solemn promises I knew how to utter. If God would just get me out of there alive, I would serve him the rest of my life; I would do anything he wanted me to do.

After a time Delos Miles did get out of that foxhole. He found about two hundred other survivors who were desperately trying to get back to friendly lines. The wounded were on trucks and those who could, were walking. Soon the convoy was stopped by a Chinese roadblock. Miles and the other wounded were left on the trucks while all who could carry a weapon and walk engaged the enemy on the ridge the road crossed over. As the battle raged Miles just happened to look to the rear of the convoy. The Chinese were fast approaching, and those fighting their way up the ridge were unaware of the Chinese attack at their rear.

Miles, whose feet were frozen up to his ankles, jumped off the truck and began to make his way up to the officer in command to warn him of the rear attack. By the time he reached him, as they turned around to look upon the convoy, the Chinese had overrun the convoy and were killing the drivers, wounded, and blowing up the trucks. They had no other option—they had to take the hill or perish. This they did and as night fell, the survivors began their long walk toward American lines. During this walk in the night, Delos Miles said that he often fell behind the others. He prayed a lot, cried a great deal, and thought much about his life. At this time he began to gain a strong sense of God's mission for his life. He also began to grow in his awareness of God's renewed presence.

Eventually, the small band of men (only twenty-five out of a whole company) were able to reach friendly lines, and Miles was able to receive the medical attention he needed. After nine months in hospitals, Delos Miles was discharged from military service at the age of seventeen. He was awarded the Silver Star for combat action in Korea and ended his military service at the rank of Sergeant First Class.

God's hand had protected the life of Delos Miles. God's purposes for this young man were set on course as he radically renewed his faith. Delos Miles left the military not only with the scars of a warrior, but with a changed heart full of passion to fulfill his promises to the Christ who had saved him from certain destruction. This mountain-top experience would serve as the launching pad for a life of devotion and service to Christ that continues today.

Ministry Years until the Present

After being discharged from active service, Delos Miles began the process of fulfilling God's call into the gospel ministry. He graduated with honors from Furman University, Greenville, South Carolina, in 1955. Shortly thereafter, he met and married Nada Lemons of Spartanburg, South Carolina. They eventually had four children: Angela, Daniel (who was born while he pastored a difficult church and named after the Bible character), John, and Miriam.

He received his B.D. degree from Southeastern Baptist Theological Seminary in 1958 and eventually earned his S.T.D. degree in practical theology from San Francisco Theological Seminary in 1973.

While in college, he began his pastoral ministry. From 1953–1963 Delos Miles served as senior pastor of four churches and associate pastor of one church. His first two pastorates were difficult. His zeal for souls was hard for stagnant congregations to stomach. Once he gathered the names of the lost in the community and printed them in the church bulletin. This did not set well with many pew sitters in his first pastorate.

His longest pastorate was in Crewe, Virginia, where he pastored Crewe Baptist Church for four years. While there he experienced his most memorable revivals. Once while preaching a revival in a bivocational church in rural Virginia, God's Spirit fell upon a service and twenty-five to thirty people were saved. Also, while serving at the Crewe church, Miles invited pastor-evangelist Rev. Dalton Ward to conduct a series of meetings. Again, God's spirit fell and forty-nine converts were baptized following the revival services.

In 1963 Delos Miles accepted a position with the Virginia Baptist General Board as associate secretary in the department of evangelism and associational missions. He served there until 1966, when he moved to Columbia, South Carolina, to accept a position as director of evangelism for the South Carolina Baptist State Convention until 1977.

Then at the age of forty-five, Delos Miles was invited to go to Midwestern Baptist Theological Seminary to serve as associate professor of evangelism. He inaugurated the department of evangelism there and served as its chair until 1981. He was then asked to come to Southeastern Baptist Theological Seminary as professor of evangelism where he once again inaugurated the department of evangelism and served as professor of evangelism until his retirement in December 1995.

During his more than twenty-six years of convention service and teaching, Miles carried on an itinerant preaching ministry. He preached revivals, taught evangelism training courses in churches, and spoke at seminaries and state evangelism conferences. In 1989 he cancelled thirty-three engagements and began to serve as interim pastor while continuing to teach at Southeastern Seminary.

Following his retirement from full-time teaching in 1995, Miles returned to the full-time pastoral ministry. He presently is residing in Wake Forest, North Carolina, and pastoring a church close enough for him to commute to the field. Although "retired," he has taught adjunctively at Gardner-Webb University in Boiling Springs, North Carolina, and at Campbell University, in Buies Creek, North Carolina. In January 1998, he began to devote all of his energies to his pastorate.

Delos Miles has enjoyed the pastoral ministry the most. He said that even as a professor and state convention staff person he tried to emphasize the pastoral aspect of ministry. To him, it is most rewarding to see the dramatic changes that conversion and personal renewal cause in individuals' lives. He said that he loved "to see people moving toward God and away from the devil."

Miles is also a prolific writer and scholar in the field of evangelism. He has published twelve books and numerous articles and reviews in theological journals. His most popular work has been his *Introduction to Evangelism* text, which has been the standard Southern Baptist introductory text in evangelism since its publication in 1983. He also has written on other disciplines as they relate to Evangelism—e.g., *Church Growth: A Mighty River* and *Evangelism and Social Involvement.*

Delos Miles has certainly had an eventful life that has been filled with much pain and sorrow, joy and happiness. Through his years of ministry, he has sought to be faithful and obedient to Christ and his call in his life. In so doing he has left an indelible mark in the field of evangelism. He has truly been used of God to stir many people to the task of making Christ known to the nations.

A Personal Word

I first spoke with Delos Miles by phone in 1987. At that time, I was president of a student ministerial organization at what was then Gardner-Webb College. I called Delos Miles to invite him to come and speak on evangelism to the ministerial students on campus. I'll never forget that first encounter with Delos Miles.

I had never before spoken with a man who was so kind, gracious, and such a "Christian gentleman" over the phone. He was hindered from that engagement by a snow storm. However, I did get an opportunity to meet him the following year, and the Delos Miles I met over the phone was true to his character in person.

Delos Miles is a genuine Christian gentleman who has always made time to encourage, counsel, and pray for/with his students. On one occasion I remember a student coming to the door of his office right at the lunch hour. I was just leaving his office and knew that he had an important lunch engagement. The student wanted to see him and talk with him concerning a pressing matter. Dr. Miles offered him the opportunity to make an appointment later in the day. The student's eyes filled with tears and said, "that will be fine."

Dr. Miles immediately sensed that the student needed to talk at that moment. Without further delay, he invited the student in. That is only one of the many occurrences that afforded me the opportunity to see the kind, caring, and gentlemanly spirit that is so much a part of Dr. Miles's Christian character.

To many, Dr. Miles is from the "old school." He is well disciplined and very well read. He seems to always be punctual with appointments, engagements, and assignments. His courses always began and ended on time. He often said to his classes, "Time is the most valuable commodity we have. I will not steal any of your time, and I ask you to do the same with my time."

Delos Miles is a Christian gentleman—devout and dedicated. I have prayed with him and cried with him. I have been with him in revival meetings and personal witnessing encounters. I have been in his home many times and he in mine, and I can say: here is a man deeply committed to his Lord.

In the fall of 1995 he lost a grandson to drowning. A few days into that very difficult time for him and his family, we talked by telephone. He said, "I have a crack in my heart and a lump in my throat, but once again I have seen the grace of God sufficient in my time of need." *What a man of the Lord!* Delos Miles is truly a man of God, a Christian who depends upon and loves his Lord.

In addition, Delos Miles is a gifted professor of evangelism. I always left his classes excited about doing evangelism, not just studying evangelism. His deep, strong voice and enthusiasm about evangelism, coupled with his unique style of using case studies make his classes interesting and challenging. He seemed to have the unique gift of encouraging the student to excellence both academically and pragmatically.

God's Word is the foundation for Delos Miles's life and ministry. He loves the Word of God. Each year he chooses a Scripture passage to be his golden text for that year. All throughout the year he meditates on, prays over, and studies this "golden text." Once in a Ph.D. seminar he commented about this practice: "This practice will prove to be a rich source of inspiration and strength for your life and service to Christ." Years ago, he chose Proverbs 3:5–6 as the golden text for his life.

This high regard for Scripture is also demonstrated by his deep commitment to making God's Word the center of all his writings and classes on evangelism.[3] Every class period he teaches begins with readings from both the Old and New Testaments, followed by a prayer. The spiritual depth of his Christlike character often surfaced during these times of prayer. Students would come and thank him for his prayers in class, which always seemed to inspire them tremendously.

Throughout his years of service Dr. Miles has always emphasized the importance of making the practice and study of evangelism the priority of one's life and ministry. He believes that an emphasis on the academic study of evangelism should be at the heart of every Christian college, university, and seminary. He also believes that without an emphasis on the discipline of evangelism, students will leave institutions and seminaries ill-prepared to lead their churches to fulfill the Great Commission. And, according to Miles, if churches are not winning people to Christ, Christian colleges and seminaries will soon run short of students to train.

Delos Miles has always sought to train his students to practice wholesome and intelligent evangelism. This is the type of evangelism that is modeled after Christ, whom Miles calls the Master Evangelist. Also, in using the terms *wholesome* and *intelligent,* he is promoting an evangelism that has integrity. His desire is that students practice an evangelism that is biblically based, ethically sound, theologically accurate, and pragmatically viable.

As grader and fellow for Delos Miles for more than seven years, I consider him both a mentor and a close friend. God has truly blessed me, my family, and thousands of seminary students through the life and ministry of Delos Miles. God has used him to encourage me when I was low, inspire me to practice evangelism daily, and to teach me much about the academic study of evangelism. Through close contact with him and his lovely wife Nada, God has taught me and my wife Tamee the importance of accepting believers in their continuum of faith, as well as encouraging them forward in their spiritual quest.

I would like to think that God would afford me the opportunity to influence a student's life in half the way Delos Miles has influenced mine. I thank God for Dr. Miles who, with his gentle yet fiery pioneer spirit, has helped to lay a solid foundation for the academic study of evangelism in theological education.

Dr. Miles, I love you and praise my Lord for your faithful service to him (Phil. 1:3–6). Shalom.

PART I

BEING THE GOSPEL

Chapter 1

Jesus Christ: Our Model for Being the Gospel

Ken Hemphill

A second principle of evangelism according to Christ is what I call the enfleshment principle. This is the principle of fleshing out the Gospel with our own flesh and blood and bones—the principle of incarnating in our lives the message which we verbalize with our lips.

The Gospel does need a voice. However it needs a body also. The Word has to become flesh in us.

Jesus not only spoke the Gospel and did the Gospel but also he was the Gospel. As John said, 'The Word became flesh, and dwelt among us' (John 1:14). If we would pattern our evangelism after Jesus Christ, somehow the Good News about the kingdom of God must become flesh in us. Not, of course, in the same unique sense as it became flesh in Jesus of Nazareth. He was the 'only begotten Son of God,' the only one of his kind. Nevertheless, the Gospel must permeate the marrow of our bones, flow through the blood of our veins, and become wrapped up with our skin so that we become living extensions of the incarnation.[1]

IT IS APPROPRIATE THAT WE BEGIN THIS *FESTSCHRIFT* in honor of Dr. Delos Miles with a section on "Being the Gospel." As the preceding quotation from *Master Principles of Evangelism* makes clear, incarnational evangelism was at the heart of Delos's teaching and life.

19

His numerous books on evangelism frequently call us back to this incarnational principle of evangelism both in principle and practice.

Dr. Miles was convinced that we must begin with Jesus to have a model worthy of imitation. In his *Introduction to Evangelism,* he entitled the first chapter on models for evangelism, "Jesus as the Perfect Model." He wrote, "Now, having said all of that, I want to go on to say that Jesus Christ is the only perfect model for our evangelizing. He is the perfect model evangelist." He then pointed the reader to John 13:15–16, "For I have given you an example, that you also should do as I have done to you. Truly, truly, I say to you, a servant is not greater than his master; nor is he who is sent greater than he who sent him" (RSV).[2]

In discussing the implications of Jesus as the model for evangelism, Delos allows us to view the passion of his own heart. "If anyone should ever ask me, What kind of evangelist do you want to be? My reply will be: I want to be the kind of evangelist Jesus was. I want to live as he lived, love as he loved, labor as he labored, and laugh as he laughed."[3]

Dr. Miles's discussion of Jesus as the model for evangelism and his own lifestyle indicates that he fully understood the implications of holding up Christ as the model evangelist. He wrote, "If we affirm Jesus as our perfect model for evangelizing and seek to pattern our evangelism after his, we shall have to flesh out the Gospel through our life-styles. We shall have to combine the deed and the word in our very lives."[4]

Dr. Miles concluded the chapter with this solemn reminder:

> The idea, if logically followed, forces us to see ourselves as an extension of the incarnation. We are indeed, the body of Christ in the world today. Such a

substantive concept also points again to our dependency upon the Holy Spirit for power to imitate the Jesus model. We cannot be like Jesus in our own strength. A power greater than ourselves is required to implement the imitation of Christ. Again we are reminded that evangelism is spiritual work which requires spiritual persons who have spiritual power.[5]

We are challenged to look again at what it means biblically and practically to look to Jesus as the model for being the gospel. We would miss the mark if we were to view this only as an academic exercise devoid of the demand for application. What we discover in the model of Christ we must be prepared to imitate in our own lives, so we can be more effective in bringing his message to a world so desperately in need of the Good News.

The person and ministry of Jesus are so rich and multifaceted that we could discover an endless number of principles to guide us in our own evangelistic ministry. I will limit my discussion to six key issues with a focus on *being* the Good News. First, let us look at Jesus as he embodied the Good News.

Jesus Embodied the Good News

The prologue to John's Gospel declares with profundity and certainty: "In the beginning was the Word, and the Word was with God, and the Word was God. . . . And the Word became flesh, and dwelt among us, and we beheld His glory, glory as of the only begotten from the Father, full of grace and truth" (John 1:1, 14). John is clear that Jesus did not simply come to herald the Good News, he was the incarnation, the embodiment of the Good News.

John makes a clear distinction between a herald of the Good News and the one who is the Good News in the testimony of John the Baptist found in John 1:19–34. The Jews sent the priests and Levites to determine the identity of this prophet in the wilderness. Apparently, their question carried the implication that John might believe himself to be the Messiah.

John immediately denied any personal identification with the Messiah (v. 20). Rather, he identified himself as the voice of one crying out in the wilderness, making ready the way of the Lord. His answers to other questions, such as his practice of baptizing his followers, afforded him the opportunity to declare that the one who came after him would be totally different than himself. "It is He who comes after me, the thong of whose sandal I am not worthy to untie" (v. 27).

When John saw Jesus coming to him, he declared: "Behold, the Lamb of God who takes away the sin of the world!" (v. 29). He then clarified that this was the one who had a higher rank since he existed before him, confirming the testimony of the prologue to Jesus' pre-existence and divinity. John related how God gave him a sign that Jesus was the embodiment of the Good News. Thus, John declared: "And I have seen, and have borne witness that this is the Son of God" (v. 34).

John, in his Gospel, presents a series of sign events which bear testimony to the veracity of the claim that Jesus is, in his very being, the gospel. The first sign event occurred in Cana when Jesus turned the water for purification into wine. Verse 11 of chapter 2 is the key verse for understanding this event. "This beginning of His signs Jesus did in Cana of Galilee, and manifested His glory, and His disciples believed in Him" (John 2:11). Remember that John 1:14 emphasized that in Jesus the Word became flesh and we beheld his glory—a glory which reflects the very presence of God.

One of the great themes of John's Gospel is the self-revelation of Christ through the great "I am" sayings. In John 6, after we are told of the feeding of the five thousand, we are allowed to listen to a conversation between Jesus and the people concerning the value of signs. Jesus seized the moment to talk to them about a food which endures to eternal life which the Son of Man alone can give (v. 27). Still seeking a sign, they reminded Jesus that Moses gave them bread out of heaven (vv. 30–31). Jesus told them that Moses was not the source of the bread; only God could give bread from heaven. They enthusiastically asked that Jesus give them this life-giving bread.

Jesus responded, "I am the bread of life; he who comes to Me shall not hunger, and he who believes in Me shall never thirst" (v. 35). Jesus, unlike Moses, is not a mere human instrument through which God gives bread; Jesus himself *is* the Bread.

In John 8:12 we find a second "I am" declaration. "Again therefore Jesus spoke to them, saying, 'I am the light of the world; he who follows Me shall not walk in the darkness, but shall have the light of life.'" The Pharisees accused Jesus of bearing false witness about himself. Jesus then referred to the law regarding two witnesses and asserted, "I am He who bears witness of Myself, and the Father who sent Me bears witness of Me" (John 8:18). The embodiment of this "I am" declaration is found in the next chapter when Jesus healed the blind man. Truly Jesus is the light of the world.

Jesus related to hearers the parable of the good shepherd, but once again they did not understand the things he was saying to them (John 10:1–6). In response he declared, "I am the door of the sheep" and "I am the good shepherd" (vv. 7, 11).

The death of Lazarus, the good friend of Jesus, provided the backdrop for one of the most powerful "I am" statements in all of Scripture. When Martha declared her conviction that her brother would rise again in the resurrection, Jesus said to her, "I am the resurrection and the life" (John 11:25). Jesus simply does not bring a message about eternal life, he *is* eternal life.

Throughout the Gospel, John illustrates how Jesus sought in word and deed to make himself known to others so they could know the Father. His self-revelation was clearly evangelistic in nature and purpose. Nowhere is this more explicit than in John 14:6. While preparing his disciples for his departure, Jesus told them that He was preparing a dwelling place for them in his Father's house (John 14:1–4). Thomas was troubled because they did not know the way. Jesus' response was simple but profound: "I am the way, and the truth, and the life; no one comes to the Father, but through me" (v. 6).

Further, Jesus promised that he would not leave them as a disconsolate and destitute group; he would ask the Father to send them another Helper (v. 16). The Holy Spirit would indwell and empower them. This in turn leads to another "I am" passage where Jesus declared: "I am the true vine" (John 15:1). The followers of Jesus are like branches on a vine. True branches will bear fruit that is consistent with the nature of the vine. The bearing of fruit will provide clear evidence that a person is a disciple of Christ. The disciple is called to bear fruit that is consistent with Christ.

Since John has made clear that Jesus' life and message are inextricably bound, it is not too much to suggest that followers of Christ in any generation are to follow his pattern of evangelistic ministry. Jesus is not only the model; but also he indwells us through his Spirit to produce his fruit.

The principle of Jesus as the embodiment of the gospel has relevance for the practice of evangelism today. First, it clearly indicates that evangelism is the natural outflow of the life of the believer who is indwelt by

Christ. Delos Miles concludes his book, *Master Principles of Evangelism,* with this challenge: "Jesus made his true identity known in order to draw persons to the Father. If we share our Christian identity in order to point others to the Father, God will bless what we unveil and use it to touch some hearts and to tingle some minds."[6] Our lifestyle must clearly reflect the gospel that we declare with our lips.

Raymond Calkins underlines this truth in an effective way as he challenges his readers to embody the qualities of Christ. For example, he underscores the importance of grace to the message of the gospel and then reminds us that Jesus' approach to people had the quality of graciousness.[7] The gospel we declare will lack conviction if it is not incarnated in our lives.

Second, we must see in Jesus, our model, that incarnational evangelism does not negate the necessity of a verbal witness; rather, it demands it. All too often people want to equate incarnational evangelism with verbal witnessing. All of us have heard the pious comment, "I witness through my life; it's not necessary for me to give a verbal witness." If the One who perfectly reflected the Father found it necessary to bring together life and witness in incarnational witness, we would do well to follow his example.

Jesus Presented the Good News

This principle flows clearly out of the first. Because Jesus embodied the gospel, his presence always made the gospel present. When we understand the full implications of this principle, we will need to ask ourselves why we are seeing so little in terms of evangelistic results through the church today. Have we made evangelism something which is done by only a few who are evangelistically gifted? Have we made it an event which can only occur when listed on the church schedule? Have we neglected to remind Christians, ourselves included, that when a Christian is *present* the Gospel is present?

I think that many of us who claim to be followers of Jesus do not win many persons to Christ precisely because we rarely make ourselves *present* with people in need or take advantage of the opportunity when it arises.

I have personally struggled with this issue since becoming president of Southwestern Baptist Theological Seminary. I am required to live on the campus that I serve. When I leave the campus, I am frequently in the presence of believers or on my way to meet with other believers. I have found that I must have an intentional strategy to be in the presence of non-Christians. Further, I find, to my own chagrin, that I am often too preoccupied to take advantage of the opportunities that come my way when I am simply "on the way."

It is instructive to note that Jesus *presented* the gospel both in planned and spontaneous meetings. Matthew 9:35–10:42 gives us a clear picture of Jesus' intentional strategy to make the gospel present. Notice the intentionality of verse 35: "And Jesus was going about all the cities and the villages, teaching in their synagogues, and proclaiming the gospel of the kingdom, and healing every kind of disease and every kind of sickness." In Matthew 10 we are told that Jesus summoned the Twelve, gave them authority and instruction, and then sent them out to do what they had seen and heard him doing. He reminded them: "A disciple is not above his teacher, nor a slave above his master. It is enough for the disciple that he become as his teacher, and the slave as his master" (Matt. 10:24–25a).

It is clear that Jesus had an intentional strategy to make the gospel present by going wherever there were people in need. Furthermore, it is equally clear that Jesus expected that his followers would continue to embrace that strategy in order to obey him and be like him.

Yet many of the stories of Jesus dealing with people about eternal issues appear to be unpremeditated and unstructured. Some people in need took the initiative to come to Jesus. We can think of the rich young ruler (Luke 18:18–30), the blind man (Luke 18:35–43), the woman with the issue of blood (Luke 8:43–48), the demoniac from the country of the Gerasenes (Luke 8:26–39), or the ten lepers (Luke 17:11–21). It is important to note that people were able to come to Jesus because he did not avoid the difficult, the lonely, the unhappy places. He went to places where people were in need, even if it took him through the graveyard or near a leper colony.

Other persons were engaged by Jesus while he was on the way. Jesus was entering the city of Nain when he encountered a funeral procession. The event provided the opportunity for an evangelistic encounter as he was moved to compassion by the scene (Luke 7:11–17). Luke tells us that Jesus was passing through Jericho when he saw Zaccheus observing him from a sycamore tree. Jesus called Zaccheus down and invited himself to Zaccheus's home, where he pronounced that salvation had come upon the household (Luke 19:1–10).

Delos Miles refers to these spontaneous witnessing events as illustrating the "principle of opportunism," stating simply that Jesus took advantage of every opportunity he had to share with people.[8] Gaines Dobbins drew attention to this strategy of our Lord and called it the "principle of seized opportunity." "The majority of instances in which Jesus dealt with persons with a view to winning them to discipleship were unpremeditated."[9]

Robert Coleman encourages us to note one other matter about Jesus' presence. He reminds us that not only was Jesus present, but also he had his disciples with him. The key to training others to do personal evangelism ministry is to have them with you when you are ministering to others.[10]

Once again we are called to examine our own lives in the light of the master evangelist. Are we intentionally present where we can encounter people in need of the gospel? We not only see the legitimacy of planned outreach strategies such as a church visitation program; we also see the necessity to sensitize ourselves to the ministry opportunities which abound if only we will seize the moment.

Jesus Personalized the Gospel

We cannot read the interviews of Jesus without being impressed by his attention to the individual—the person being confronted by the Good News. Jesus was concerned about the individual, and therefore he always personalized the gospel. Inviting himself to the home of Zaccheus was no gimmick to embellish the story; it was a personal touch that took the wealthy tax gatherer out of the eye of the public and put him in the comfortable surrounding of his own home. It enabled Zaccheus to hear the gospel unimpeded by the uproar of the marketplace and the potentially angry stares of those whom he might have defrauded while collecting taxes.

Gaines Dobbins compares Jesus' ministry to Nicodemus with that of the Samaritan woman. He writes: "We think of his respect for Nicodemus as 'the teacher of Israel,' and at the same time of his utmost courtesy shown to the Samaritan woman who had lost respect for herself." Dobbins referred to this personalizing of the gospel as "the principle of respect for personality."[11]

Whatever title we give it, the ministry of Jesus clearly demonstrated the need for the evangelist to make the gospel personal. Personalizing the gospel will call us to place the needs of the individual over all extraneous concerns. The priority Jesus placed on persons kept the religious establishment off balance, as the story in Luke 13:10–17 makes clear.

Jesus healed in the synagogue on the Sabbath a woman who had been bent double for eighteen years. Jesus placed his hands on her, and she stood erect and began glorifying God. You might think this event would be the catalyst that would spark revival in the synagogue—but not so. The synagogue official became indignant and issued a lecture about working on the Sabbath. Jesus responded by reminding them that they would take care of their animals on the Sabbath. Then He asked, "And this woman, a daughter of Abraham as she is, whom Satan has bound for eighteen long years, should she not have been released from this bond on the Sabbath day?" (Luke 13:16).

A reading of the Gospels reveals that numerous occasions of ministry occurred in a setting where it juxtaposed the need of an individual with some Jewish institution, tradition, or regulation. In each case Jesus demonstrated a priority for caring for the needs of an individual. Jesus' concern for persons does not in any way trivialize his love for the temple, the synagogue, or the law. An event such as cleansing the temple of the traders indicates that Jesus had the highest regard for the temple because it represented God's presence.

Jesus articulated this principle of personalizing the gospel clearly in Mark 2:27: "And He was saying to them, 'The Sabbath was made for man, and not man for the Sabbath.'" Religious institutions and regulations were designed to bring people to God, not separate them from him.

In his book, *How Jesus Won Persons,* Dr. Miles underlines the need to value persons if we are to be effective in winning them to Christ. "One of the very first things we have to settle in order to be effective witnesses to Jesus Christ is our attitude toward persons. If we don't believe persons are worth saving, we shall not so much as lift one little finger to save them." Speaking of Jesus he notes, "He sets an infinite value upon every human being. Persons are more important to Jesus than are profits and property and things."[12]

If we are to follow Jesus' model, we must value people, build effective witnessing relationships, and expose our true selves to people.[13] These are risky and frightening thoughts for many persons today. Issues such as abortion and assisted death, along with the depersonalization of society, have called into question the value of persons. The pressures of our busy schedules and the temptation toward cocooning in what little free time we have has made the building of relationships for evangelism even more challenging. The thought of exposing our true selves with the accompanying risk of vulnerability always creates the fear of possible rejection. But these are risks worth taking and challenges to be overcome for the sake of the gospel.

Jesus Contextualized the Gospel

These great principles of evangelism taken from the life of Jesus flow naturally from one to the other. It stands to reason that for Jesus to personalize the gospel, he must also contextualize it. Dr. Miles makes the point that God contextualized our salvation in the incarnation. He writes: "God, in other words, offers us salvation in our particular cultural setting. We don't have to conform to some other person's cultural image in order to be saved. The only image to which we need to conform is the image of God's beloved Son."[14]

Jesus never compromised the content of his message, but he suited it to the need of his hearers. Jesus understood what the potential barrier was in the life of the rich young ruler that could keep him from responding to the gospel. Therefore, he challenged him to forsake his wealth for a much greater wealth. He talked to the woman at the well about water that would fully satisfy, and then he inquired about her husband. He challenged Nicodemus, the religious intellectual, with the message that he must be born again. In each case Jesus suited his message to the unique circumstances of his hearer.

In commenting on this principle of contextualization, Dr. Miles notes: "Surely, we can see how Jesus began with persons where they were. He began with them where they were socially, morally, religiously, educationally, physically, and so forth. While he sought to lead them into the kingdom, he did so by relating what he said and did to their unique personalities and to their particular needs and peculiar circumstances."[15]

Paul's statement in 1 Corinthians 9:19–23 is better understood in terms of contextualization of the gospel than it is in terms of accommodation. For Paul there could be no compromise of the message, but there was flexibility in the presentation of the message. Paul could with clear conscience declare, "I have become all things to all men, that I may by all means save some" (1 Cor. 9:22b).

To apply this principle will require that we come to understand people and their circumstances. This in turn requires that we spend time with the people we are attempting to lead to a saving knowledge of Jesus Christ. We will be willing and desirous of developing relationships with them because they are a unique creation of God who needs to hear his redemptive word.

We will need to listen to people and to develop relationships with them through which the gospel can flow with power and authenticity. It will require that we look at witnessing as a dialogue and not a monologue. Applying this principle will force us to see evangelism as a way of life and to look for every opportunity to contextualize the gospel. This will require that we treat people with dignity and that we separate the sin from the sinner.

Jesus Universalized the Gospel

When Jesus gave the Great Commission, he made it abundantly clear that the mission field was the world. The Book of Acts begins with the ascended Lord reiterating the global reach of the Gospel: "You shall receive power when the Holy Spirit has come upon you; and you shall be My witnesses both in Jerusalem, and in all Judea and Samaria, and even to the remotest part of the earth" (Acts 1:8).

Here once again the Gospel narratives tell us that Jesus embodied the gospel he presented. Jesus evangelized Jews and Gentiles, rich and poor, the religious and not-so-religious, officials and common people. You cannot read the Gospels without seeing that Jesus was the man for all people. He universalized the gospel by befriending people from every walk of life. He was willing to eat with a Pharisee or a tax collector. He healed the centurion's servant and the widow's son. Jesus was no respecter of persons.

This principle of universalizing the gospel is brought into stark relief by the story of the meal in the home of Simon, the Pharisee. Simon was a well-to-do, well-educated leader of the religious establishment who invited Jesus to dine with him and some of his select friends (Luke 7:36–50). The appearance of an uninvited guest created a level of drama.

The woman who came without invitation was declared by Luke to be a sinner. The truth is that both the woman and Simon were sinners, but only the woman was aware of her sinful condition. She was so overwhelmed with her sin and guilt that she was unconscious of her own immodesty when she took her hair down and kissed the feet of Jesus. Jesus was willing to eat with the Pharisees, and he was also receptive to the plight of the immoral woman. He embodied the universal scope of the gospel.

It is easier for us to talk about the universal scope of the gospel than it is to embody the implications of its universality. If we believe that the Good News is for every people group of every nation, we must be willing to go to the dangerous and difficult inner city as quickly as we go to the wealthy suburbs. We must be as interested in targeting those on welfare as we are those in the country club. We must give and go with the world in view.

We must call into question the spending patterns that have provided too little resources to develop and fund a strategy for evangelizing the world. We must challenge North American evangelical spending patterns which have allowed us to spend 94.5 percent of all monies given to Christian causes on 4.7 percent of the world's population.[16]

Jesus Empowered the Good News

"Jesus never made a disciple, preached a sermon, or worked a miracle until the Holy Spirit came upon him at his baptism."[17] The Gospel writers make it clear that Jesus' ministry was empowered by the Holy Spirit. Luke tells us that "Jesus, full of the Holy Spirit, returned from the Jordan and was led about by the Spirit in the wilderness" (Luke 4:1). Mark states that "the Spirit impelled him to go out into the wilderness" (Mark 1:12).

Speaking of Jesus' dependency on the Holy Spirit, Delos Miles draws particular attention to Luke 11:14–26. You will recall that Jesus had been accused of exorcizing demons by the power of Beelzebul, the prince of demons. Jesus answered this false accusation with several points, but the key point is stated clearly in Luke 11:20: "But if I cast out demons by the finger of God, then the kingdom of God has come upon you."

Dr. Miles writes: "Make no mistake about it. Jesus was claiming to lay waste to the kingdom of Satan by the power of the Holy Spirit. He was implying that all evil spirits are cast out by the Holy Spirit. He was claiming that the power which he has is greater than all the demonic powers."[18]

Jesus' ministry of evangelism was accomplished in the power of the Holy Spirit. He promised his followers that they would be empowered to witness by the same Holy Spirit who indwelt him (Acts 1:8). The powerful and convicting preaching of Peter on the day of Pentecost bears testimony to the veracity of his promise. But the power of the Spirit was not given to Peter alone: "And when they had prayed, the place where they had gathered together was shaken, and they were all filled with the Holy Spirit, and began to speak the word of God with boldness" (Acts 4:31).

As believers we have received the promised Holy Spirit, and we have been entrusted with a gospel which has supernatural empowering. "For I am not ashamed of the gospel, for it is the power of God for salvation to everyone who believes, to the Jew first and also to the

Greek" (Rom. 1:16). Why then, we must ask, are we seeing such meager results in terms of evangelization?

Some church growth statisticians indicate that as
many as two-thirds of all evangelical churches have
either plateaued or have begun to decline. Many
churches will go an entire year without seeing anyone
confess Jesus Christ as personal Savior. What is the
source of our problem? Could it be that we have become
so obsessed with our man-made methods and models
that we have neglected the supernatural power of the
Holy Spirit made available through prayer and the sharing of the gospel?

I would like to end this short essay in honor of Dr.
Miles as I began—with a quote from Dr. Miles which
will serve as a challenge to all of us: "When we get to
feeling powerless and impotent in the face of our mam-
moth task of world evangelization, we need to remember
that there is enough power in our Gospel to save every
one who will believe. God has passed down to us
through faithful witnesses a constructive power which
can liberate the world from its bondage to all the powers of this present and passing age."[19]

Chapter 2

A Theology of Evangelism
Paige Patterson

IN STEPHEN KING'S BEST-SELLING APOCALYPTIC NOVEL,
The Stand, most of the population of the United States is
decimated as a result of a mistake in the laboratory of a
military facility producing agents to be employed in bac-
teriological warfare. The small surviving population that
was immune to the super-flu virus finds that surviving
the plague is not enough. When one survivor has sudden
need for an appendectomy, everyone realizes that there
are no available physicians. While the nature of the
problem is easily diagnosed, the clumsy effort to perform
the surgery by non-physicians results in the death of the
patient. Those wishing to save the patient meant well,
but even locating a book on surgery at the last minute
proved insufficient.

Sal Sberna is now the illustrious pastor of
Metropolitan Baptist Church in Houston. Before he was
converted, he was sitting on a stool in a bar one evening
accompanied by an inebriated Christian. The conversation
turned to spiritual matters when the drunk believer
informed Sal that God would punish them both, but that
it would be worse for Sal since he would go to hell.
Wishing to avoid this result, Sal went home, got a Bible,
read it, and came to Christ.

These two incidents, one fictitious and one actual,
serve to demonstrate important truths about evangelism.

First, if a person is to do invasive spiritual surgery in the heart of another, he needs to understand all he possibly can about the nature of the malady and the procedures for effecting a cure. Otherwise, however well-meaning he may be, he may inflict harm rather than healing.

On the other hand, the second incident reminds us that truth is truth even when it arises from an unlikely or unworthy source. Furthermore, God's power is such that he can take the most meager and ineffective effort to share Jesus and produce the miracle of salvation. But this last story of God's remarkable providence should not blind us to the lesson of the first story. When dealing with the eternal destinies of humans, sensitive Christians will want to comprehend what evangelism is and how and why it works. This is the theology of evangelism.

To develop a theology of evangelism might seem to some people a superfluous enterprise. A systematic presentation of the great doctrines of the faith should include anthropology and hamartiology, disciplines which discover the purpose of man and document his fall, together with its deleterious consequences. Soteriology and ecclessiology should explain the nature of salvation and the missionary strategy of the church. Where then is the need for a separate theology of evangelism?

The answer to this query is not determined by the need to access information hitherto unavailable in other good theologies. Rather, the rationale for a theology of evangelism develops from the need of accentuation. A theology of evangelism is necessary as a result of an unexpected development in the life of the postmodern church. Elton Trueblood caught the gist of it when he said:

> Part of the paradox of our time lies in the double
> fact that we are now ready to listen to witness but are
> hesitant to give it. We avoid the witness stand insofar
> as our religion is concerned, with the odd result that

although religion is popular its dominant mood is apologetic. Christian colleges want, in many areas, to hide the basic Christian commitment of their institutions, for it is something of which they are slightly ashamed. Many persons are terribly fearful of seeming pious. Something must have occurred in their childhood for them to develop what is essentially a phobia on this point. The strangest result of this phobia is that great numbers of people continue to fight against a danger which may once have been real, but is so no longer. A little realism in observation would teach us that the genuine danger *we* face, whatever our ancestors may have faced, is that of a mood in which people are so terribly apologetic that they refuse to witness at all.[1]

With this warning before us, four questions can be proposed, the answers to which will provide an introduction to a theology of evangelism and give accentuation to the task of evangelizing the world for Christ. (1) What is evangelism? (2) Why is evangelism necessary? (3) What is it that actually transpires in the doing of evangelism? And finally, (4) What is acceptable evangelistic strategy?

What Is Evangelism?

Definitions for evangelism are as many as the monographs on the subject. Many of these are adequate and helpful. My purpose here is neither to review a myriad of such definitions nor to propose some revolutionary new perspective. Rather, I wish to call to the attention of the reader salient emphases of the Scriptures that stake out the parameters of biblical evangelism.

First, *the church must see its evangelistic task as above all a continuation of the mission of Christ.* Scripturally, the reasoning proceeds like this: (1) Jesus defined his own mission as having "come to seek and to save that which was lost" (Luke 19:10 NKJV). (2) He further commissioned his disciples by saying, "As the Father has sent Me, I also send you" (John 20:21 NKJV). (3) This task is to be viewed by the church as that which "fill[s] up in my flesh what is lacking in the afflictions of Christ" (Col. 1:24 NKJV). Because of the unusual providences of God, we are to God the fragrance of Christ among both those who are saved and those who are perishing. "To the one we are the aroma of death leading to death, and to the other the aroma of life leading to life" (2 Cor. 2:16 NKJV).

The ministry of our Lord was multifaceted—healing the sick, feeding the hungry, etc. But when he sought to define his mission, he did so in terms of the spiritual lostness of humanity and his determination to seek the lost and save them. He expects and even commissions his disciples to continue that task. That such an assignment is costly becomes apparent in the passage that speaks of finishing up his sufferings.

This suffering of believers arises from no inadequacy in the atonement of Christ, which in any case could only have been efficaciously accomplished by one without sin, but from the fact that all of Christ's ministry involved "suffering." This suffering continues in the witness of the church today sometimes even to the point of martyrdom. To get the message out is costly!

The cost of this ministry of evangelism is apparent since not everyone likes the way it smells. After all, no matter how the evangelist may sugarcoat the message, he is still announcing God's judgment to wayward people, the savor of death unto death. And even in salvation proffered, the savor of life unto life, the approach is humiliation, repentance, and faith—not the sort of thing most people are eager to hear.

In fact, a plausible definition of evangelism from the perspective of the witness might be, "the act of making oneself totally vulnerable in order to bear witness to the truth and to save some." As Trueblood states it, "The call to witness is a call which men can answer affirmatively or negatively, but one who answers it negatively, however kind and pious he may be, is not in the company of Jesus."[2]

In Western jurisprudence, witnesses are not infrequently in danger and sometimes must be accorded special protection by the courts. The two witnesses of Revelation 11 found that the heavenly court protected them until they had finished their assignment. Then their witness cost them their lives. Only afterward followed the martyr's reward. The contemporary church must overcome the idea of "easy witnessing," inoffensive to all. Such inadequate framings of the task will never succeed in mobilizing a witnessing army.

Some years ago, we all watched the television in horror and amazement as the story of an Air Florida flight from the nation's capital unfolded. A brief rise from the runway at Washington's National Airport was followed by a plunge into the ice-capped waters of the Potomac River. That was the horror. The grandeur was watching rescuers leap into the icy Potomac at great risk to themselves. They knew they could not save all, but they took the ultimate risk to save some. Today, they bask in the gratitude of the families whose loved ones they plucked from almost certain death. This is the picture of the task of the church, including both its risks and its rewards.

Although the next matter broached will challenge one of the most popular dictums in contemporary Christianity, it, nevertheless, must be noted. *Popularly, evangelism is distinguished from what is called "discipleship."* This unfortunate trend is not heretical, but it is in error exegetically. In this construct, evangelism refers to witnessing leading to conversion and regeneration; whereas "discipling" takes the mantle of teaching.

Consider by contrast the Great Commission of Christ.

> Then the eleven disciples went away into Galilee, to the mountain which Jesus had appointed for them. When they saw Him, they worshiped Him; but some doubted. And Jesus came and spoke to them, saying, "All authority has been given to Me in heaven and on earth. Go therefore and make disciples of all the nations, baptizing them in the name of the Father and of the Son and of the Holy Spirit, teaching them to observe all things that I have commanded you; and lo, I am with you always, even to the end of the age." Amen (Matt. 28:16–20 NKJV).

Note here that the only imperative in the verse is *mathēteusatē*, or "make disciples." This is followed by participles, which receive their mandatory status from the strength of *mathēteusatē*. These words command that the disciple be baptized as a public statement of his faith and then taught (Gk. *didaskō*). Note that baptizing and teaching *follow* the act of "making disciples." In other words, "discipling" is not a process but an initial act in which a person chooses to follow Christ and become his disciple. He then declares that act publicly through faith-witness baptism and begins a lifetime process of being taught exactly what is involved in the discipleship to which he has committed himself.

Why Is Evangelism Necessary?

Why then must the church be wed to a task that has danger and suffering associated with it? Is the Lord not an ark of safety for his people?

First, evangelism is necessary because of the *nature of Christ and His mission*. Already we have noted Jesus' own definition of his mission in Luke 19:10. In

Philippians 2:5–11, Paul provides a theologian's perspective by picturing the eternal Christ as he "emptied Himself" (v. 7) to appear on earth as a man and there to accept the cruel death of the cross so that he could, as the author of Hebrews adds, "taste death for everyone" (Heb. 2:9 NKJV).

It is hardly necessary to assess the various theories of this self-emptying (Gk. *kenosis*) to get the drift of ultimate sacrifice on the Savior's part. If both the incarnation and the atonement were demanded by the significance of the plan of God and the predicament of man, can the church afford to do less than give its best, yes even its all to the dissemination of this great truth?

Second, evangelism is essential because of the *nature of the mandate and example of Christ.* No stories in God's Word are any more poignant or revealing than those of our Lord's personal encounters with people. He encountered and shared with the monied aristocracy (Mark 10:17–27), the religiously committed (John 3:1–12), and to the openly sinful and disdained (John 4:1–42). He called men down from trees (Luke 19:1–10), paused to speak with a wild man at Gadara (Mark 5:1–20), sought out a man disenfranchised from the synagogue (John 9:35–38), talked to a woman at a well (John 4), demanded that roadside beggars be brought to him (Mark 10:46–52), insisted that hated tax collectors follow him (Matt. 9:9–10), and broke up a lucrative fishing business on the Sea of Galilee (Luke 5:1–11). While Jesus certainly preached to the gathered throngs, the most enlightening insights into the character of Jesus and the spiritual needs of the human family are drawn from those one-on-one witnessing encounters of our Lord.

Already, the mandate of our Lord to take his message to the world has been discussed in terms of the Great Commission and other passages. It remains to remind the reader that from the outset of the incipient church, the call of Jesus was to people who would learn to be "fishers of men." In Luke 5:1–11, Jesus used an object lesson to prepare Peter and others. A fisherman reported to Jesus that a night of fishing had produced nothing. Following the command of Jesus, the fishermen made a last attempt resulting in a huge catch. Jesus' words follow: "Do not be afraid. From now on you will catch men" (v. 10 NKJV).

The metaphor is hardly difficult. In following Jesus, the task of the disciples would be to be "fishers of men" or "to catch men." Never was there a faith (from the day of its inception) more immersed in the task of seeking adherents than was Christianity. And if Pentecost is cited as the "birthday of the church," it is worthy of note that not tongues or any other miracle but the conversion of three thousand is the major focus of the story.

Common nowadays is the affirmation that the first work of the church is to worship God. On the surface such an avowal sounds good—even noble. But the truth is different. The truth is that it is the first assignment of *all* people to worship God. The first assignment of the church is to show the world how to worship God in a way that brings redemption—to make all people disciples by being fishers of men. And, by the way, few acts of worship are any more significant than introducing someone to Christ, someone for whom he died!

Third, the *nature of lostness* demands evangelism. The scriptural mosaics that picture lostness are frightening to the careful reader. The Luke 15 trilogy depicts items of increasing value: a lost sheep, a lost coin, and a lost boy. The value of these items, as well as the tragedy of lostness, are vividly revealed against the backdrop of an earnest, almost panicked, search and unbridled rejoicing when the lost is found. The discovery of that which is lost, "one sinner who repents," is the only thing mentioned in the Bible that causes all of heaven to rejoice.

This whole picture is accentuated by the awesome lists of the actions of lost people found in Romans 1, Ephesians 2, and Titus 3. In those passages, lost people are "filled" with unrighteousness, sexual immorality, covetousness, murder, strife, and deceit. They are haters of God, unmerciful, untrustworthy, disobedient to parents, and unforgiving. They are by nature the children of wrath, dead in trespasses and sin, strangers from the covenants of promise, without God, and without hope in the world. The lost are foolish, slaves to lusts and pleasures, hateful, and hating one another. Such a litany may not be very appealing, but it certainly establishes the extent of lostness and provides the mandate for evangelism. If for no other reason, gratitude to God for deliverance from such a lifestyle should prompt aggressive evangelism.

No wonder that even atheist Bertrand Russell said, reflecting on what he viewed as the origin of religion, "only on the firm foundation of unyielding despair, can the soul's habitation henceforth be safely built."[3] For this reason, Mark McCloskey concluded, "I am convinced that only those who have made the effort to develop firmly rooted biblical convictions about evangelism will be able to overcome the cultural undertow of convenience."[4]

Finally, evangelism is critically important because of the *nature of eternity*. As I often say to my faculty and students, the logic is obvious. If heaven is real and hell is real, and all five-plus billion people on the earth will spend *eternity* in one of these, and if Jesus and his atonement constitute the only way to avoid one and get into the other, then whatever in our lives is second in importance to evangelism is so far behind that it may as well not be in the race.

Now the threat of an eternal yawning abyss known as hell is hardly pleasant. Furthermore, the exclusivity of Jesus as the only way of salvation is not only politically incorrect in contemporary society, but also even Christians are embarrassed by such claims and do all they can to soften them. Elton Trueblood again addressed this issue memorably. Speaking of the words of Jesus in Matthew 7:14, "Because narrow is the gate and difficult is the way which leads to life, and there are few who find it" (NKJV) he notes:

> If we could have a renewed understanding of these unequivocal words of Christ, we should have a brave start on Church Renewal. The lines are beginning to be drawn and this may be a good thing, for there is a world of difference between the frank acceptance of a narrow way, and the popular notion that one way is as good as another. The pressure to conform to the broad way is now very strong and is getting stronger. For example, there are cities in which the YMCA is urged to drop the word "Christian" from its name, and at least one financial drive has failed because of refusal to do so. It is important to note that the chief pressure has not come from Jews, but from those whose only religious expression is a vague goodwill. The resistance is not specifically to Christianity, but to anything which has a sharpness of outline. Before Christians succumb to such pressures they are wise to note that there is no cutting edge that is not narrow. There is no likelihood whatever that Christianity could have won in the ancient world as religion in general. It survived very largely because it accepted the scandal of particularity. It could not have survived had it not been sufficiently definite to be counted worthy of persecution.[5]

Trueblood goes on to note that "a tolerant panthe-ism, which is the real core of some of the self-styled new theology, will never be persecuted because most people will never oppose anything so vague."[6]

In 2 Corinthians 5, the apostle Paul turns to the vocabulary of state to emphasize the evangelistic man-date. Believers are said to be Christ's ambassadors to bring the message of reconciliation to an estranged world. The urgency of the task is presented against the backdrop of the imminent appearance of every believer before the judgment seat of Christ. Furthermore, knowl-edge of "the terror of the Lord" results in ardent activity to persuade people. Some interpret this terror to be a threat to believers who fail to persuade persons. Others take the terror of the Lord to be the experience of those facing God in judgment. In a sense both ideas are true even though it is likely that the last idea was in the mind of Paul. In any event, God's impending judgment is a fre-quent theme in the Bible.

Add to this picture the fact that the Lord himself often spoke of hell. His rehearsal of the story of the rich man and Lazarus constitutes one of the most arresting accounts in the Bible. In Luke 16, the rich man is described as being in torment, having memory, being aware of the favorable status of Lazarus, and being eternally separated from God. The belief that anyone who fails to come to Christ experi-ences such an eternity ought to be compelling, next only to the love of Christ, as motivation for witness.

What Is It That Transpires in Evangelism?

In Romans 10:13–15 Paul connects a sequence of events that is instructive for comprehending what tran-spires, theologically speaking, in evangelism. Beginning with the availability of Christ, Paul promises that anyone calling upon Jesus' name for forgiveness will be saved.

But, of course, the apostle notes that no one would call on the name of Jesus without believing in him. Further, how would it be possible to believe in someone about whom the needy sinner had never heard?

The sequence culminates with a focus on the evangelist. How can the lost hear about Jesus unless there is a preacher, and how can one preach if he is not sent? This leads the mission-minded apostle to cite Isaiah 52:7 about the beauty of the feet of those who bring good news.

Here in a nutshell is evangelism and the evangelist. Jesus is God's only ordained way of salvation. But to believe in him and call upon him, one must know of him. This he can do only if God sends an evangelist. An evangelist, or a preacher in this case, might be one speaking to a multitude, but, more often, just one witness sharing the moving story with one who is perishing. The witness, by his faithfulness, sets in motion a further sequence which continues into eternity.

Some months ago I needed to make atonement with my wife for having taken her on a float trip down the Amazon River. So, I agreed to a train ride through the Canadian Rockies. She loves trains. I hate trains! Did you ever try to read on a herky-jerky train? Just outside of Banff we passed a sign that read "Continental Divide." Everyone knows that this spine of the Rockies is the point from which all waters are divided flowing either east or west.

So also, there is a "continental divide" in religion. Buddhism, Islam, Hinduism, Animism, Shinto, New Age, natural religion, free-thought, most of Christendom— and, tragically many self-styled evangelicals—agree on one critical idea. This idea suggests, either implicitly or explicitly, that a person can do something, or perhaps a combination of some things, that will somehow make him or her acceptable to God.

Over against all such human reasoning, the faith and witness of the New Testament declares man's finest efforts to gain acceptability with God as wholly useless (Rom. 3:28). Titus 3:5 reminds us that it is not by works of righteousness but by God's mercy that we are saved. Ephesians 2:8–9 dramatically contrasts saving grace with failing human works. The Reformation principles, *sola gracia, sola fide,* are indeed the continental divide of all human thinking in religious matters.

In Mark 10:26–27, the disciples asked Jesus, "Then who can be saved?" He replied that "with men it is impossible," but that with God "all things are possible." In Luke 18:9–14, a Pharisee robed in sincere religion and morality prayed but went to his house unjustified; whereas a tax collector pleaded with God for mercy and, as a result, went to his home right with God.

Paul explains the rationale of God's salvific work in Romans 3:23–26. All have sinned. There are no exceptions save Jesus. However, the saved are justified through the redeeming blood of Christ. The cross of Christ demonstrates his righteousness in that through his atoning death he is both just (dealing with sin according to justice) and the justifier (this by grace) of those who trust in Christ. With this atoning sacrifice as foundation, it is now possible to observe the events which are set in motion by the Holy Spirit, using the evangelist.

God sends the evangelist who bears faithful witness to those who will hear (Rom. 10:13–15). The Spirit of God uses the testimony of the evangelist to awaken the hearer to God's call to salvation (Rom. 8:30). Sensing this call of God to redemption, the unbeliever sees his own sinfulness and unworthiness. He sees this in the light of the holiness of God (Isa. 6:1–5). This produces in the unbeliever heartbroken sorrow for his sin and rebellion against God which leads him to repentance (2 Cor. 7:10).

This is a critical point at which we must pause for reflection. Consider carefully this verse: "For godly sorrow produces repentance leading to salvation, not to be regretted; but the sorrow of the world produces death" (2 Cor. 7:10 NKJV). Our pause here is because this aspect of salvation is seldom emphasized. Yet, the verse suggests that repentance leads to salvation, and repentance is not possible without godly sorrow for sin, which the older theologies spoke of as "contrition."

Matthew even cites Jesus as saying to his own contemporaries that when they heard John, they "did not afterward relent and believe him" (Matt. 21:32 NKJV). This statement suggests that trust or saving faith cannot precede but rather logically follows contrition and repentance. Even though this verse uses the less emphatic Greek word, *metamelomai,* for repentance, the meaning of the verse is not obscure.

Further, not just any sorrow will do. The sorrow of the world results only in death. The repentance of Judas is a splendid example of this kind of sorrow. This sorrow actually produces bitterness toward God and further rebellion against him. But godly sorrow (sorrow induced by the convicting power of the Holy Spirit) leads to repentance (John 16:8).

One of the most difficult problems faced by the contemporary church is the problem of unregenerate membership. It is difficult, if not impossible, for the church to act like the society of the redeemed or to witness as it ought if large segments of church people have never been saved. Without ever having been broken before God in godly sorrow for sin, there can be no genuine repentance leading to salvation. Much of this problem is the result of the desire of many churches to be

respectable in postmodern society. Marketing strategies
have replaced messages on sin and judgment. Depicting
the counsel of the devil for the contemporary church, I
have elsewhere imagined Satan as musing,

> You surely must know that we have utterly failed
> to destroy them with the evil of liberalism; so I am left
> with no other alternative but to induce them to accept
> the good in the place of the best. We will substitute
> bulk for nutrition, junk for substance, activity for
> holiness, methods and formulas for the power of God.
> In so doing, we will weaken the body and render it
> susceptible to every disease.
>
> We will induce the thoroughgoing Calvinist to
> accuse the less-Calvinistic of Arminianism, and the
> less-Calvinistic to accuse the thoroughgoing Calvinist
> of unconcern for evangelism. We will entice them to
> substitute multiple repetitions of *Get All Excited* or
> Kum Ba Yah for psalms, hymns, and spiritual songs
> brim-full of strong theology. We will allure them to
> address the surface-felt needs of people by getting
> them tacitly to believe that a 2,000 to 3,500-year-old
> book like the Bible cannot and does not address the
> deepest, often unidentified, longings of the human
> heart. We will above all things convince their preach-
> ers, especially the 200 or 300 strongest pulpiteers,
> never to preach about such politically incorrect sub-
> jects as hell, the wrath of God, or impending judg-
> ment. We will convince them to believe in these, but
> rarely if ever to mention such shocking topics to an
> "I'm okay, you're okay" society. We will secure their
> commitment never to address subjects such as femi-
> nism, through which we can ultimately destroy the
> fabric of families and eventually the churches and all
> of society. We will occupy the minds of the pastors
> with increased readings on leadership, technology,
> self-help, and pop psychology, and thereby insure their
> neglect of the reading of substantive theology.[7]

Godly sorrow having asserted itself in the heart of the unbeliever, repentance follows (2 Cor. 7:10; Luke 13:3). Repentance is a translation of the Greek word *metanoia,* meaning literally to be "after-minded." A monumental change of mind and heart has been effected, which results in a turn from trust in oneself to faith in Christ alone. Without faith it is not possible to please God (Heb. 11:6). This faith is understood not in terms of mere intellectual consent but rather in terms of trust or commitment.

Repentance toward God and faith in Jesus seems to occur almost simultaneously. Even these are not generated out of the impulses of man's goodness, but are the results of the convicting work of the Spirit (John 16:8). As a result, the new birth, or regeneration, occurs. Nicodemus was instructed by Jesus that unless a person is born again (Gk. *gennēthē anōthen*), or born from above, he cannot see the kingdom of God (John 3:3, 5).

The metaphor of new birth for the experience of salvation is flush with significance. As a physical birth has a nine-month gestation period in humans, so many things may lead up to and precede the new birth (i.e., opportunities to hear the gospel). Just as growth and maturation follow the physical birth, so, too, should spiritual growth and eventual maturation follow the new birth (1 Pet. 2:2). And just as a birth takes place in a particular place and moment, so also the new birth is a once-for-all experience that takes place in a particular moment and a stated place.

As a part of this new birth, a number of salubrious developments take place for the new believer. He is forgiven for his sins (Eph. 1:7). Since he has been estranged from God by his sin, he is also now reconciled to God and is no longer viewed as an enemy of God (Rom. 5:10; 2 Cor. 5:19). He is also justified, i.e., he is accorded legal status as accepted with God even though his own works would have condemned him (Rom. 3:24; Rom. 8:30).

He is sanctified or placed safely in Christ Jesus (1 Cor. 6:11; Heb. 2:11). This is positional sanctification, which also marks the beginning of progressive sanctification in which the believer grows in holiness (John 17:17) until the moment of glorification, the final redemption of the body (Rom. 8:30). In Romans 8:30, this glorification is so certain, though awaiting the return of Christ, that it is spoken of in a past tense along with justification, etc.

Finally, the prominence of the concept of "salvation," the necessity of being "saved," and the title and office of "Savior" all testify to at least three crucial truths.

First, all people need to be saved (1 Tim. 2:4; Rom. 5:9), attesting to the fact that something has gone radically wrong in the human family, so wrong, in fact, that a Savior is necessary to salvage man.

Second, saving people is that which prompted the incarnation of Christ and is the overriding purpose of his atoning sacrifice (1 Tim. 1:15; Matt. 1:21; 18:11).

Third, salvation is the melody in the symphony of all of God's work and hence becomes the most important standard by which to judge the viability of the professed Christianity of church or individual. Those persons and churches which place their major emphasis on salvation and on the Savior are by far the most likely to model New Testament Christianity (1 Cor. 9:22).

This whole evangelistic and soteriological process may be summed up as follows:

> A Christian is a person who confesses that, amidst the manifold and confusing voices heard in the world, there is One voice which supremely wins his full assent, uniting all his powers, intellectual and emotional, into a single pattern of self-giving. That voice is Jesus Christ.[8]

A concluding word needs to be said about the doctrine of election since Romans 8 and Ephesians 1:3–7, as well as other passages, make it clear that the entire process we have been describing is somehow bound up in the electing providences of God. Twenty centuries of concerted effort on the part of theologians has failed to produce much consensus. Therefore, it is unlikely that the present author can, in a few sentences, or for that matter in a lifetime of books, resolve the tension in the issues of God's sovereignty and man's responsibility. So, instead, let us take a slightly different approach by asking why such a difficult doctrine as election is even offered on the sacred page?

Here four answers emerge.[9] As long as the doctrine of election is in the Bible, it is clear that salvation is the work of God and God alone from initiation to termination (Rom. 8:29–30). This being the case, it follows that salvation is an act of God's grace alone into which human merit can never enter. Furthermore, election ensures that we can never forfeit salvation (Rom. 8:33). God will not later lose any of his elect. Finally, the doctrine of election assumes the providential oversight of God for all his saints, including the ultimate triumph of good (Rom. 8:20–23, 28).

No matter how one resolves the difficult issues associated with the electing providences of God, *any construal of those doctrines that results in a curtailment or lessening of zeal for the soul-winning enterprise is either erroneous altogether or else dangerously out of balance with the whole of New Testament truth.* No matter how Paul, John, Jesus, and the Synoptic Evangelists understood those truths, it had the effect of spurring them on to more aggressive evangelistic and missionary endeavor. Both the example and the express mandate of Christ and the apostles establish forever the critical importace of aggressive evangelistic effort!

What Is Good Evangelistic Strategy?

Some Christians find an excuse for not witnessing in the poor methodology of others. Of course, this is like saying that because there are disreputable physicians who are guilty of malpractice, I will never visit a doctor! To be blunt, this is foolishness. Nevertheless, there is a theology of methodology in the New Testament. While remembering the example of Sal Sberna and the resultant truth that even bad methodology is sometimes used of God, there does seem to be a "right way" to present the claims of Christ.

Jude, our Lord's half-brother, noted that different people and situations have to be approached in different ways. "And on some have compassion, making a distinction; but others save with fear, pulling them out of the fire, hating even the garment defiled by the flesh" (Jude 22–23 NKJV).

Paul counsels care in speech while sharing the faith. "Let your speech always be with grace, seasoned with salt, that you may know how you ought to answer each one" (Col. 4:6 NKJV).

In a previous *Festschrift* in honor of Lewis Drummond, I illustrated this proposal of varying methodology by asking a simple question regarding building a basketball franchise. Does the owner need to draft big inside men or quick darters with the ability "to hit from downtown?" To change the analogy to a military illustration, what was needed in the Gulf War—air forces, tanks, or ground troops? The obvious answer is that no attempt would have been successful that did not include all three.

As long as "methods" are honest and violate no biblical guidelines in letter or spirit, much of the discussion of methodology is a waste of time. Jude says that the message never changes, but the methodology is marked by elasticity.[10]

Basically, the Scriptures seem to encourage three ideas in methodology. First, confrontation should be without condescension. People know the difference between condescension and conviction, and they pick up on it quickly. Watch the different approaches of Jesus to Nicodemus, the rich young ruler, and to the woman at the well. Each was accorded respect and dignity even though Jesus pulled no punches.

Second, witness should be offered in gravity without glumness. The subject matter is deadly serious—eternally serious! But you and many of life's circumstances are hysterical. Be serious about the gospel, but do not check your smile or your sense of humor.

Finally, exercise witness in compassion without coercion. One searches in vain for a single passage in the Bible where anyone is ever forced to embrace the Lord. While there indeed will come a day when every knee shall bow, this implies only the triumph of Christ and not the coercion of anyone. On the other hand, note the compassion of Jesus as he wept over Jerusalem (Matt. 23:37). Listen to Paul as he agonized over his Jewish countrymen even to the point that if it were possible he would agree to be cursed of God if only they could be saved (Rom. 9:1–3). No element is any more responsible for the failure of the church to witness and to evangelize than the absence of compassion—genuine love for the wayward souls!

One of the best ways to assess methodology and expectation arises from our Lord's parable of the sower (Matt. 13:1–23). The "sower" is one who disseminates seed (the word about Christ). Four things happen to the seed, three of which are undesirable, but one of which is glorious. The various soils represent the hearts of hearers.

Sometimes the gospel message is heard but not understood. Before reflection takes place, the wicked one absconds with the seed. Some seeds fall on stony ground and cannot penetrate to take root. There is an initial response, but there is no permanence. Because there is no root (there is profession of salvation without possession of salvation), persecutions arise and the "professed" Christian stumbles. Some seeds fall among thorns. This category also seems to be one of apparent, but not real, receptivity. This is because worldly pursuits, "cares," and the "deceitfulness of riches" choke out the gospel. Finally, some seeds fall on good ground and brings forth fruit in varying quantities.

Jesus never intended to suggest that only about twenty-five percent would respond. He was doing three important things. First, He was emphasizing to his followers that the Word of God must be disseminated. Second, Jesus anticipated the sorts of responses that sowers could expect. This way his followers would be discerning rather than disappointed at rebuff and apparent failure. Finally, Jesus was promising that faithful sowing would find receptive soil in significant numbers and that these, in turn, would produce varying proportions of fruit.

Several times in the above essay, I have cited Elton Trueblood's two wonderfully incisive works, *The Incendiary Fellowship* and *The Company of the Committed*. This whole chapter can be concluded with a statement from each work that will provide provocative summary.

The renewal of the Church will be in progress when it is seen as a fellowship of consciously inadequate persons who gather because they are weak, and scatter to serve because their unity with one another and with Christ has made them bold. This is the only kind of Christianity that can stand up to the challenge of the militant paganism and the fanaticism of the New Left. It will win, in the long run, because it is more revolutionary than they are.[11]

And finally,

A little self-analysis reveals the fact that what we call humility is actually fear of involvement which is costly in time, in money, and in peace of mind. We avoid witnessing because we recognize that it comes at a high price! . . . The person who says naively, "I don't need to preach; I just let my life speak," is insufferably self-righteous.[12]

Chapter 3

Prayer and Presence Evangelism
Lewis A. Drummond

ONE OFTEN HEARS IN THE "HALLOWED HALLS" OF
theological institutions the well worn cliché, "evangelism
is caught—not taught." No mistake, evangelism certainly is caught. As theologian J. I. Packer declared,
believers must "get in step with the Spirit." In that
dynamic context, evangelism becomes exceedingly contagious. An intimate walk with Jesus Christ in the fullness of the Holy Spirit will inevitably result in a fervor
for evangelism. But that is not the whole story. Our
cliché is only half true: Evangelism is also taught. Hence,
the expression should really read, "evangelism is caught
and taught."

The teaching of evangelism may appear simple, if not
simplistic, to those with only a surface understanding of
the grand enterprise. Yet, in the final analysis, there is
nothing more profound than becoming adept in leading
and guiding others into the sharing of the gospel of our
Lord Jesus Christ. It demands far more than just a fervent
spirit, as essential as that is. Other considerations are also
vital: the absolute necessity of understanding the exact
nature of the gospel, the biblical facts concerning the
operation and work of the Holy Spirit in a person's coming to faith in Jesus Christ, a demographic sensitivity to
people's needs and the culture in which the Good News

of Christ is communicated, along with many other attending practical and theological skills.

These matters must be mastered. And that is not simplistic. Consequently, an intense relationship exists between the challenge of the Holy Spirit and the discipline of learning how to work out that challenge in effective evangelism. Nowhere is this more true than in the preparation of those called to full-time ministerial vocations. It is to this role that the professor of evangelism fulfills his or her ministry.

Through the years, Dr. Delos Miles has filled that role beautifully. As a state director of evangelism for many years, then moving into the field of theological education, he has personified the principle. For decades he has inspired and taught young men and women to share the message of Christ with spiritual insight and skill. Thus I find it a joy to write in this *Festschrift*, and say to the glory of Christ, that here is a man of God who has caught and taught all that evangelism means. And in the area of "prayer and presence" in the teaching of evangelization, he has excelled.

Now what do we mean by the phrase "prayer and presence," and why do we contend that it has a vital place in evangelizing? To that question we now turn our attention.

A central aspect of effective evangelization for the individual personally, and for the church collectively, revolves around two primary principles: Prayer and Presence. Without both, the Holy Spirit may well be in some sense "hindered" in his role of conviction and enlightenment (John 16:7–11). As paradoxical as it may appear, the sovereign, immutable God often "limits" himself to the prayers and presence of his people.

Prayer in Evangelism

The Shantung Revival

The year was 1927. The place was Chefoo, a seaport city in Shantung Province, China. The missionaries had been laboring faithfully for decades in that part of this country. They met opposition, resistance, ridicule, apathy, and discouragement at every bend of the road. They were forced to travel a rugged terrain. The churches were carnal, many of the members being no more than "rice bowl" Christians. They joined the church and professed faith in Christ in order to receive some sort of handout or perhaps even a job at the hands of the missionaries. The little Baptist seminary in Shantung had five students enrolled. Missionaries were almost to the point of despair.

Right at that junction Nanking fell at the hands of the armies of Chiang Kai-shek. Along with communist influence, the entire populace of that large northeast province of China plunged into chaos. The unrest grew so severe that the United States government informed all the missionaries that they should proceed at once to the seaport city of Chefoo and remain there until the unrest settled down. It was a bleak time for the discouraged missionaries.

The Baptist missionaries, some twenty in number, were crammed into a small mission compound of only two buildings. Missionaries in those early days of the Christian mission were "high-powered" personalities. They spent their days in fervent activity and labor. With much time on their hands and in such cramped quarters, something was bound to explode. They were very aware of the tension that would rise. So they decided to have a prayer meeting every morning. Perhaps that would keep tension and tempers under control. It was surely the thing to do, not only because of their needs, but they were vitally concerned about the spiritual well-being of the Chinese believers they left behind on their respective fields. So they gathered together for an hour's prayer each morning.

In that setting Miss Marie Monsen, a Norwegian Lutheran missionary, was invited to share her testimony. Through her testimony, along with some very able Bible studies delivered by another missionary, God began to stir their hearts. The morning prayer meetings soon began to last two hours, then three—then the entire morning was given over to prayer. The burden of the missionaries' prayers shifted from the believers back on the field to their own spiritual needs. All began to sense a deep awareness that God desired to do a profound reviving work in their lives.

As the dynamic moving of the Spirit drove them more and more into fuller commitment and profound prayer, Dr. Charles Culpepper, one of the Baptist missionaries, tells the thrilling story of what God began to do through those hours together in prayer. He should be permitted to tell it in his own words:

> As Miss Monsen gave her testimony, Ola (Charles' wife) began to be impressed with the fact that she should go and talk to her about the eye damage. (Ola suffered from optic neutritus.) We made an appointment and went to her apartment. As she met us at the door, Miss Monsen's first question was, "Brother Culpepper, have you been filled with the Holy Spirit?" I stammered out something less than a definite reply. Then, recognizing my uncertainty, she carefully related a personal experience fifteen years earlier when she had prayed for and received the promise of the Holy Spirit as recorded in Galatians 3:14. After visiting with her for two hours, we urged her to come to our home to pray for Ola's eyes.

That night we were deeply troubled. Prayer for healing seemed unorthodox for Baptist people. But in private we read James 5:14–16 and were greatly encouraged. The words "confess your faults" particularly pierced my heart. A consuming realization that our hearts must be completely open to God pervaded all our senses. I began to feel the Lord was going to undertake a great thing for us.

The next morning about twenty people came to our home for prayer. We felt an electric excitement, a feeling that God was preparing us for something we had never known before. After praying for several hours, we all seemed in a complete spirit of communion. Suddenly Ola took off her glasses and laid them on the mantle. Following the instructions in the Book of James, I anointed her with oil. Then we all knelt and continued praying. It was as though God had walked into the room. Everyone prayed aloud. We felt that Heaven came down and Glory filled our souls.

As we prayed, the male Chinese cooks from both missionary residences in Chefoo walked into the room. Their hatred for each other was common knowledge. But, as the power of God's Holy Spirit worked, they went to each other, confessed their hatred, sought forgiveness, and accepted Christ as personal Savior.

In the midst of our joy for the cooks' salvation we had completely forgotten Ola's eyes. Then someone remembered and asked her, "What about your eyes?" She replied, "They feel all right and the pain is gone."

It never returned. This was the most wonderful experience in our lives. We had never known such spiritual joy.[1]

Then Dr. Culpepper read from James, chapter 5, and put olive oil on his ailing wife's head and invited the missionaries to lay their hands on her and pray for her healing. However, before they could lift up their voices in prayer, Bertha Smith, another Baptist missionary, suddenly broke in and related a very significant principle. But she too should be allowed to tell it in her own words:

I had gone into that room, so far as I knew, absolutely right with the Lord. I would not have dared to go otherwise. But when I stretched my hand out to Mrs. Culpepper's head, I had to bring it back. There stood facing me a missionary (Anna Hartwell) with whom there had been a little trouble. In her early years she had been head of a girls' school, but for several years she had been teaching illiterate women to read.

I had been asked to serve as principal in our boy's school in Chefoo while the missionary principal was on furlough. I had majored in education, and by that time had had ten years' experience in teaching and thought that I was "the last word" in education! I had recommended Miss Hartwell to lead daily worship in that school. After a few weeks, I asked another missionary to tell her that methods for teaching old women were not appropriate for high school boys. She was hurt, of course.

But what about my proud self? I did not have a particle of sympathy for her. Right there before everyone, I had to say, "Miss Hartwell, I did not have the proper attitude toward you about that school affair. I beg you to forgive me!" My hand then joined the others and we prayed.

Had I refused to confess that sin, and joined in the prayer with it covered, I believe that I would have hindered the prayer of the others, and the eye could not have been healed.

Because all were right with God and of one heart, heaven came down! We did not have to wait to see whether or not Mrs. Culpepper's eye was healed! We knew in our hearts that she would never have another attack. The Lord had heard the prayers of such human frailty and had performed a miracle in healing one whom we so loved! She did not put her glasses back on. While the sight was not restored completely in the weak eye, both were strengthened and not once has she had any more pain, though using her eyes steadily for reading and needlework.

Walking around the room rejoicing and praising the Lord, we were all on a mountaintop of ecstasy. Then I had to be the joy-killer. There came over me such a sense of our inconsistency, that I had to speak of it.

"What kind of missionaries are we?" I asked. "We have gone through a week of heart-searching, humbling ourselves before each other and before the Lord, in order that we might be altogether right with Him, so that He could hear our prayers and heal the physical eye of one of our own number. Yet we have never gone to this much self-negation for preparation to pray for the opening of the spiritual eyes of the Chinese to whom we have been sent." Our mountaintop of ecstasy suddenly became a valley of humiliation. We all went to our knees in contrite confession for having been so careless as to have gone along supposing that we were right with the Lord, while holding all kinds of attitudes which could have kept the Lord's living water from flowing through us to the Chinese.[2]

That moment birthed the beginning of the great Shantung Revival of 1927. What took place in those dynamic days is all but indescribable. The seminary flourished. Almost immediately over 150 students enrolled. The churches filled to overflowing as many of the apathetic Chinese believers found new life and spiritual vitality in their Christian walk. Above all, multitudes were brought to saving faith in the Lord Jesus Christ. The number who were actually "born of the Spirit" in that revival period could only be recorded in heaven. Evangelism flourished as it had never done in the history of the Christian mission in that part of China. They were glorious days indeed.

The significant thing to note in this great revival is that the awakening with its tremendous evangelistic results all began in prayer. This is a fundamental principle that always exerts itself. Whenever the Spirit of God sets about to do a profound work, whether it be in just one person's life, or in an individual church, or for an entire area or nation, he always lifts up prayer warriors who will stand in the gap and intercede for the salvation of the lost. It cannot be emphasized too strongly: Prayer is an essential ingredient of great evangelism. Little prayer—few people saved; much prayer—multitudes brought to Christ. It is that simple. History is replete with this basic principle.

The John Hyde Story

One of the giants of prayer in evangelism was John Hyde, American missionary to India. After graduating from McCormick Theological Seminary in Chicago, young John made his way to the West Coast ready to sail to his missionary assignment in that so called "sub-continent of misery." As he prepared to board the ship, a friend handed him an envelope. He put it in his coat pocket and made his way to his room. After getting settled in, he opened the letter, thinking it must be a bon voyage message from a friend. It was a farewell note from an old preacher friend. But it read rather strangely. The letter said: "Dear John, are you filled with the Holy Spirit?"

That pungent, short message did not set well with young John. From a rather proud heart, he declared to himself that he was a seminary graduate and was on his way to pour out his life on the mission field. What did this old preacher mean by asking him if he were filled with the Spirit? In something of a fit of anger, he crumpled up the letter, threw it on the floor, and paced out on the deck.

Back and forth he paced on the deck. God's convicting barb had pierced his proud young heart. Finally, God broke his heart, and when young John Hyde stepped off the ship on India's coral sands, he disembarked as a different young man than when he set sail in America.

Through the years of missionary service, the Spirit of God gave this young Presbyterian missionary a most profound ministry. God made of him a great prayer warrior. Through those years of service his prayer life deepened until he found himself praying four hours a day. One may think that is excessive. But the four hours for missionary Hyde was certainly not too much; in the context of praying those four hours a day, God also granted him four Indians won to faith in Jesus Christ every day. Prayer does precipitate conversions.

John poured out his life in India and became very ill. God called him to his eternal home as a relatively young man. What a loss for the great nation of India! But when the eulogies that went up over that vast country were sounded at the death of their beloved missionary, the words heard were not words of praise for *John Hyde,* but rather for *Praying Hyde,* the name India knew and loved him for, because he had moved that nation Godward on his knees. That's what prayer can do in evangelism.

The Hebridies Revival

It was 1949 in the Hebridies, the windswept islands off the northwest coast of Scotland—a bleak part of the British Isles. But the spirituality of the churches proved more chilling than cold winds off the North Atlantic. The churches were virtually empty, and those members who did attend had very little fervency for Jesus Christ. Many of the churches had not registered a true conversion for some time. Evangelism had virtually dried up.

On the island of Lewis a small handful of men grew deeply burdened and concerned for the spiritual climate of their community. They gathered outside the village in a dirt-floor barn and began to intercede for a real touch of the Spirit of God upon them. They devoted themselves to prayer. Night after night they interceded. At times they would pray into the early hours of the morning. This went on for months. Yet, the heavens seemed as brass. The churches remained in their state of apathy and no one showed concern except the little handful of interceding men.

Then one night, one of the younger men of the praying group stood and said, "Men, this is futile. We have been praying and praying and nothing has happened. Could it be that we, the very ones most concerned for a fresh touch from God, are the very ones standing in His way? God has laid upon my heart a passage of Scripture." He then read Psalm 24:3–6:

> Who may ascend the hill of the LORD?
>   Who may stand in his holy place?
> He who has clean hands and a pure heart,
>   who does not lift up his soul to an idol
>   or swear by what is false.
> He will receive blessing from the LORD
>   and vindication from God his Savior.
> Such is the generation of those who seek him,
>   who seek your face, O God of Jacob (NIV).

As these pungent, penetrating words fell from the lips of the young prayer warrior, the Spirit of God fell upon the group in overwhelming power. They sank to the dirt floor of the barn as they caught a glimpse of the holiness of God, like Isaiah of old (Isa. 6:1–13). Seeing themselves in the light of the holy God, they poured out their heart in broken confession. Then God poured out upon them the spirit of joy. They exalted Christ and thanked God for his cleansing touch upon their lives. When they were able to contain themselves, they made their way back into the village. It was early morning.

As they entered the village, they saw the lights in many of the small homes were on. They also discovered a multitude of people gathered at the police station. Thinking perhaps some tragedy had occurred, they began to inquire. To their utter astonishment they discovered that the very moment the Spirit of God had fallen upon them in the barn, the Holy Spirit had likewise fallen upon virtually the entire community. People were awakened out of their sleep under deep conviction of their need of salvation. They did not know what to do. They got up, dressed, and gathered at the police station, hoping to find someone to tell them how they could find forgiveness and relief in the salvation of Christ.

Before dawn broke on that small community, scores had come to faith in the Lord Jesus. Then the Spirit of God moved throughout all the Hebrides Islands. This revival had its beginning there in the barn on the Island of Lewis when just a few men determined to pray.

A local pastor, after much prayer, invited evangelist Duncan Campbell from Scotland to come and preach. However, Campbell informed the pastor that he was completely booked up for a year, but he said he would be happy to come if he had a cancellation. To the evangelist's surprise, virtually every engagement almost immediately cancelled. He began to discern that the Spirit of God was leading him to the Hebrides. He went and spent a protracted period on the Islands and saw thousands of people evangelized and brought to faith in Jesus Christ. In historical retrospect, we now call this movement the Hebrides Revival. And prayer brought it all about.

America Is Touched

How can Americans forget the impact of the Holy Spirit in our history? Most people know of the First Great Awakening under the ministry of Jonathan

Edwards, George Whitfield, the Tennants, Theodore Frelinghuysen, and a host of others. America was transformed in those days of revival. But then the American Revolutionary War erupted. The moral decay that so often accompanies such an event set in, and the churches found themselves in dire straits.

As Christians longed for God to do a significant work among them, an early Baptist historian, Isaac Backus, along with some twenty other pastors, sent a letter to every minister and church in the newly formed United States. They urged every pastor to set aside the first Monday of each month as a day of prayer for a fresh awakening. And the churches responded. Prayer went up all over the new republic. God heard these prayers, and the Second Great Awakening burst on the scene.

The revival began in New England as had the First Great Awakening. It then spread down the east coast. By this time, the westward movement had begun and settlers were streaming through the Cumberland Gap in eastern Kentucky. Two pastors, James McGready and Barton Stone, were such pioneers. McGready became pastor of the Red River and Gasper River meeting houses in Logan County, Kentucky. Barton Stone took up the pastorate of the Cane Ridge meeting house in Bourbon County in the same state.

In 1800, McGready asked people to come for a four-day protracted meeting to be culminated with the observance of the Lord's Supper. To his amazement, six thousand people arrived. The settlers came in wagons, on horseback, and by every way possible. They brought bed rolls and slept in tents, their wagons, or on the ground. This actually gave birth to the camp meeting movement. Thousands of people, as a consequence, ultimately came to faith in Christ.

Barton Stone was a participant in the Logan County meeting and the next year he called for a similar meeting at the Cane Ridge meeting house in Bourbon County. The astounding thing is the multitude that came. They had to call in the army to help with crowd control. Army documents record that some twenty thousand people arrived. The Cane Ridge meeting house could seat only two or three hundred people at the most. The masses were scattered all over the cane breaks of Bourbon County hearing the gospel.

Thousands were brought to faith in the Lord Jesus Christ as the Second Great Awakening burst on the American frontier. It so vitalized the westward movement with the presence of the Spirit of God that the nation was shaken from one end to the other. It actually wove the so-called "Bible Belt" in the southeastern part of America. Once more God was glorified as thousands were evangelized.

This all began in the prayer of the churches as they sought God, who alone can bring people to faith in the Lord Jesus Christ. From this short historical survey one principle stands as an inescapable reality—there will be little effective evangelism without prayer. Prayer and evangelism are inseparable.

What the Bible Says

This leads to what the Bible has to say about the vital ministry of prayer. Six issues must be addressed:

1. *The biblical mandate for prayer.* Space forbids the multiplied number of biblical passages that mandate prayer. But here are a few of the central passages:

> And I say to you, ask, and it shall be given to you; seek, and you shall find; knock, and it shall be opened to you. For everyone who asks, receives; and he who seeks, finds; and to him who knocks, it shall be opened. Now suppose one of you fathers is asked by

his son for a fish; he will not give him a snake instead
of a fish, will he? Or if he is asked for an egg, he will
not give him a scorpion, will he? If you then, being
evil, know how to give good gifts to your children,
how much more shall your heavenly Father give the
Holy Spirit to those who ask Him? (Luke 11:9–13).

Until now you have asked for nothing in My
name; ask, and you will receive, that your joy may be
made full (John 16:24).

With all prayer and petition pray at all times in the
Spirit, and with this in view, be on the alert with all
perseverance and petition for all the saints (Eph. 6:18).

There can be no doubt that God expects his people
to pray. As emphasized earlier, in one sense of the word,
God, the unlimited one, has limited his activity to the
prayers of his people. This always remains something of
a mystery, but it is nonetheless true. Our Lord Jesus
Christ himself constantly prayed. If it were vital for him
and his ministry, how much more for us! That truth has
been constantly repeated, but it often goes unheeded.
The Bible simply mandates prayer.

2. *The sovereignty of God.* Tension always arises
when we talk about the sovereignty of God. What does it
mean? Does it imply that God has everything, in minute
detail, mapped out so there is no opportunity for anything to change no matter what we do? Are we victims of
an unchangeable fatalism? What do we understand about
the sovereignty of God and how do we see that operating
in the setting and in the context of prayer?

Let it first be said that God is sovereign. Nothing
happens that he does not know or in his sovereign will
he either decrees or permits. He is sovereign and we are
not to question it. God in his sovereignty does decree
some things and they are immutable; they will happen,
regardless.

But God does permit some things to occur that are not necessarily in his perfect will, sin being a classic case in point. Moreover, the Father's will is that none should perish but that all should come to repentance. Nevertheless, many people do perish. The Lord Jesus Christ himself said: "Enter by the narrow gate; for the gate is wide, and the way is broad that leads to destruction, and many are those who enter by it. For the gate is small, and the way is narrow that leads to life, and few are those who find it" (Matt. 7:13–14).

3. *Human freedom.* God has made us for himself and he has graciously endued us with his image. Through Adam and Eve's fall into sin, that image has been bludgeoned. We thus inherit a sinful, perverse nature. Yet, the divine image has not been completely obliterated. We still bear the marks of the divine upon us, one of the central features being our freedom. We have freedom of will. We can choose to do God's will or we can choose not to do God's will. If human freedom is just a superficial non-entity, the whole concept of moral praise and blame falls in utter contradiction. We are free. Yet, at the same time, we realize that God is sovereign. Thus we have to bring these two principles together. Consequently, we face a classic paradox.

From a finite, human, rationalistic perspective, it is impossible to resolve this paradox. One day, a puzzled person came to the great preacher, Charles Haddon Spurgeon, who freely preached the absolute sovereignty of God and the absolute freedom of human beings. He asked the preacher, "How do you reconcile these two ideas?" Spurgeon simply replied, "I do not try to reconcile friends." Spurgeon had it right.

Remember, God is infinite and ultimate; we are limited. Human, limited reason cannot scale the mountain of God's infinite reason. We live in the tension and in the paradox and thank God for his sovereign grace and also for our freedom to choose him.

This is exactly where prayer plays an essential, central role. God wants people saved, and God can save them in his sovereign grace. But we have learned from the Scriptures and from history that prayer plays a vital role in effective evangelism. And here human freedom exerts itself. We can choose to pray or not to pray. We can get before God and intercede for the lost, or we can refuse to do so. But souls depend on it. And the consequence is we are held responsible if we fail to do so. May God give us grace to be a praying people.

4. *An evangelism of integrity.* We must have an evangelism of integrity. Much is going on in the name of evangelism today that brings reproach on the enterprise. We are disturbed by the superficiality, gimmicks, excessive emotionalism, and a thousand other problems we see in some contemporary evangelizing. The result is that many churches today have carnal Christians or those who do not know Jesus Christ. Our Lord spoke to this issue. He told some of the superficial followers of his day: "Many will say to Me on that day, 'Lord, Lord, did we not prophesy in Your name, and in Your name cast out demons, and in Your name perform many miracles?' And then I will declare to them, 'I never knew you; DEPART FROM ME, YOU WHO PRACTICE LAWLESSNESS'" (Matt. 7:22–23). May God save us from engaging in an evangelism that lacks biblical integrity. True evangelism brings about true disciples.

Perhaps we are all guilty to some degree of relying upon our human ingenuity, our abilities, or some other humanistic approach in bringing people to Christ. But prayer can save us from that. Prayer will force us to realize that true conversions come about only by the convicting work of the Holy Spirit and the faithful proclamation of the full gospel of Jesus Christ. People who become genuine disciples come to Christ on the basis of biblical and spiritual principles. Those principles must be fully declared and permeated with prayer.

5. *Evangelism is "kingdom business."* True biblical evangelism centers in the kingdom of God and its extension. The kingdom of God is the central motif in all evangelism. John the Baptist and our Lord himself preached, "Repent, for the kingdom of heaven is at hand" (Matt. 3:2). Jesus Christ was the great revealer/redeemer who offered new life in the kingdom of God. Evangelism is inviting people to leave the kingdom of death and darkness and enter the kingdom of life and light. It takes a person of prayer and insight to recognize the centrality of the kingdom of God in the evangelistic enterprise. May God drive us to our knees until the kingdom shines in all of its eternal glory as we invite people to enter this kingdom.

6. *All for God's glory.* All evangelism culminates in the glory of God. The Westminster Confession states: "The chief end of man is to glorify God and enjoy him forever." That stands true today as always. Paul put it this way: "Whatever you do, do all to the glory of God" (1 Cor. 10:31). There is only one motivation, one goal, one final objective: to bring glory to God. Few will seek God's glory except through much prayer. Prayer is a vital and essential ingredient for an effective evangelism of integrity.

Practical Issues

How can we engage in the kind and quality of prayer that precipitates great movements of God in kingdom extension?

1. *We must have a genuine commitment to pray.* We must commit ourselves to a ministry of intercession. All Christians should have a vibrant, alive, personal prayer

life. In such a commitment the Spirit of God will surely lay on believer's hearts friends, loved ones, acquaintances, and others who do not know the Lord Jesus Christ. We must pray for the lost personally and individually.

2. *Christians should also recognize that they are not in this ministry of prayer alone.* They are part of the body of Christ. The church as a body must engage collectively in prayer. There are many ways that God's people can come together in corporate prayer. The church as a whole can meet for prayer. Prayer partners can be organized. Even if people can only pray together over the telephone, this can be significant. Prayer breakfasts for men and prayer teas for women and special prayer meetings of various sorts can be implemented in the life of the church. Young people and children can be organized to pray. Some churches even have instituted around-the-clock chains of prayer. They intercede continually for needs and especially for those who are lost.

The innovative, thoughtful pastor or leader can devise, under the direction of the Holy Spirit, the kind of programming that will lead to an effective prayer life for the entire church. Prayer ministries are multiplying across the land, and it is one of the signs of great things in the future.

Some Personal Prayer Principles

A few words are appropriate concerning praying itself. First, prayer must always be directed to the praise and glory of God. Further, specific individuals and needs should be prayed for. So often our prayers sound so generalized and non-specific that they really say very little. Definite requests and specific people should be objects of intercession. And it must never be forgotten that a believer is to pray from a pure heart with all of his or her sins confessed up to the moment. This results in walking in the Spirit. That forms a key ingredient—praying in the

Spirit. The New Testament makes the principle abundantly clear (Eph. 6:18).

Finally, all prayers must be prayed in the name of Jesus Christ. He is our righteousness; he is our justification; he is our sanctification; he is our life. We have no right to stand before the throne of grace, apart from the righteousness of Christ. To pray "in Jesus' name" is not a pious platitude that we append to our prayers. It is recognizing our complete inadequacy, but the complete adequacy of Jesus Christ. Therefore, we pray in his name, knowing that God will hear when we come to him through his Son.

Presence in Evangelism

I was attending a summer session at Augustana College in Rock Island, Illinois, between my graduation from high school and my induction into the Air Force. I had been in the enlisted reserve of the air cadet program for some time. I knew my call to active duty would not arrive until I could squeeze in a summer session, so off to Augustana I went. I enrolled in this particular college because they had a course in advanced mathematics and physics that I thought would suit me well for a military air career. When I arrived on campus, I discovered that it was a church-related school—a fine small college sponsored by the Augustana Synod of the Lutheran Church in America.

The air cadets who had already been inducted had filled the men's dormitory, so we who were still civilians were housed in what they called the seminary dormitory. A small Lutheran theological seminary was attached to Augustana College at that time. I did not even know what a seminary was. But when I arrived in my room in the dormitory with one of my good friends from my hometown in northern Illinois, we met some men who were, to say the least, very different from us.

One of the men I met was Bob Pearson. He failed to live up to my expectations of what a sharp young guy ought to be. He didn't go where I went, didn't do what I did, didn't think like I thought, and he certainly didn't have the ambitions I had. Yet, at the same time, there was something so incredibly winsome about his lifestyle. I couldn't put my finger on it. There was an attractiveness and something of a "presence" about him that really grabbed my attention. I found out that he was studying for the Lutheran ministry. I was not irreligious. I had been a member of the church in my hometown for some years and attended every Sunday. Yet, for all practical purposes, church life was meaningless to me. But when I met Bob Pearson, I began to sense something that struck a deep responsive chord in me.

My life at that time was wrapped up in two things: music and flying. I could not remember when I did not want to be a pilot, and I had been playing in various musical groups around my hometown area. But when I met Bob Pearson I began to question certain things about life.

One day Bob asked me if I ever read the Bible. To be frank, never once in my life had I picked up the Bible seriously to see what God had to say to me. But I did start to read the Scriptures, and strange things began to take place. I began to pray with some seriousness rather than just asking God to help me here and there in a selfish manner. Those "strange things" deepened in my life.

I found out that Bob was a "born-again" Christian. Although that term meant very little to me at that time, God was beginning to do a deep work of conviction— and finally conversion—in my life.

I can remember very little of what Bob Pearson said to me about the Christian faith. I am sure that he did share the essence of the gospel with me, but I cannot recall it. But it was the incredible "presence" of his life that impressed me.

To make an intriguing tale of a spiritual journey short, I came to faith in the Lord Jesus Christ. My life was radically altered. Everything changed. Many of my friends and family were aghast. Life would never be the same; I had entered the kingdom.

If there were a human instrument that became the key person in my conversion, it was that Lutheran ministerial student, Bob Pearson. It was not only what he said; it was the combination of his life yielded to Jesus Christ and his real concern for me. Simply put, he was there; he was a presence of Christ for me. Presence and evangelism, like prayer and evangelism, are inseparable. Someone must "be there."

Being There

One of the great glories—and responsibilities—of the Christian witness is to "be there." Simply put, no one witnesses for Christ, if no one personifies and proclaims the gospel. If believers fail in this task and do not relate to people in order to impact them for Christ, what will happen? We cannot retreat into God's sovereignty and avoid our responsibility. We must be there. We must relate to unbelievers in a myriad of ways and share Christ. I wonder what my lot would be if Bob Pearson had not shared Christ with me. If the church had not sent missionaries worldwide, what would the world be like? Jesus said, "You shall be My witnesses" (Acts 1:8), and that is all there is to it.

Of course, the Bible makes it clear that the entire church is to engage in evangelism: individually and collectively as the body of Christ. And it is also clear that there are a multitude of ways in which the evangelistic enterprise, the global declaration of the kingdom, is to be carried out. We must find every way possible to be there for people who need Christ, regardless of who they are or where they are. World evangelism hangs in the balance—eternal souls hang in the balance.

But being there in itself is not enough. We must "be something" while "being there."

The Necessity of "Being Something"

All of us project an image. People see us and draw conclusions by the presence that we exude in our lifestyle. It is vital that we "be something" that exemplifies the Lord Jesus Christ. Our presence when we evangelize or do any service in Christ's Name should speak of him as loudly and clearly as our words and works. Presence is as essential to effective communication of the message of Christ as our words.

What is this "something" that we ought to be? We are to personify the spirituality of the Lord Jesus Christ. This we all know quite well, but it seems that often it is not as central in the thinking of the church as it ought to be. We can be so involved in "our ministry" that we fail to recognize that if our lives do not speak of Jesus Christ, then all of this ministry may fall upon deaf ears and unresponsive lives.

Thus, genuine spirituality becomes the goal. We are to have our eyes fixed on that which is eternal and not temporal as we give ourselves to what has lasting consequences. We are to learn what it means to abide in Christ and walk in dynamic fellowship with Jesus and with our fellows. We must have the aura of Jesus Christ. This is the "something" that causes our "presence" to exude the life of Jesus Christ.

A Clarification

Our lives are not, strictly speaking, an *imitation* of Jesus Christ. We can attempt to emulate him and try to mold ourselves into his image endlessly, and find ourselves finally frustrated and failing. Rather, we should be an *embodiment* of Jesus Christ. It is not so much our "living for the Lord"; it is Christ living his life through us. That is the New Testament principle. That is what Paul was saying in Galatians 2:20: "I have been crucified with Christ; and it is no longer I who live, but Christ lives in me; and the life which I now live in the flesh I live by faith in the Son of God, who loved me, and delivered Himself up for me."

To learn that principle is not always easy. We like to "whip our own lives into shape." But God says that we are simply to rest in Christ by faith and let him live his life through us. We are saved by grace through faith; we are also sanctified by grace through faith. We should not, after we have received salvation by grace, then thrust ourselves under the Law. It is faith all the way.

The presence that we seek is the presence of Jesus Christ within us as by faith we take our position in Christ as crucified with him so that he might now live through us (Rom. 6:1–12). He becomes the One who makes the impact for himself to the glory of God and the salvation of souls.

Implications

This basic principle implies many important truths relative to self discipline.

1. *Our lives must be absolutely abandoned to the lordship of Jesus Christ.* We call him Lord; we must make him Lord in our daily lives. Our will becomes his will. Paul caught the spirit of that when he said in Romans 12:1–2: "I urge you therefore, brethren, by the

mercies of God, to present your bodies a living and holy sacrifice, acceptable to God, which is your spiritual service of worship. And do not be conformed to this world, but be transformed by the renewing of your mind, that you may prove what the will of God is, that which is good and acceptable and perfect."

Above all, God wants our unequivocal obedience. A classic biblical illustration of this principle is found in the encounter between King Saul and the prophet Samuel. As Saul came back from the battle with the Amelakites, he was rejoicing that God had given him a great victory. The prophet Samuel went out to meet him. The King said to the prophet as he approached, "Blessed are you of the LORD! I have carried out the command of the LORD" (1 Sam. 15:13).

Then from the other side of the camp, there came the lowing of cattle and the bleating of sheep. The old prophet said, "What then is this bleating of the sheep in my ears, and the lowing of the oxen which I hear?" (1 Sam. 15:14).

Saul was on the spot. Samuel had given him explicit instructions that everything that breathed should be obliterated, and this meant the cattle and sheep. So Saul attempted to escape the sting of the prophet's rebuke by saying, "The people spared the best of the sheep and oxen, to sacrifice to the LORD" (1 Sam. 15:15). Perhaps he thought that he could squirm out of his predicament by blaming the people or "getting religious."

The prophet then spoke a word that should ring in the heart of every true believer in Jesus Christ. Samuel said, "To obey is better than sacrifice, and to hearken than the fat of rams" (1 Sam. 15:22 KJV). God demands our obedience. He will never be able to live his life out through us if we are not yielded and obedient to him.

2. *A disciple who exudes the presence of Christ is a disciplined person.* He is disciplined in prayer, disciplined in being found in the Scriptures, disciplined in keeping one's heart thoroughly right with God through the cleansing blood of Christ; disciplined in walking in the fullness of the Holy Spirit; disciplined in walking in fellowship with Jesus Christ. There will be no "presence" if there is no discipline.

3. *A believer must have a serving life.* God saves us to serve him. There remains much to do in the kingdom of Christ. Our Lord has given us the privilege and responsibility of being "God's fellow workers" (1 Cor. 3:9). To think that the great, infinite, ultimate, omnipotent, omniscient, holy God of the universe, the creator and sustainer of all life, invites us to engage in kingdom service with him is incredible. Yet, that is our privilege. Moreover, he bestows the ministering "gifts of the Spirit" on us so we can effectively serve him. If the world does not see us faithfully serving our Lord, exercising our "gift," there will be little in our presence that will impress them. We must "be filled with the Spirit" (Eph. 5:18).

4. *A believer must have a compassionate life.* If anything exemplified our Lord, it was his unreserved and unfettered love. Jesus had compassion for all people. How the world longs to see this compassion in a believer's life. This is why Paul told the Romans, "The love of God has been poured out within our hearts through the Holy Spirit who was given to us" (Rom. 5:5).

By human ingenuity we can never attain to the *agape* love of God. But God's quality of love is given to us by the Holy Spirit. That is why Paul wrote the Galatians, "The fruit of the Spirit is love" (Gal. 5:22). We love because Jesus loves in us and through us. By his Holy Spirit he expresses himself in compassion in meeting the

needs of people through believers who have an understanding, loving spirit and a graciousness that Jesus
exemplified in all of his interpersonal relationships.
These are the things that make us "something" that the
world wants to see, because it projects the very presence
of the living Christ.

Presence Demands Sharing

How easy it is to claim that as long as we are living
a godly Christian life, meeting needs, etc., this is all God
requires. This is not true: we are to speak. Jesus Christ
personified in his incarnation all that God is. No one
could question any aspect of his life or service. He was
God ministering among us. The Presence was there in all
fullness. Yet, Jesus constantly taught and spoke, urged
people and pleaded with them to come to him. He threw
out His gracious loving invitation time and time again:
"Come to Me, all who are weary and heavy-laden, and I
will give you rest. Take My yoke upon you, and learn
from Me . . . and YOU SHALL FIND REST FOR YOUR SOULS"
(Matt. 11:28–29). The presence in evangelism is essential, but the communication of the gospel is vital as well.

One other caution is mandatory. In the West, especially in America, we tend to see our spiritual experience
in the "rugged individualism" motif. We are so tuned in
on our own individualism that we sometimes forget that
we are one among many. We are simply one member in
the whole body of Christ. And God works primarily
through the entire body. This is why the Lord Jesus
Christ said, "Upon this rock" (namely, Peter's confession) that he would "build My church" (Matt. 16:18).

The entire church is essential in the concept of presence in evangelism as well as individual believers. When
the whole body of Christ comes together, a dynamic
emerges and an entity forms that is more than the sum of
all the parts. When church members are brought

together in the Spirit and function as they were designed to function, they become something more than just scattered individuals. This implies several truths.

First, individuals must see themselves as members of the body and subservient to the body. We live in the body, to serve the body, that the body then in turn, as a whole, may serve and glorify Jesus Christ.

We also draw upon one another's sustenance. I cannot live a Christian life totally by myself. We must see ourselves as a member of the body, mutually dependent upon one another. Furthermore, the body can do far more than the individuals who make it up can do. This has been implied above, but it needs strong emphasis. The church must be the church in the full biblical sense of the word.

Finally, the church serves as the bride of Christ. Believers are so united to him that as a bride and her groom are made one, so Christ and the church are inseparable. This does not mean we lose our individual distinctiveness. It does mean, however, that we are so united in fellowship that we personify the very body of Christ, which means his presence. Therefore, the church as a whole plays an essential role in evangelism.

In the light of all these principles, it is clear that to be a true evangelist we are to be present to bring Christ to the world. In addition, the living Christ must live through us and radiate from us in such a way that the world is gripped by his presence. Apart from this, there will be little effective winning of the lost.

Conclusion

To sum the matter up, we must be there and we must be there on our knees. Presence and prayer, prayer and presence—exemplifying and shining forth and communicating Jesus Christ in a life of dedication, love, commitment, and prayer. This is evangelism. May God drive us to our knees and may we find ourselves in such an intimate walk with Jesus Christ that his presence is lived out through us. Then as we share his great Good News, we will see many people won to saving faith in our Lord Jesus Christ, the kingdom extended, and our gracious God glorified.

Chapter 4

Evangelism and Personal Holiness
Henry T. Blackaby

THE VERY HEART OF THE LIFE AND MINISTRY OF JESUS (IN fact, the heart of the Father, also) is seen clearly in Jesus' prayer in John 17. The entire prayer is immersed in the holiness of God that is reflected in the life of Jesus and his activity with his disciples. Here, in this prayer, he reveals the vital connection between holiness and evangelism:

> Sanctify them by Your truth. Your word is truth.
> As You sent Me into the world, I also have sent them into the world. And for their sakes I sanctify Myself, that they also may be sanctified by the truth . . . . that they also may be one in Us, that the world may believe that You sent Me. . . . that they may be made perfect in one, and that the world may know that You have sent Me, and have loved them as You have loved Me (John 17:17–19, 21, 23 NKJV).

Holiness Is the Work of God

Jesus prayed to his Father that he would sanctify the disciples. The Amplified Bible gives clarity to what he meant: "Sanctify them—purify, consecrate, separate them for Yourself, make them holy" (John 17:17 Amplified Bible).

Holiness is the work of God that prepares a servant of God, for God to work mightily through him to redeem a lost world. God himself must separate his servants for himself. In doing so, he must make us holy and he must

86

purify us. According to Jesus in this prayer, the Father will do this by the Truth, that is, by his Word.

The disciples had to be immersed in God's Word, which the Father would use to separate them, consecrate them, and make them holy for himself. All through Jesus' ministry, he took what he heard from the Father, and made it known to the disciples (John 15:15). And, as Jesus shared the Father's Word to them, the Spirit of God was revealing to them all the Father wanted them to know (Matt. 16:17; John 16:12–15).

With each word from God, the disciples were drawn closer to Christ (John 6:44–45, 65). They were made more available for God to accomplish his work through them, for the sake of a lost world. One of the clearest and simplest pictures of the profound impact God's Word (Truth) had on the evangelism of the disciples is found in Luke 24. In this text Jesus "opened the Scriptures" (Luke 24:32 NKJV), and "He opened their understanding, that they might comprehend the Scriptures" (Luke 24:45 NKJV). This was Jesus' final preparation of the disciples for global evangelism. Truth, i.e., God's Word, cleanses and purifies God's people (Eph. 5:26) so God can work mightily through them in a lost world. But this is the work of God, in the hearts and lives of his people.

In the Old Testament, every time a servant of God heard a word from God, he was face-to-face with the heart, mind, and will of God. This encounter would draw them into the activity of God—allowing God's heart of redemption for a lost world to be conveyed to his servant. Over and over again, we read: "The Word of the Lord came to . . ." When God spoke, the servant of God was more and more separated unto God, and his mighty purpose in and through them.

This was true of Abraham, Moses, David, Jeremiah, Isaiah, Amos, the disciples, and the apostle Paul. Unless God shares his Word (Truth) with a person, they will never be separated to God. And when he does share the Truth (his Word), it immediately has a deep, cleansing, purifying, and separating effect on the one receiving it. Then they are his, cleansed to fulfill his redemptive purposes in the world.

Apart from the Word of God, there will be very little holiness, and therefore very little evangelism. This has been eminently true in my own life and the lives of the people God gave me to pastor. The more the Word of God was shared with the people of God, in the power of the Holy Spirit, the more the people of God would become involved personally and as a church in evangelism.

The Word of God pierces to the very heart of a child of God (Heb. 4:12), and draws him or her into the will of God redemptively. It is not human reasoning, or the needs of the lost, but the Word of God that draws God's people and separates them unto God. It is a cleansed and pure life that can pray (James 5:16b; Ps. 24:3–5), and thus bring about the salvation of multitudes of lost people.

Prayer is not an additive to the Christian's life, *prayer is his life*. Holiness is crucial to an effective life of prayer, and thus to effective evangelism. Such a life of prayer is the work of God in the life of the believer.

Highway to Holiness[1]

A call to the cross is a call to holiness and a rejection to sin. Scripture clearly demonstrates that holiness is greatly affected by a person's attitude toward personal sin. In 1 Peter 1:15–16 believers are called to be holy as God is holy. What a call, what a responsibility, what a demand of discipleship! Yet, without a proper attitude toward personal sin, the holy, set-apart lifestyle believers are called to is only a dream.

I have begun to sense with increasing intensity that the highway over which God comes is a highway to holiness. Our generation has little if any reference point in experiencing revival and almost no reference point to experience the holiness of God.

You cannot talk about the holiness of God without at the same time having the refiner's fire touch every corner of your life and leave it absolutely exposed to him. When you read the Word of God, it is like a hammer. The Word of God is like a blaze—everything in your heart and life is exposed. The holy God does not play games. But if our hearts are hard, we will be able to walk into God's presence with minds filled with videos and television. It will not concern us—no grief, no sorrow, no turning it off.

The psalmist asks, "Who may stand in His holy place?" (Ps. 24:3 NKJV). James 5:16 says it is the very active prayer of a righteous man that is powerful. I believe one of our greatest dangers is that we have it all in our head, but it is not in our heart. Do you know how you can tell if it has touched your heart? Jesus said it is spiritually impossible to have your heart in one condition and the fruit of your life in another. If we can say that we believe the things of the Word of God and say that they are in our hearts but see no evidence of the implementing of those truths, then the Scripture has been in our heads but has never hit our hearts.

I have said, "Lord, I believe correctly." God replied, "That is true, but it is still in your head. Henry, you will know when the truth has gone from your head to your heart. When there is a change in your life, that change is obvious to everyone else. It is not in your heart until it is bearing fruit in your life. When it bears fruit in your life, then it will bear fruit in the world around you."

We have conditioned ourselves to think that, once we believe correctly and fill our heads with truth and thought, these truths are automatically implemented in our lives. I ask many pastors, "Do you believe in prayer?" They say, "Absolutely." Then I ask, "Do you pray?" They reply, "Well, that has been the weak point in my life."

There is your problem: *You do not believe in prayer!* You do not believe in a God who issues a summons to come before him. Has God ever summoned you into his holy presence? If so, did you come into his presence? Did you feel that God had transformed you with his Word? Did this so change your heart that you wondered what in the world had happened to you? That is when the truth from the mouth of God moves from your head to your heart. Jesus said what you see coming out of a person is indicative of that person's heart. We keep walking in the truth.

Can you examine James 5:16–20 and say, "Lord, would you make certain that I am righteous, that I have holiness as a pattern in my life, so that I can speak for you? Have you dealt with my life radically about sin and holiness? When I stand in your holy place, are my ears open and my heart tender before you? Is sin there? Do my eyes understand what you are doing? Then I can go from that moment knowing there is a word from the Lord and that you will respond. Then the people will know that you are God and that at least one person is serving you and listening to your Word." When you prayed like this, what was God's response?

That is the point at which I want us to be accountable. Throughout Scripture there is a highway over which God moves and over which his people travel, especially when God brings to our minds what he wants us to do in praying. And when we do it, God initiates holiness. When the life is clean to receive it, then we will respond.

John the Baptist preached: "Prepare the way of the LORD; make His paths straight" (Luke 3:4 NKJV). That highway is a highway of holiness. God uses a clean mind, a clean heart, and a pure heart. "Blessed are the pure in heart, For they shall see God" (Matt. 5:8 NKJV). This is the kind of walk that God uses as a highway on which he will move mightily in revival.

God says, "You will know it is in your heart when you have met the criteria of holiness. Then I will start to move in mighty power in your life, your church, and out to the ends of the earth."

Holiness says that God is holy, and the Scriptures give us abundant evidence of the nature of that holiness. Esau "for one morsel of food sold his birthright. For you know that afterward, when he wanted to inherit the blessing, he was rejected, for he found no place for repentance, though he sought it diligently with tears" (Heb. 12:16–17 NKJV). That is connected with the holiness of God.

The Scripture says we need to pursue holiness. We must let the full measure of the nature of God become the pattern of our character. We need to let him form in us the full measure of the righteousness of Christ. We need to let him take every part of our minds and our hearts and keep them holy unto himself.

Does the holiness of God overwhelm you? Do you find yourself trembling when God speaks? The other day, I turned in the Word. When I read it, a trembling came over my life from top to bottom. I found myself spontaneously weeping. I said, "O God! Suddenly you have made me aware of how holy you are and how sinful I am.

How much is at stake when I handle the sacred things! When I take the Bible, how much of eternity hangs in the balance! When I speak with people, how much you have in your heart! Lord, I am totally unworthy of that! O God, if this is true, never let me speak again in your name! Your holiness and my sinfulness are far apart!"

I laid there with no strength. I said, "O God, how could I possibly speak?" He said, "I will do in you what I did in Isaiah. He had no right to speak. I took coals and put them on his lips. You will know when I have done that." Then I said, "O Lord, hold me accountable for holiness. Lord, do not let me merely talk about it. Do not let me just read about it. You say it is the highway of holiness that will bring the people back to you. The people will rejoice, and they will sing."

No one can stand before God without clean hands and a clean heart. The pure in heart will see God. May the Spirit of God teach us to pray, "O God, help me to see you," but only when we also pray, "O God, give me the conditions of heart that are prerequisite to seeing you. I cannot ask you to do a work in me unless I also ask you to do a work in my heart and in my mind and in my will." Without the prerequisite, this prayer is absolute foolishness.

Why have we cried to the Lord and seen so little? Could God be waiting for his servants to walk over the highway of holiness? The unclean will not walk on it. Others will—those whom the Lord has ransomed and redeemed from sin, and dressed in his righteousness, now free in heart and mind before him.

Holiness Is for Evangelism

In Jesus' prayer (John 17:18), he connected holiness and evangelism. Having asked the Father, he affirmed to the Father, "As You sent Me into the world, I also have sent them into the world." Jesus told the disciples that "the Son of Man has come to seek and to save that which was lost" (Luke 19:10 NKJV). Since this was his mission, it would now be the mission of his disciples— not in the uniqueness of the cross, but sharing his cross (suffering), for the redemption of the world.

Later, in John 20:21, Jesus, in his resurrection appearance with the disciples, asserted: "'As the Father has sent Me, I also send you'" (NKJV). The Father had set his Son apart for the redemption of the world, and sent him (John 3:16), and now Jesus affirmed to the disciples that he had set them apart, and was sending them into the world to "preach the gospel to every creature" (Mark 16:15 NKJV).

It is incredibly important to remember that the call to salvation is at the same time a call to be on mission with God redemptively in our world. *Holiness is for evangelism!* The apostle Paul knew this, at the moment of his conversion. He was told *immediately,* "I am Jesus . . . I have appeared to you for this purpose, to make you a minister and a witness . . . to open their eyes, in order to turn them from darkness to light, and from the power of Satan to God, that they may receive forgiveness of sins and an inheritance among those who are sanctified by faith in Me" (Acts 26:15–16, 18 NKJV).

Paul, standing before King Agripa, confirmed this: "I was not disobedient to the heavenly vision, but declared . . . that they should repent, turn to God, and do works befitting repentance" (Acts 26:19–20 NKJV).

The Effect of Personal Holiness on the People of God

Jesus, knowing his own obedient relationship with the Father would dramatically affect the disciples in their obedience to the Father's assignment in the world, affirmed: "And for their sakes I sanctify Myself, that they also may be sanctified by the truth" (John 17:19 NKJV).

Jesus was well aware that his holiness (his pure walk with the Father in unbroken relationship, love, and obedience) would dramatically affect each of the disciples. He would always be the supreme pattern for every disciple to follow. His initial invitation was, "Follow Me, and I will make you fishers of men" (Matt. 4:19 NKJV), and "Do not be afraid. From now on you will catch men" (Luke 5:10 NKJV). *Set apart for God!* That was supremely the life of Jesus, and because of his life before the disciples, they, too, would be forever set apart for God.

This has always been God's pattern. First, Jesus! Then us! Paul knew this, and was keenly aware that his life of holiness and separation to God would affect those around him. He was able to encourage others, saying, "Pattern yourselves after me [follow my example], as I imitate and follow Christ (the Messiah)" (1 Cor. 11:1 Amplified Bible). Just as Jesus taught, and lived out before his disciples all he taught, so did the apostle Paul.

There is a leavening effect of one life touching another life, and that life touching yet another. Holiness in one encourages and develops holiness in others nearby. This can be seen in and through Peter's personal response to Jesus' invitation in Luke 5. In this text, Peter responded to Christ's invitation to cast the net once again in the same location in faith and obedience. He let down his fishing nets. The amazing catch of fish convinced Peter not only of who Jesus was but also convinced him to follow Jesus.

Notice that Peter's first verbal response to Christ's command related directly to holiness: "Depart from me, for I am a sinful man, O Lord!" (Luke 5:8 NKJV). Notice also that Jesus called him to follow him (i.e., let God set him apart for his use). Thus, when Peter denied self, took up a cross, and followed Jesus, it had an extraordinary effect on Peter's closest family and friends. The Scriptures record, significantly: "For he and all who were with him were astonished . . . so also were James and John. . . . So when they had brought their boats to land, they forsook all and followed Him" (Luke 5:9–11 NKJV).

Therefore, Scripture demonstrates that personal holiness not only affects the person set apart by God; it also affects all those close to that person for evangelism. Peter, James, and John together became the closest friends of Jesus for the rest of his ministry. Their lives continued to affect the reaching of the lost multitudes to the end of each of their lives. They, along with others, "turned the world upside down" (Acts 17:6 NKJV).

Lives, truly separated to God, cleansed from sin, and walking in holiness with the Lord, are awesome instruments of evangelism in their world. The Holy Spirit fills, uses, and empowers for witness those who walk in holiness. The writer of Hebrews states it this way: "Pursue . . . holiness, without which no one will see the Lord" (Heb. 12:14 NKJV). James said, "Draw near to God and He will draw near to you" (James 4:8 NKJV).

Holiness has always been God's condition for his presence working in and through his people. God instructed King Asa with this word: "The LORD is with you while you are with Him. If you seek Him, He will be found by you; but if you forsake Him, He will forsake you" (2 Chron. 15:2 NKJV).

In these days, when sin runs rampant in both our nation and among the people of God, we must remind God's people that evangelism, *effective* and *powerful* evangelism, waits on the holiness of God's people. The multitudes of lost and hell-bound people wait on the holiness of God's people. It is only through God's people, sanctified by the Truth, in the hands of the heavenly Father, that the prayer and promise of Jesus will be fulfilled in his high priestly prayer:

> Sanctify them by Your truth. Your word is truth.
> As You sent Me into the world, I also have sent them
> into the world. And for their sakes I sanctify Myself,
> that they also may be sanctified by the truth . . . that
> the world may believe that You sent Me (John
> 17:17–19, 21 NKJV).

Chapter 5

Revival/Spiritual Awakening and Incarnational Evangelism

Alvin L. Reid

"I BELIEVE THAT THE WORLD IS UPON THE THRESHOLD of a great religious revival, and I pray that I may be allowed to help bring this about. I beseech all those who confess Christ to ask Him today, upon their knees, if He has not some work for them to do now. He will lead them all as He has led us. He will make them pillars of smoke by day and pillars of fire by night to guide all men to Him."[1]

Evan Roberts spoke these words during the Welsh Revival of 1904–1905. Roberts passionately shared the Good News of Jesus Christ and the message of revival. "I felt ablaze with a desire to go the length and breadth of Wales to tell of the savior," he exclaimed on another occasion, "and had that been possible, I was willing to *pay God for doing so.*"[2] Evan Roberts epitomized the passion of a man consumed by the fire of God in revival. He had a vision for one hundred thousand people to be saved in Wales, and within six months this number was in fact converted.

Partnering Revival and Evangelism

Recently I heard Sterling Huston of the Billy Graham Evangelistic Association comment on a twofold need in our day: effective *evangelism,* and a great *awakening.*

Huston recognized the vital link between the two. The relationship between revival or awakening[3] and evangelism is evident in Scripture. In the Book of Acts, when the lives of the early Christians were transformed by the outpouring of the Spirit at Pentecost, the unbelieving world marveled at the changed lives of Christians even as they heard the clear preaching of the gospel. Even the religious leaders could not deny the impact Christ made (Acts 4:13). At one point Luke records that people outside the church were filled with wonder and awe (Acts 2:43, 47).

Even as we see the critical relationship between revival and evangelism, we must remember the two are not synonymous. Genuine revival comes when God touches the hearts of believers, causing brokenness for sin, repentance, and a new sense of the presence of God, allowing for unusual effectiveness in ministry. In short, revival brings the church back to the wonder and awe of God. Evangelism is the communication of the gospel to lost people. Here is the critical point: the most effective evangelism historically has occurred in times of great revival.[4]

Perhaps the greatest impact our culture has had on the American church is that it has robbed us of a sense of wonder toward God. In times past, when God has moved in mighty awakening, the wonder, the majesty, the sovereignty of God has been so real that not only was the church revived, but the lost world was amazed as well. Thus, one of the marks of great awakenings is a huge influx of new converts.

We live in a day marked by a growing awareness of the need for a sweeping, national revival in America. Across the globe, record numbers of conversions are being reported, but in the United States the church's impact is far from what it could be. But in increasing numbers believers are developing a hunger, a yearning for the Lord God to "rend the heavens and come down" (Isa. 64:1).

Signs indicate a growing possibility for a great awakening. The Promise Keepers movement has raised the spiritual thermostat in the lives of thousands of men. As many as two million people have studied the *Experiencing God* materials, which describe how a believer can encounter God in a continuous, life-changing way. Several leaders have issued calls to prayer for national revival. Bill Bright, founder of Campus Crusade for Christ, International, has led in hosting an annual three-day conference on fasting and prayer. This emphasis grew out of Bright's own forty-day fast in 1994 for spiritual awakening.

A North American Convocation on Revival met in 1995 and 1996 to emphasize the need for, and a description of, biblical revival. Pastor's Prayer Summits beginning in Oregon and spreading across the nation have changed the lives of scores of church leaders. At the annual meeting of the Southern Baptist Convention in 1996, keynote speaker Ronnie Floyd called upon the Southern Baptist Convention to set apart a special time in the fall for fasting and preaching on revival. On October 30, 1996, thousands of Southern Baptists set aside a day of fasting and prayer. Also, on October 4, 1997, the largest-ever gathering of evangelical believers in America met at the Washington, D.C. "Stand in the Gap" day of prayer and repentance for revival.

One of the most encouraging signs of revival began in January of 1995 when revival came to the Coggin Avenue Baptist Church in Brownwood, Texas. The revival which began there spread to Howard Payne University and then to campuses and churches across the nation.[5] The movement has been marked by prayer, spread by testimony, and guided by clear, biblical preaching. The church witnessed more conversions in the months following the revival's genesis than at any other time in its history.

The growing burden for revival is quickened by an understanding of past awakenings. At times over the centuries God has shaken his church in mighty revival. The First and Second Great Awakenings and the Layman's Prayer Revival of 1857–59 are examples of such movements. Studying the activity of God in the past is awe-inspiring. Entire cities were gripped by the hand of God. Multitudes were converted, and society was changed.

Personal Soul-Winning and Revival

Across the past four centuries, God has occasionally poured out his Spirit in a marvelous way upon his church in spiritual awakening. Many have read about the First Great Awakening—of men like John Wesley, George Whitefield, or Jonathan Edwards. However, one of the more overlooked aspects of these leaders is their commitment to personal soul-winning.[6] A burden for revival exhibits itself not in introverted, spiritual navel-gazing, but in an outward focus to fulfill the Great Commission. And, the evangelism that results from awakening is not centered on a method, but on a life consumed by God. A hunger for awakening should not supersede a passion for fulfilling the Great Commission.

To state it succinctly, my conviction is that the key to reaching the present generation is a return to an awe toward God, and this awe can best be seen in the lives of a revived people.

Key leaders in historical awakenings were people whose passion for God was expressed in abundant zeal for personal evangelism. We can learn from these people, for there is a key linkage biblically between who we *are*, reflecting a passion for God in our lives, and what we *do* to fulfill the Great Commission. Delos Miles has well noted that evangelism is actually three dimensional. He explained his concept:

> [Evangelism] is being, doing, and telling the gospel. That *being* corresponds to what the Bible calls *koinonia,* the *doing* to the biblical *diakonia,* and the *telling* to the biblical *kerygma.* What we are, along with our deeds and our words, reveal the three faces of evangelism.[7]

Keeping the three dimensions of evangelism in proper harmony helps to facilitate effective, biblical revival. Those touched by great revival were more likely to demonstrate such a balance. In times when the Spirit of God is hindered from free reign in the church, evangelism may still take place. But it is often a malnourished form of evangelism which underachieves for the glory of God. Some churches effectively teach their people to tell the gospel, to the negligence of living and acting out the implications of the message we share. But a life transformed by the power of God in true revival breeds believers who share verbally, in how they act, and in the very life they live. *That* is effective evangelism!

True revival always leads to a deep commitment to evangelism and a concomitant effectiveness in reaping a gospel harvest. As we begin the twenty-first century, we must see the need more than ever to live passionately for God; this passion will be reflected in our soul-winning. What can we glean from the lives of those transformed in great awakening?

Passion for God

Often I am asked why most American Christians do not actively witness. There are many reasons—fear of failure, fear of rejection, theological compromise, carnality, a lack of commitment to the gospel in the church at large, to name only a few. But I am convinced that many of these are symptoms rather than the root problem. The root cause lies in a misunderstanding in our day of the essential nature of the Christian faith. For some, Christianity is a simple system of dogma. Make no mistake: doctrine is critical, particularly in our pluralistic world which sees tolerance as a virtue and conviction as a vice. But an emphasis on doctrine apart from devotion to God leads to dead orthodoxy.

For others, Christianity is an experience. Again, this is true, because the Christian faith is based on a personal relationship with God through Christ. Still, an over-emphasis on experience too often leads to subjective interpretations of Scripture and ultimately to heresy.

We must maintain a proper balance. *Christianity is a life-changing relationship with Christ guided by the unchanging teaching of the Bible.* Why then do most Christians fail to witness? To put it simply, the reason most Christians do not witness is because they have been changed by the power of the Gospel, but they've gotten over it! That was the problem of the church at Ephesus (Rev. 2). What a great church, birthed at the height of the Spirit's work in the first century. But by the end of that century the church had lost its passion for Jesus; it had abandoned its first love. What is the key to linking our life (demonstration) with our lips (explanation) in communicating the gospel? The key is a *passion for God.*

When revival grips a person, a church, a region, or a nation, a renewed passion for God results. The leaders of the great awakenings were committed soul-winners, not because of a tool or technique, but because they had personally experienced a life-changing personal revival which brought them kneeling at the foot of the cross and standing to preach the Word of God. For them,

Christianity was not a Sunday-only, part-time commitment. Instead of a pastime, it was a passion!

Listen to Theodore Frelinghuysen, the Dutch Reformed pastor in the First Great Awakening criticized for his ministry of personal evangelism and his emphasis on biblical preaching. His response to his critics demonstrates his passion for God: "I would rather die a thousand deaths than not preach the truth."[8] John Wesley once said that he would take one hundred men who feared only God and hated only sin, and with them he could set up the kingdom of God on earth. He understood the role of passion for God.

In reading the biographies of men of God used in revival: Wesley, Whitefield, Edwards, Finney, Nettleton, Moody, and others, one quickly recognizes they differed in significant ways. A common thread remains: leaders in revival have been deeply *passionate* about the Lord. Their passion did not lead them to a stale detachment from the real world; rather, it led them to confront their culture with the life-giving gospel.

Jonathan Edwards confronted the town of Northampton, Massachusetts: socially by challenging their negligence of the Sabbath and "company keeping," and theologically by preaching a series on justification by faith. A mighty revival resulted, a revival that saw a total transformation of the town in the span of one year.

A genuine hunger for God produces an apostle Paul, a Stephen, a Moses. It creates believers who not only know *about* God, but they *know* Him. And they not only *know* him; they are passionate about *making him known*. Witness the circuit-riding preachers in the Second Great Awakening. Half of them died by age thirty-three because the task was so vigorous.

How can a believer develop a passion for God that will lead to a passion for evangelism, one might ask.

Here are suggestions gleaned from examining the lives of revival leaders.

1. *Make much of the wonder of your personal salvation.* One of the things I say to my students about a commitment to evangelism is that your *soteriology* will determine your *evangelism.* So many who have been catalysts in revival which led to countless conversions had for themselves a conversion experience they never forgot, which birthed a continuous passion for God.

Peter Cartwright, (1785–1872), circuit rider in the Second Great Awakening, was converted after a period of deep soul-searching. A camp meeting under the leadership of James McGready experienced a stirring revival. Cartwright attended the meeting: "As there was a great waking up among the churches from the revival that had broken out, many flocked to [the meetings]. The church would not hold the tenth part of the congregation."[9]

The power of God manifested at the meeting overwhelmed the young Cartwright. Its impact on his conversion is clear:

> To this meeting I repaired—a guilty, wretched sinner. On the Saturday evening, I went with weeping multitudes and bowed before the stand and earnestly prayed for mercy. In the midst of a solemn struggle of soul, an impression was made on my mind, as though a voice said to me, "Thy sins are all forgiven thee." Divine light flashed all round me, unspeakable joy sprung up in my soul.[10]

Other revival leaders had dramatic conversions—including John Wesley and Charles Finney. They never got over what God had done through Christ for them.

What about the believer who has lived many years in a state of mediocrity, apathy, or perhaps in ignorance of the possibility of knowing God intimately? There is yet hope. Witness the men who, though already converted, experienced a personal revival resulting in a transformed life. Although already born again, R. A. Torrey, D. L. Moody, J. Edwin Orr, Bill Bright, and countless others encountered God in a life-changing way. These encounters transformed their ministries.

Evan Roberts was studying for the ministry when he encountered Christianity in a real way. The transformation was evident to all who knew him as well as strangers. He immediately shared four tenets for personal revival. These were doubtless a reflection of his own experience: (1) confess every known sin, (2) put away every doubtful habit, (3) obey the Holy Spirit promptly, (4) proclaim the Lord Jesus publicly. If you have lost a passion for evangelism, lost your passion for God, why not consider using the four points of Roberts to search your heart, to seek a renewed passion for God?

2. *Give a high priority to personal holiness.* One aspect of a life consumed by a passion for God is a passion for holiness. Not merely seeking some form of experience, but a desire for a holy life marks such individuals.

For some, the desire to deepen their walk with Christ eventually leads them down a path to introversion. Personal devotion becomes a spiritual litmus test, in extreme cases a devout "rabbit's foot" rather than intimacy with God. Some people become more excited about an experience than an encounter with the living God.

Today there is much talk about revival. Revival is needed to reform culture, we are told. Family values have fallen on hard times; surely, revival is the remedy. "Ethical norms have all but evaporated—give us revival to prove the lost world is wrong and prove us right," some have even ventured to say. While all these emphases are needed, revival is *not* a moral reform plan, a church growth technique, or a series of evangelistic meetings. Revival is a return to God based on the holiness of God. It is Isaiah encountering a holy God in the temple in Isaiah 6, and expressing contempt for his personal sin and that of the nation.

Leaders in awakenings have desired to live holy lives. John Wesley, George Whitefield, and others formed a small group while at Oxford which emphasized holy living. In fact, they were called the "Holy Club" in derision. Wesley himself deeply desired a holy life, as seen in this statement made in 1734, four years before his conversion: "My one aim in life is to secure personal holiness, for without being holy myself I cannot promote real holiness in others."[11] Wesley's desire following conversion was "to reform the nation, particularly the Church, and to spread scriptural holiness over the land."[12]

Robert Murray McCheyne, whose church in Dundee, Scotland, experienced revival, prayed in 1839, "God, make me as holy as a saved sinner can be."[13] Duncan Campbell was wounded during World War I. While being transported to safety, Campbell reflected on his life. He considered even his Christian life to be empty. He prayed McCheyne's prayer, "Lord, make me as holy as a saved sinner can be." His full surrender commenced in a clear sense of the Spirit of God. Years later Campbell would be the catalyst for the Hebrides Revival beginning in 1949. Campbell said the focus of true revival is holiness, and holiness is better than happiness.

3. *Immerse yourself in the Word of God.* Brian Edwards has said that "total acceptance of Scripture as the Word of God, and instant obedience to its commands, has characterized those whom God uses in revival."[14] It is also true historically that a person's view of Scripture has had a strong relationship with his or her commitment to evangelism.[15] It is no wonder persons of revival are

committed to evangelism, for the imperative to evangelize is paramount in the New Testament. The *Great Commission* for such leaders is not the *Great Suggestion.*

The great awakenings were characterized by a great love for the Scriptures. Jonathan Edwards said the Bible was like a new book after revival came to his people. That helps to explain why converts during revival remain faithful at a higher rate than at other times. The love for Scripture in the church gives an example to the new believers.

The Holy Club mentioned earlier had another nickname: "Bible Bigots," because of their unashamed commitment to Scripture. After his conversion George Whitefield wrote in his journal, "I got more true knowledge from reading the Book of God in one month, than I could ever have acquired from all the writings of men."[16] Jesus said, "Why do you call Me, 'Lord, Lord,' and do not do what I say?" (Luke 6:46).

Earlier I mentioned the revival beginning in Brownwood, Texas, in January 1995. On that day a college student read Joel 2 and began to weep. People streamed down the aisles. The service continued into the early afternoon. Interestingly, the day revival began pastor John Avant was beginning a sermon series on the Ten Commandments. In successive weeks his preaching on key absolutes of the faith served to strengthen and deepen the growing revival.

Jonathan Edwards wrote that one of the distinguishing marks of true revival is a great esteem for the Scriptures. People are drawn to the Word of God and to the God of the Word. That Sunday in Brownwood a ranch hand heard testimonies of revival on the radio. He immediately fell under conviction and was converted, drawn by the sounds of a passionate people!

Passion for People

These leaders in revival did not become so consumed with a passion *for* God that they overlooked the passion *of* God—the salvation of sinners. The leaders in great awakenings were also keenly committed to evangelism. This is seen in their devotion to spreading the gospel. Jeremiah Lanphier models this principle. Those who know of Lanphier recognize his role in inaugurating the New York City union prayer meetings in the Layman's Prayer Revival of 1857–1859. What is not as well known is his passion for evangelism. In fact, his evangelistic passion led him to establish the prayer meetings, and helped to keep the prayer meetings focused on evangelism.

George Whitefield first preached the Good News outside the church building at Kingswood. He so desired the common man to hear the gospel that he preached despite inner turmoil over the practice of field preaching (quite an innovation for an Oxford man!) and the ridicule he heard. Kingswood was an area near Bristol where coal miners lived. These rough, primitive workers were looked upon with contempt by others. "Why go to America to preach to the Indians?" some asked Whitefield, "Go to Kingswood."[17]

In 1739, Whitefield showed his passion for the lost and rejoiced in their response to the gospel:

> My bowels have long since yearned toward the poor colliers, . . . After dinner, therefore, I went upon a mount, and spoke to as many people as came unto me. They were upward of two hundred. Blessed by God that I have now broken the ice! I believe I was never more acceptable to my Master than when I was standing to teach those hearers in the open fields. Some may censure me; but if I thus pleased men, I should not be the servant of Christ.[18]

Personal soul-winning characterized such preachers as Whitefield. Whitefield's itinerant ministry fanned the flames of revival into the inferno of the First Great Awakening in the American colonies. "God forbid," Whitefield stated, "That I should travel with anybody a quarter of an hour without speaking of Christ to them."[19] D. L. Moody imagined an "L" on the forehead of those he met, reminding him that unless they had met the Savior they were lost. Circuit riders preached at points along their circuit, but also spent much time talking to individuals or families about their souls.

During the Second Great Awakening Finney emphasized "much prayer, secret and social, public preaching; *personal conversation, and visitation from house to house.*"[20] The focus of about forty prayer meetings across Dundee during the revival associated with Robert Murray McCheyne was on the conversion of sinners.

Be wary of those who talk about revival without a concomitant passion for biblical evangelism. Historically the two are not separated. Neither must we relegate evangelism to preaching only; the evangelism we need today must focus on personal encounters with lost people in which the gospel is shared from a passionate, revived believer. The key to personal soul-winning in our day is to be *real.*

A revived saint demonstrates a close proximity between how they *live* and what they *say* about the gospel. Believers in need of a touch from God easily position biblical priorities such as evangelism to second-rate status in their life, or at best program it into a method. In short, serving God becomes a *pastime* rather than a *passion.* Such living demonstrates the *need* for revival, not the experience of it. Let those of us who call the name of Christ live radically changed lives that give glory to God and reach sinners for the kingdom.

PART II

DOING THE GOSPEL

Chapter 6

The Urban Challenge: Developing Ethnic Churches in the United States
David F. D'Amico

WHEN I SERVED AS EXECUTIVE DIRECTOR OF THE METRO New York Baptist Association, I was able to experience the excitement, joy, and frustrations of ethnic ministry in an urban setting. During one of his sabbatical study leaves in 1985, Delos Miles went to New York to research the Bronx Baptist Church for his book *Evangelism and Social Involvement*. It was a privilege to meet this author, teacher, and colleague in ministry. I am honored to write an article related to urban evangelism for this *Festschrift*. Miles's commitment to all aspects of evangelism embraces the burgeoning field of ethnic congregations in urban areas of the United States.

The purpose of this essay is to sensitize and inform the reader about the complexities and challenges of ethnic ministry in urban settings of the United States.[1] I will attempt to describe and analyze from an urban ethnic missiological perspective the realities of church life and portray the mission challenges of the cities of the United States to the evangelical community. The literature available for the task is found mostly in periodicals and journals. I will present several case studies to illustrate some models of ethnic churches in selected cities. I

113

choose to circumscribe my discussion to evangelical local congregations and omit from the central thrust of this article the significant and exciting phenomena of the growth of African-American congregations and the inestimable contributions to the kingdom of social ministries of all types in urban settings.[2]

Statistical Overview

To understand the context related to ethnicity in the United States a few facts are necessary. The 1990 census reported that there are 51 million persons of European descent in the United Sates, excluding English, Welsh, Scottish, and Irish, constituting the largest ethnic population in the country. Hispanics rank second with at least 23 million. The Asian population numbers 4 million. The Native American population is 2.8 million and the North African and Middle Eastern population accounts for 1.3 million. Other ethnic groups such as Caribbean, Pacific Islanders, Sub-Saharan African, etc. add to a total ethnic population of 84 million.[3]

The Language Church Extension Division of the old Home Mission Board, SBC, reported 5,624 language units (congregations) across the country representing 101 ethnic groups and 97 American Indian tribes worshiping in 98 different languages in addition to American English.[4] The largest concentration of ethnic congregations in urban settings among Southern Baptists are in Los Angeles (208), Dallas-Fort Worth (201), Houston (156), Miami (125), New York (62), San Antonio (53), Chicago (40), San Francisco (23), New Orleans (23), and Boston (21).[5]

I have not considered statistics of ethnic congregations of American Baptists, Assemblies of God, Nazarene, Church of God, charismatic and independent groups. I can venture a conservative estimate of at least

3,000 units across the United States, representing these denominations.

The reader can surmise the potential of the "ethnic church force" in the life of Christianity in the United States. These congregations present a mission thrust which includes evangelism, church growth, discipleship, and the challenges of new forms of church life that will revolutionize the status quo in many parts of the country during the twenty-first century.[6]

Patterns of Ethnic Ministries

I present some generalizations to set the stage for the following discussion about ethnic congregations in urban centers. It is a well-known fact in church growth circles in the United States that evangelical denominations have lessened their decline during the last two decades by the eruption of ethnic congregations in urban areas. One source for the growth of ethnic congregations has been the increase of immigrants.

Moreover, the seizing of the opportunities by Southern Baptists, Assemblies of God, Nazarenes, and Church of God to assist in the development of ethnic congregations has been considerable. Catholics and mainline denominations have been responsive to the changes in some areas and have adapted their church life to accommodate an enlarging ethnic population. The city of Boston provides an exciting example of ethnic church life in urban centers of the United States.

> In Boston and Cambridge there are 532 churches spread across 110 denominations. The church worships in 33 different languages . . . People from over 106 nations are represented in our city's churches.
>
> The number of churches in Boston has grown from approximately 300 in the late 1960s to 459 in 1993 . . . The ethnic Protestant churches of Haitian, Hispanic,

and Asian backgrounds have a combined growth of an estimated 12,000 to 14,000 new members.

The Protestant group which has grown the most is the Pentecostal, Pentecostal-Holiness, Charismatic churches.[7]

How can one explain the surge of ethnic urban congregations? There are multiple patterns of church development. I have observed the following: (1) spontaneous beginnings, (2) Roman Catholic and mainline denomination adaptations; (3) evangelical denominational sponsorship and assistance; and (4) Anglo local church initiatives.[8]

Case Studies of Effective Ethnic Urban Congregations

There are a considerable number of ethnic congregations effectively adapting to the multicultural contexts in cities of the United States and ministering as bulwarks of the kingdom. I perceive effectiveness by stating that an effective ethnic congregation is one that has recognized its uniqueness in mission, has confronted the external factors that affect "doing church" in the 1990s, has set forth a mission agenda, and through its leadership is actively working to fulfill it. Effectiveness as I see it does not relate necessarily to numerical growth but to obedience to the call of Christ to be the church with faithfulness to the gospel message.

I have chosen to describe briefly, from the many available cases, the ministry of four ethnic congregations in Chicago, San Francisco, New York, and Houston as examples of effective urban ministry. Two churches are multicultural and two are monocultural. They provide different patterns of development and growth and will serve as types of many others scattered through the urban landscape of America.[9]

Uptown Baptist Church, Chicago

The Uptown Baptist Church in Chicago was organized in 1978 as a response to the needs of the neighborhood and in harmony with the tender feelings of ministry in the heart of its founding pastor, Jim Queen. Queen, a Chicago resident since his youth, was brought up as a child of a single parent. He went to the army, attended Southern Baptist Theological Seminary in the 1970s, and moved back to the city to minister as a church planter under the sponsorship of the Home Mission Board, SBC.

During the early 1980s the community known as Uptown comprised about ten square blocks or an area of two miles long by one mile wide, and a few blocks away from the shore of Lake Michigan. About 130,000 persons inhabited the community, including a large number of Native Americans, 14,000 senior citizens, and 10,000 to 13,000 mentally disabled persons. The area is multiethnic in population with Asians (Vietnamese, Laotians, and Cambodians), Hispanics, African-Americans, and other groups. In the 1920s, Uptown was America's first film capital; Charlie Chaplin made movies there. But the posh neighborhood gradually deteriorated. Today old hotels have been converted into apartments for the elderly and former patients of mental institutions.

How did Uptown develop as a congregation? Jim Queen believed that the needs of the people of the community provided a ready agenda for mission. Ministry to the elderly, the homeless, and the poor combined with ethnic population concerns congealed into a congregation that began as a store front and was able to move to a church building previously owned by a Congregational church. The Metro Chicago Baptist Association, the Metropolitan Department of Evangelism of the Home Mission Board, SBC, and a group of persons known as "Friends of Evangelism"—these significantly interested in urban mission—became partners in assisting the fledgling group to buy the property.

The church had a core of English-speaking members, mostly students and senior citizens. Then it became a facilitator for ethnic congregations desiring to meet in its facilities—Vietnamese, Cambodian, Spanish, and Hmong.

There have been some significant components in the ministry and programs of the Uptown Baptist Church that are indicators of effectiveness.

For one thing, the congregation is *multicultural* in its membership, whether one examines the White Anglo component or the other language congregations. Multiculturality is ingrained in Uptown as in many other urban ethnic congregations. The church thus mirrors the community in its population. *Needs-based ministry* leads persons to come for help, both physical and spiritual. The congregation makes an honest effort to present the gospel together with "a cup of water and a piece of bread in Jesus' name," and evangelizes the needy. Those assisted in turn become part of the team to assist others, bringing them to the worship services in addition to any program of assistance such as tutoring, refuge for abused women, and programs for the elderly and infirm.

If an ethnic congregation grows and the facilities in Uptown are not adequate for future ministry potential, then the ethnic group may move to another location more favorable to growth. A *family type of consensus* guided the congregation under the aegis of a "benevolent father figure," that of Jim Queen. Worship services under his pastorate were spontaneous and informal with testimonies as to what Christ had done in the lives of people during the week, contemporary music, an evangelical sermon, and an appeal to follow Christ.

Another significant element in the effectiveness of Uptown as a multicultural congregation is its ability to use hundreds of "partners of the gospel" in its ministries and mission. Besides the networking mentioned above related to the purchase of the building, the church has consistently availed itself of mission groups from churches, especially youth, who come to assist its programs during the summer months. These groups perform valuable ministries and services to the church.

A summer missionary from Texas, after spending ten weeks in Chicago assisting the Uptown church, declared: "I can't reach the whole world but I can go to one section and knock on all those doors. If every Christian did this, the world would really know about Jesus Christ."[10] Each year, during the last decade, the church has created partnerships for ministry with at least twenty visiting groups and has provided urban mission experiences to ten to twelve student summer missionaries.

The commitment of the congregation to assist the development of ethnic units continues under the leadership of Tom Maluga, who became pastor in 1995. Under his leadership the church has added a second Sunday morning worship service and is seeking ways to enhance lay discipleship and more interaction between white Anglos and the ethnic groups. The congregation facilitates the ministry of five ethnic congregations and a Bible study cell that are listed with the approximate number of participants: Cambodian (25); Vietnamese (150); Hispanic (30); Russian (50); African (60); Bulgarian (15).

Two of the congregations use the facilities, contribute to cover expenses, and function independently. The other four units are in a stage of development under the guidance of the Uptown congregation. During a typical Sunday morning worship service, the Uptown church gathers a total of between 400 and 500 participants, including the ethnic and Anglo congregations. During its brief history the Uptown Baptist Church has facilitated the development of fourteen different congregations.[11]

Nineteenth Avenue Baptist Church, San Francisco

This church was organized in 1958 and soon after was open to the cross-cultural mission opportunities of the city's ethnic groups. The main role of the congregation during its thirty-eight-year history has been facilitator for the development of ethnic units. The mission heart and mind of Professor Francis DuBose of Golden Gate Baptist Theological Seminary provided the initial impetus during the late 1970s. DuBose has been one of the few professors of missions among Southern Baptists who has devoted his teaching career to sensitize American Christians in general and Southern Baptists in particular to the global nature of mission and the imperative of consistent and holistic evangelism in cross-cultural settings.[12] Bill Smith led the church from 1978–1988 and solidified the commitment of the congregation to develop what came to be known as the "Church of the Nations."

The possibilities to assist evolving small ethnic congregations without a place to meet was a moving factor in the beginning. Later the mission and evangelistic opportunities these ethnic groups envisioned charged the hearts of the congregation to organize a multicultural congregation. The view that ethnic groups in the city of San Francisco constituted a mission field permeated the commitments to share facilities, to enable new units, and to become an example to others in California of what a multicultural congregation can accomplish.

Since 1968, the church has sponsored Arabic, Korean, Cambodian, Cantonese, Mandarin, Japanese, Estonian, and Vietnamese language ministries. The ethnic units that the congregation has enabled include a Mandarin congregation, the San Francisco Mandarin

Baptist Church, that began as a Bible class in 1968, developed into a full-grown congregation, and purchased property to become autonomous in 1982.

In addition, a Japanese unit was started in 1973 and met in the facilities of the church for twenty years. It became the Japanese Baptist Church of San Francisco in 1992. During 1994 the church, as a multicultural congregation, housed Arabic, Cantonese, English, and Vietnamese congregations.

The name "Church of the Nations" describes the relationship of all four congregations, although the Nineteenth Avenue Baptist Church has taken the lead because it owns the facilities and has the most members.

> The separate congregations exercise autonomy within the bounds of certain agreed upon practices and principles. Each congregation has its own pastor, budget, calendar, and programs of worship and ministry. Each group contributes to the Cooperative Program of the Southern Baptist Convention and to the local association of Southern Baptist work.[13]

The implementation of these principles includes a very systematic plan of sharing facilities.[14] The pastors meet periodically to pray, plan, and consult on calendar activities, attempting to avoid conflicts. The congregations meet together on a quarterly basis for worship and fellowship. The advantages of this model of church are many. Christians can celebrate their unique gift in language and culture. They exalt the unity which binds them together in Christ. They rejoice in unity amid diversity.

The membership and staff of Nineteenth Avenue Baptist Church have been involved through the years with diverse social ministries in the city of San Francisco, ministering to the homeless, the poor, and the children of the city. The effectiveness of the church in evangelizing, enabling, and ministering in such a challenging setting has brought the congregation recognition from the community and the denomination. The progressive nature of the church was illustrated by the fact that from 1993 to 1998 the congregation was led by a woman minister, Julie K. Pennigton-Russell.

French Speaking Baptist Church, Brooklyn, New York

This church represents an effective monocultural model of ministry. It was started in the early 1970s under the leadership of Jean Baptiste Thomas. He arrived in New York City in the early 1970s, fleeing from the oppressive and dictatorial politics of Haiti. He had pastored churches in Haiti. When he arrived in Brooklyn he began to evangelize and develop a congregation that would meet the needs of recently arrived refugees. Together with other fellow workers, pastors who had attended the Baptist seminary in Haiti, Thomas gathered a significant congregation.

In French Speaking Baptist Church, *strong pastoral leadership* is shared with laypersons who are trained in preaching and teaching and are ready to lead a new unit soon after it is started. The Brooklyn church provides lay and ministerial training through a center sponsored by Boyce Bible School of Southern Baptist Theological Seminary in Louisville, Kentucky. The center, under the direction of Pastor Thomas, has enrolled approximately thirty-five students per year during the last eight years. They are taught in French. The program of studies is contextual, practical, and basic for the needs of Haitian congregations.

Indigenous worship forms are practiced. Because a large portion of the membership is originally from Haiti, the music, worship style, preaching, and congregational participation are designed to meet their needs. The hymnody is traditional, and the choirs follow the patterns of European hymnody learned by Baptist churches in Haiti. To reach the younger generation, English choirs are also an active part of the worship.

A biblical, conservative theological stance is part of the worldview of the church. Evangelism and missions are central. Educational development as practiced by some white Anglo Southern Baptist churches is still in its rudimentary stages. The congregation is more concerned with the content of Bible study than with methods such as a graded Sunday School structure.

Social ministries are an integral part of the evangelistic strategy. The congregation provides assistance to the needy of the community. The Brooklyn church has a medical clinic once a week in the building staffed by physicians and nurses who are members of the congregation. Annual benevolent collections of money and goods are part of the church's program to assist their underprivileged countrymen in Haiti.

Denominational missionary strategy works well in the development of evangelistic and missionary plans. The church has been an enabler in developing other ethnic congregations in the New York area, New England, Florida, and Canada. During Harvest Sunday in September 1986, the church commissioned five Haitian congregations with a combined membership of 750 members to become autonomous congregations. These five congregations had been sponsored by the Brooklyn church and at that time were ready to function independently.

The location of these congregations provides an idea of the territorial influence of the church. They are located in Stamford, Connecticut; Manhattan, New York; Asbury Park, New Jersey; Far Rockaway, New York; and Jamaica, New York. Of these congregations the church at Stamford, Connecticut, has at the present three units or "mission chapels" in Norwalk and Bridgeport, Connecticut, and in White Plains, New York.

The church has enabled the beginning of other Haitian units in Maryland, Florida, and Missouri. Former members of the church who are transferred to different areas of the country and find Haitian enclaves are equipped as laypersons to start new units.

The congregation gathers about 1,500 participants on Sunday morning worship services. They meet in a large sanctuary that formerly was a Jewish synagogue which the church bought and refurbished. The church is the largest Southern Baptist congregation of the Baptist Convention of New York. In the Metropolitan New York area there were in mid-1996 at least forty Haitian congregational units cooperating with Southern Baptists and between thirty-five and forty congregations cooperating with American Baptists.[15]

Houston Chinese Church

The story of the Houston Chinese Church is one of the most fascinating accounts of ethnic church life in the United States. The congregation had its beginnings with a group of Chinese believers and students at the University of Houston in the early 1970s. The church was formally organized in 1974 as an evangelical non-denominational congregation and used the facilities of the South Main Baptist Church from 1975 to 1983, when the Chinese congregation moved to a new building. There are a number of significant elements in the life of this congregation that serve as a pattern of effectiveness for other Chinese churches in the United States.

The congregation has been evangelizing and ministering consistently to newly arrived immigrants of the Chinese world. One interesting fact is that attendance at worship services exceeds the number of members, indicating spiritual hunger and possibilities for evangelistic growth. Evangelism and missions are high priorities in the vision of the church. The membership of the congregation grew from 240 in 1977 to 520 in 1987.[16]

In addition to the evangelization thrust, discipleship of new converts is an integral part of the functions of the church. As a result, a high rate of retention of new members is experienced. The church ministers to persons by assisting with matters related to settling in a new country such as learning the English language, immigration and health matters, and a strong commitment to family life.

The membership of the congregation can be classified as upper middle class sociologically and economically, with a considerable number of persons working in the service area, merchants and business persons, and many professionals. Two-thirds of the members of the congregation have an educational level of master's degree and above.[17]

Houston Chinese Church emphasizes discipleship. Spiritual giftedness and skills are the bases for laity involvement. The congregation is organized to minister according to five basic gifts. Pastor Chan described the process:

> We identify people orientation, task orientation, artistic orientation, enterprise orientation, and content or investigative orientation . . . Those who are people oriented, we want to train them to be, first of all, small group leaders for caring ministries. We define the office of elder as a caring ministry and not as administrative ministry . . . Those with task orientation are trained for the teaching ministry. Those with artistic orientation are leading in the worship ministry. Those with enterprise orientation are leading the administrative ministry. Those with content or

investigative orientation are leading the planning and visionary ministry.[18]

The congregation is able to minister effectively as a metropolitan church because it has intentionally adopted the fellowship/congregation strategy. Each fellowship group is composed of between fifteen and fifty members, following the homogeneous principle of church growth. The congregation is trilingual—Mandarin, Cantonese, and English—and the fellowships follow the language pattern. During 1994 the church had between thirty and thirty-five fellowship groups meeting weekly in diverse neighborhoods of the Houston metropolitan area and coming to worship at the worship center on Sundays.

The administrative aspects of the congregation are also interesting. Pastor David K. Chan has been the senior pastor since 1978. After graduating from the Alliance Bible Seminary in Hong Kong and Southeastern Baptist Theological Seminary in Wake Forest, he served as dean of the Singapore Bible College before moving to Houston. He leads a staff of four ministers—two associates for the Chinese ministries and two associates for the English ministries. The church had a plant built and paid for by the congregation through the issues of bonds for $2.7 million in the early 1980s. The annual budget of the church is approximately $1.5 million. Of the total budget, about 40 percent is targeted for evangelism, missions, and ministries.[19]

Another significant aspect of the effectiveness of the Houston Chinese Church is its multicultural character. The membership represents persons from at least six different countries of the Chinese world (China, Hong Kong, Taiwan, Malaysia, Singapore, and the United States). In the training function of the church, the different languages/dialects are used. In the worship services all persons come together and the languages are interpreted. By doing so the church is avoiding the exodus of the ABCs (American-Born Chinese). They are an integral part of the church, with two staff members ministering to their needs.

Pastor Chan, a multilingual and multicultural leader, has inspired the two major groups of the church, Chinese and Americans, to work together in a strategy of ministry that keeps families together and keeps the church as the center of activities for all of its members, the older and the younger generations. He views the division of Chinese congregations into Mandarin/Cantonese-speaking and English-speaking as detrimental to evangelistic growth. The success of his congregation gives credence to that view.

In Houston, there are between twenty-five and thirty-five evangelical Chinese churches. The five that are growing steadily are those that have adopted a multicultural pattern of church life.[20] The Houston Chinese Church is the largest of all these congregations, with a worship attendance of 1,200 in two locations.

The congregation is also committed to world missions. Because of the high socioeconomic level of the membership, the desire to increase training, and the understanding of the missionary task, the congregation has sent numerous candidates for theological education to Dallas Theological Seminary and other evangelical institutions. It has also commissioned numerous short-term and long-term missionaries to different cities of the United States and Canada and to other areas of the world. The church sends an average of twenty to thirty short-term missionaries to diverse mission fields every year, including Boston, New Mexico, Mexico, Taiwan, China, and Hong Kong.[21]

Summary and Analysis

In analyzing ethnic urban congregations, some significant issues must be raised to determine whether their effectiveness can be sustained with shifts of population, diminishing denominational loyalty, variety of styles of pastoral leadership, and above all the fact that buildings in metropolitan areas will not be available to accommodate worshipers if patterns of worship requiring persons to attend a central location continue. For future research and analysis—which will generally originate not from the practitioners but from missiologists, denominational leaders, and others interested in the burgeoning ethnic evangelical population—certain issues are outlined below. These may help those interested in studying and celebrating the growth and development of ethnic urban congregations.

One important factor is the lack of history. Most ethnic congregations are in an incipient stage of development in American Christianity, having less than three generations of history behind them. Some congregations among Hispanics in Texas, California, and Florida and some Chinese congregations in California have a longer history but have not been able to propagate patterns of evangelization and ministry to others for differing reasons. The patterns of church life are extremely fluid. The potential institutionalization will come under the pressure of the prevailing American culture or the denomination with which the congregation is affiliated.

Another element worth studying is the future of ethnic congregations as they move from first to second and third generations. It is my conviction that most ethnic leaders will not plan ahead for these changes. The changes are too threatening for some who have not been able to become acculturated to the American milieu. Instead of planning, there will be reaction. In the process, the younger generation may be lost from the church to a secular world.[22]

Leadership training for pastors of ethnic congregations will also become a significant factor for the effectiveness of these churches. Accredited theological education is available in English for leaders of these congregations at the master's level in most urban centers. The strategy to train those who are not able to complete a professional degree will provide significant challenges to theological institutions in the future. It is my considered opinion that for sustained growth in urban areas, leaders for the twenty-first century will have to be biprofessional.

The ability to experiment with different forms of church life, such as cell groups, will also measure the effectiveness of these churches. For the future the concept of cell groups in urban areas may not be a missiological or ecclesiological issue but a pragmatic issue. Churches will not be able to afford new or used buildings, and sharing spaces will become the norm.

The issue of cooperation among ethnic churches of evangelical persuasion is worthy of consideration. Evangelicals are very fragmented. The goal of reaching urban multicultural peoples for Christ with the gospel is too important to be left to the whims of some of the most influential leaders who, holding a strong leadership position because of years of ministry in the city, do not wish to cooperate with others. In all other aspects of city life, coalitions are imperative. Should they be less important in the fulfillment of the mission of the church?

In the Third World all types of congregations are rising to fulfill the Great Commission. The urban centers of the United States provide a comparable type of Third World patterns of church life. The leaders of the First World will have to face the challenges of urban ministry with creativity and vision if the church is to remain viable in urban centers of the United States.

Chapter 7

Community Ministries and Evangelism
Thom S. Rainer

I am reasonably sure that evangelical churches
which give priority to the evangelistic mandate are in
the long run actually doing more for the poor, the dis-
possessed, the exploited, and the marginal citizens of
America's cities than more liberal ones. . . . Study a
major metropolitan area and see where the physically
and mentally handicapped are attending churches in
considerable numbers. Locate the churches that have
active and growing programs for the deaf. . . . Most
likely such churches will be of an evangelical nature.

—C. Peter Wagner

THE MYTH EXISTS AND PERSISTS: A CHURCH MUST CHOOSE TO BE
either a community-ministry church, or social-ministry
church, or an evangelistic church—it cannot be both.[1] Or
so we have been told. Yet, studies of the past two decades
have not only dispelled the myth; they have shown that a
direct correlation exists between evangelistic growth and
the level of ministries offered by a church.

For example, a recent study by C. Kirk Hadaway
found that newly growing churches are more likely to
be involved in community ministries than declining
churches. Hadaway spoke of these as "breakout
churches," churches that reversed a pattern of numerical decline to achieve numerical growth. Hadaway

unhesitatingly says, "It is clear that breakout churches (and growing churches generally) tend to have a greater presence in their community."[2]

Hadaway's study found that the outward focus of an evangelistic church engenders an outward concern for ministry as well. Evangelistic churches "are less inward looking and see the role of the church as helping people, whether they are members of their congregation or not. As a result, persons in the community are aware that the church exists and that it is available in time of need."[3]

But Hadaway's research also showed that the growing churches did not provide community ministry as simply a means to add to their membership roles. "The goals of providing ministry to the community were not designed to produce growth in these churches, but it would appear that growth can be seen as an unintended consequence."[4]

Indeed, the community's perception of an evangelistic church is often significantly improved as the church reaches out in both evangelism and ministry. "The ministering church is seen as an open, accepting congregation, rather than a restricted social club. Those who have received help or support and those on the outside who have worked on joint ministry projects with the church may establish relationships with the pastor or members, come to know Christ (if they do not already), and eventually join the fellowship."[5]

Our study affirms and concurs with Hadaway's research. The evangelistic churches in this study are very ministry-minded and community-oriented. Why then do misperceptions still abound? Why do many well-intentioned people still see a dichotomy between evangelism and social ministries? The roots of the misperceptions are found in a historical reality.

A Historical Excursion

As the nineteenth century came to a close, the understanding of mission shifted dramatically. The social gospel movement was influencing churches, and mission changed in perception from the simple task of winning converts to the complex task of social justice, betterment, and reconstruction.

Evangelicals began to build defenses against the social gospel. In doing so, evangelicalism was rightly affirming the importance of evangelism but wrongly avoiding any recognition of social ministries as being a part of missions. A dichotomy emerged in which conservative evangelicals raised the flag of evangelism and liberals touted the cause of social ministries. For conservative church leaders, an outspoken position on involvement in social ministries would have been tantamount to theological treason.

After nearly six decades of debating about evangelism and social ministries, evangelicals began to recognize that they were overreacting against social ministries. Scripture favors an evangelistic priority, they argued, but not to the neglect of temporal needs. Signs of the more balanced and biblical change were noticeable at the Berlin Congress of 1966, but the shift was explicitly stated at the International Congress on World Evangelization, held in Lausanne, Switzerland, in 1974. The Lausanne Covenant affirmed "that evangelism and sociopolitical involvement are both part of our Christian duty. For both are necessary expressions of our doctrines of God and man, our love for our neighbor and our obedience to Jesus Christ."[6]

If the evangelical world was returning to a more balanced understanding of missions, the word about the return was not spreading rapidly. Evangelistic churches, most all of which were conservative, evangelical churches, were still stereotyped in the minds of many. They were perceived as single-faceted, "notch-belt" evangelistic machines with little concern for people who are hurting. But as Hadaway, Wagner, and others have shown us, evangelistic churches have taken up the banner for social ministries. Our study only enhanced those observations.

Consider Town 'n' Country Baptist Church in Tampa, Florida. It is one example of a church that seeks biblical balance. Look at their ministries in both evangelism and community involvement.

Evangelistic Ministries:

• Continuous evangelism training program designed by pastor.

• Program focuses on three graduated levels of involvement: visiting, witnessing, and soul-winning.

• Teaching and preaching of lifestyle evangelism.

• Deacons, Sunday school leaders, and their spouses expected to spend one and one-half hours per week in soul-winning.

• Every morning at 8:00 A.M., the pastor meets with some of the laity to pray specifically for lost people to be saved.

• Wednesday night prayer meetings include a time to pray for lost people specifically by name.

• An ongoing ministry where a trained soul-winner takes an apprentice on visitation until that person is ready to train someone else.

• Youth of the church receive soul-winning training.

Social and Community Ministries:

• Prison ministries.

• Backyard Bible clubs.

• Ministry in retirement homes.

- A Spanish mission was recently meeting in this church's facilities, but they have moved into their own facilities.
- Ministry to troubled youth through the local sheriff's department.
- Philosophy to meet people where they are and meet their needs.

Town 'n' Country Baptist has seen consistent growth through its balanced ministries in the community and in evangelism. Today most of its growth is conversion growth.

An Attitude of Caring

In the survey, we asked some questions about community and social ministries. Two of these questions related directly to an attitude of caring for those in need. We asked leaders to respond to this statement: "Everyone who loves Jesus will have a heart for the poor, sick, lost, widowed, and homeless." Over 53 percent agree without equivocation that such is the attitude of all Christians.

In our follow-up interviews we spoke to leaders who responded "do not agree" or "somewhat agree." Their responses in no way indicated an aversion to social ministries. They simply did not believe that all who love Jesus will *naturally* have a heart for the poor, sick, lost, widowed, and homeless. Said a pastor in Oklahoma, "I wish that everyone *did* have that kind of compassion. It certainly is the model of Jesus. Unfortunately, I don't think our love for Christ is always reflected in our love for the down-and-out. It should be, but it's not."

We also asked leaders to react to another statement: "Non-Christians may not remember what they have been told regarding God's love, but they always remember what they have experienced as God's love." Many leaders related this statement to ministries in their churches. A minister of education from California told us, "We began a ministry in 1991 similar to big brother and big sister ministries. The greatest reward that we receive on earth is the look of gratitude of the children and their single parents. It's a tough world for them, and I thank God that we are helping just a little. That's the ministry I recall when you mentioned experiencing God's love in the survey."

As we discovered in our interviews, the responses are more indicative of the attitudes of these leaders. They truly have a heart for people who are hurting. They are leading their churches to diverse community and social ministries. And they are seeing balance in ministries between temporal and eternal needs.

Diverse Ministries

No one type of community or social ministry is dominant among these evangelistic churches, though we found that almost every church was involved in some kind of intentional social ministry. Since our survey did not ask respondents to name the ministries in which they were involved, we cannot with confidence convey a level of involvement with any particular ministry. We can, however, name some of the ministries that were mentioned in our interviews or in the miscellaneous portion of our survey.

Benevolence Ministries

Many churches mentioned a significant involvement with benevolence ministries. Some were as basic as providing budgetary funds for emergency needs. Others were much more complex and involved. When we asked one pastor the key to his church's growth, he responded: "Ministry! A church is effective evangelistically when it is reaching out in compassion to a hurting community.

Recovery groups, food assistance, clothing, shelter, and other services are an excellent way to model the love of Jesus. The gospel embodied is essential to the gospel proclaimed if people are going to be reached."

We also heard leaders frankly assess their own churches' involvement or lack of community involvement. "We are committed to providing benevolent ministries," said an Arkansas church layperson. "But our commitment has been greatly tested since some of the recipients of our ministry began attending our church. These people are of a lower socioeconomic status than the membership, and some folks are not sure about 'those kind of people.' Our pastor is leading us to work through some of those issues and to learn to accept all people as God's creation."

Ministries to Military Personnel

Some churches in the study are located near military bases. The turnover of membership is high, but we received several rewarding testimonies from church leaders who are trying to lead their churches to make a difference in the lives of these military personnel.

Ministry to Women

If this study is indicative of future trends in ministry, we should see a continued growth in ministries specifically for women. Numerous churches in this study were in some manner involved in pregnancy ministries. For example, Christopher Road Baptist Church in Shelby, North Carolina, is a relatively new church started in 1987. Among the numerous ministries in which they are already involved is a crisis pregnancy ministry led by the Baptist Women, a missions group in the church.

Though fewer in number than the churches involved in crisis pregnancy ministries, some of the churches are also involved in meeting the needs of abused and battered women. A few of the churches even have their own facilities for these ministries.

Support Groups

As many as one-fourth of the 576 churches had some type of ongoing support group. The most commonly mentioned support group was for divorce recovery. Others were formed for alcoholics, persons with eating disorders, single parents, compulsive spenders, and those with drug addictions, to name a few. Though these groups meet at a variety of times on every night of the week, the most frequently mentioned meeting time was Sunday evening.

Ethnic Ministries

Several of the churches (130 of the 576) have begun ministries to ethnic groups. The most common expression of these ministries has been the availability of church facilities to a particular ethnic group. First Southern Baptist Church in Garden City, Kansas, worships each Sunday morning while a Vietnamese mission worships at the same hour in the same facility.

Bus Ministries

In the 1960s and 1970s bus ministries were among the key evangelistic methodologies for many churches. Some larger churches purchased entire fleets of buses to bring lost children and adults to Sunday school and worship services.

As we will see later in this chapter, bus ministries are used infrequently today for specific evangelistic ministries. Several of the churches in this study, however, utilized bus ministries as a community or social ministry.

We were surprised that 165 of the 576 churches still had some type of busing ministry in operation. Church leaders indicated that these ministries were largely social or community-oriented rather than explicitly evangelistic. "We pick up senior adults who have no way to get to church," said an Alabama minister of education. A Georgia pastor commented, "The purpose of our bus ministry is to pick up children and youth at a local children's home. We view these efforts as part of our ministry to the community."

Interestingly, our study clearly depicts the more frequent use of busing ministries in the smaller churches. A pastor of a megachurch shared with us that an effective busing ministry would require an expenditure of resources that the church was not prepared to make. "I wish we had the money to send buses to every corner of the city. A small church can make an impact with just one bus going to one place in their community. We wouldn't know where to begin!"

Busing ministries may not be the impact ministry of two and three decades earlier, but they have not completely faded away. Nearly 30 percent of the churches still had some type of busing ministry, with the greatest concentration in the smaller churches.

Family Ministries

Family ministry is a broad term that can refer to a number of different ministries. For some churches, family ministry simply refers to a wide range of activities including recreational activities. For other churches the term means in-depth spiritual and emotional resources specifically designed to strengthen the family. Because of the varied ministries that were placed in this category, nearly 90 percent of the churches indicated an involvement in family ministries. Beyond the statistical indicators, we heard from these churches that they are committed to helping strengthen the family. "We believe that, as the family goes, so goes the nation," a Maryland pastor said. "In almost everything we do we ask the question: Can this help our members and the community to strengthen the family? We don't automatically eliminate a ministry if the answer is no, but that question is asked quite a bit."

The churches mentioned family ministries more as an avenue to strengthen Christian families rather than to offer a specific evangelistic outreach. Only a small minority of the churches spoke of family ministries as first being evangelistically motivated.

Counseling Ministries

Seventy percent of all churches surveyed say that they offer some kind of counseling ministry for the church and the community. Of course, a counseling ministry can range from a meeting with a bivocational pastor to an appointment with a full-time counseling minister on a megachurch's staff. Many of the counseling ministries, especially in the middle-sized churches, were "staffed" by laypersons. Some of the laypersons had received rather extensive training while others were acting as counselors because of their life's experiences.

But Are the Ministries Evangelistic?

Our study was designed specifically to ask questions about evangelistic methodologies. We asked the respondents to evaluate twenty-three methodologies in terms of their evangelistic effectiveness. Before we reveal the perceived evangelistic value of these methodologies, we will share with you three major conclusions about ministries and evangelism.

Ministries Should Be Evangelistic

An overwhelming sentiment we heard in our follow-up interviews is that social and community ministries should be evangelistic. "We have an average of four or five community ministries going on in a particular week," a Texas pastor said. "We make certain that the workers are trained in ways that they can share their faith with the recipients of our ministries."

Since we heard from 576 of the most evangelistic churches in America, we fully expected this sentiment. Because of their evangelistic intentionality and evangelistic attitude, the strong feelings about evangelism in ministries was no surprise. Perhaps the surprise came in our next discovery.

Most of the Ministries Are Not Evangelistically Effective

Later in this chapter we will share with you the perceived evangelistic effectiveness of five broad categories of ministries. As a rule the pastors of the 576 churches were disappointed if not frustrated with anemic evangelistic efforts in most of the social and community ministries. "We are doing everything we know how to do to see evangelistic growth in our ministries," a Texas megachurch associate pastor told us. "We have trained workers, provided evangelistic literature, conducted follow-up visits in the home, attempted to establish relationships, you name it! But very few of our baptisms come as a result of these ministries."

The nature of this study is such that we received many responses that were perceptual. While we did not necessarily believe that the respondents' perceptions and reality were in conflict, we did discern that the leaders evaluated their churches and themselves ruthlessly. The comments we received about ministry ineffectiveness in evangelism was but one example of their vigorous and continuous evaluative process.

Ministry Will Continue Regardless of Evangelistic Effectiveness

Rarely did our research team hear a comment about discontinuing a ministry because of its evangelistic ineffectiveness. Listen to the insightful words of a Kentucky pastor: "Fewer than 2 percent of our baptisms each year come as a direct result of the community ministries we offer. We are not proud of that statistic, and we will do everything we can to make our ministries more intentionally evangelistic." The pastor paused and continued, "But we don't see involvement in helping hurting persons as optional. We are constantly reminded of the One who said 'whatever you did for one of the least of these brothers of mine, you did for me.' That's our source of motivation to be involved in ministry."

Though I cannot predict the future, I believe their social and community ministries will become more evangelistic. Though the church did not participate in our survey, First Baptist Church of Leesburg, Florida, is being highlighted by Southern Baptists as a model for doing ministry with evangelistic effectiveness. Churches like First Baptist, Leesburg, and the churches in our survey indicated that an eagerness to learn and an attitude of evangelistic zeal in ministry will enable them to transform ministries into true opportunities for evangelism.

Evaluating Five Categories of Ministries Evangelistically

We now turn to the churches' own assessment of the evangelistic effectiveness of their social and community ministries. Despite less-than-enthusiastic evaluations of themselves, there were no indications that these ministries would be discontinued. To the contrary, many of the churches were looking for greater ministry involvement with heightened evangelistic efforts.

Weekday Ministries

Weekday ministries were mostly defined as day care, Christian schools, moms' day out, and similar ministries. Several churches indicated that day care was a financially subsidized ministry for single mothers in the community. Only slightly above 10 percent of the churches viewed weekday ministries as evangelistically effective. Most of the leaders saw value in the ministries, but lamented their minimal impact for evangelism.

Ethnic Ministries

Only 130 of the 576 churches had any type of involvement in ethnic ministries—less than one-fourth of the total churches in the study. Therefore, we are not surprised that, overall, relatively few churches in the survey considered ethnic ministries to be evangelistic.

Most of the churches that did not view ethnic ministries as a factor in their evangelistic effectiveness were those that did not have such ministries. Forty-five of the 576 churches (7.9 percent) cited ethnic ministries as a main or contributing factor to their evangelistic outreach.

Bus Ministries

Though nearly 30 percent of the churches in this study were involved in busing ministries, most of these ministries did not focus on evangelism. As we saw earlier in the chapter, most of the churches involved in busing ministry viewed it as a way to meet the needs of Christians. Senior citizens were mentioned frequently among those utilizing this ministry. But fewer than 8 percent of the churches considered busing ministries as a contributing or major factor in evangelism.

Family Ministries

Because of the significant number of churches with some kind of family ministry, nearly 40 percent of the respondents indicated that these ministries had an evangelistic thrust. Among the social and community ministries, this factor was among the highest for evangelistic effectiveness.

Due to the diversity of these ministries, however, we were unable to identify any specific group of ministries that were more evangelistic than others.

Perhaps more significant is the fact that only 11.6 percent of the respondents indicated that family ministries were *not* a factor in their churches' evangelistic effectiveness. We believe that the level of evangelistic activities in the family ministry category warrants future study.

Counseling Ministries

Counseling ministries included a considerable variety of activities. Still, only 18 percent of the respondents indicated that counseling ministries were a contributing or main factor in their church's evangelistic efforts.

One Florida church had an extensive counseling ministry that was staffed fully by laypersons. The laypersons had received extensive training, but they were instructed to refer any difficult assignment to one of nine professional counselors on the church's referral list. The counseling ministry of this church had a strong evangelistic thrust.

The associate pastor, who has primary responsibility for the ministry, shared their philosophy: "We believe that a person cannot begin to deal effectively with his or her problems without the presence of Christ. All of our counselors are trained to confront everyone with the claims of Christ. We make no pretense about it. We tell them that they are to go to a secular counselor if they are offended by our confrontational approach. But they have come to us knowing that we are a Christian counseling ministry."

While family ministries were overall more evangelistically effective, counseling ministries apparently could become more evangelistic with greater intentionality. Many church leaders indicated that counseling is the perfect opportunity for witnessing. Said an Illinois pastor, "You have someone who is seeking you out because he or she has a need. You have the ultimate Truth in the person of Jesus Christ. You have the perfect setting to share that Truth with someone. It is the single best opportunity for evangelistic sharing."

Another pastor, this one from Alabama, had similar sentiments. "The problem with most counseling ministries is that they aren't intentionally evangelistic. Nearly one-fourth of our baptisms last year came directly from a counseling session. We have discovered that a large number of counselees referred to us aren't Christians. We would be clearly disobedient if we didn't witness to them."

Conclusion: Ministries Grow in an Atmosphere of Love

More than any programmatic attempt to start community ministries in a church, the most effective ministries are those that develop from an atmosphere of love and concern. The most successful ministries to which we were introduced were not those formed in a committee seeking to justify its existence. To the contrary, the most effective ministries were begun somewhat unexpectedly. Believers in a church saw a need and began to find ways to meet that need. Before long, an entire ministry had developed with an impact far greater than anyone imagined.

The following are additional comments from pastors and other leaders in the leading ministry churches in our study:

- "The attitude of our church is positive, enthusiastic, and loving. We emphasize reaching out to others on a continual basis."
- "We have learned to love people as Christ did—unconditionally. Our Sunday school teachers have first responsibility to let us know of needs in their classes and in the community."
- "Our church tries to let everyone know that they are loved by God within our 'family' of God."
- "We strive to embody the gospel in all that we do through love and concern."
- "We have been told that the environment of our church is loving and accepting."
- "If there is any one factor that makes our church what it is today, it is that we are a church that loves people. We have heard that from visitors and people who are ministered to by our church many times over."

Love is the common denominator. But how does a church create a loving atmosphere that is conducive to meaningful ministry? We received many responses to this question, but three answers stood out because of their frequency.

One key factor for an atmosphere of love is strong biblical preaching. "You cannot be in the Word very long without hearing about the amazing love and grace of God. Our church began truly to see that love when we received 'meaty' Bible preaching from our new pastor," an Arkansas layperson said.

A second significant factor that engenders an environment of love is a season of prayer and fasting. We heard many testimonies from church leaders about the miraculous work of God after a new corporate prayer emphasis was begun, or after the leadership of the church called the people to an extended time of prayer and fasting. Not only did numerical and evangelistic growth result, but new ministries often began as well. These new ministries were born out of renewed hearts that expressed love and concern.

The third key factor is that these churches demonstrate love and acceptance because the pastor models love and acceptance. "We were a church divided before our pastor came here," a Georgia layperson shared. "His example of unconditional love and acceptance has not only helped us to heal old wounds; it has also been a model for us to emulate."

Evangelistic churches are involved in ministries for their communities. They demonstrate the love and concern of Christ. Not all of their ministries are explicitly evangelistic, but most of their ministries are born out of hearts of love and concern. The love of Christ compels the people of these churches to share the gospel and minister unto the least of these.

Chapter 8

Pastoral Models for Doing the Gospel

Danny Forshee

THERE ARE SOME FUNDAMENTAL PRINCIPLES IN THE area of pastoral evangelism that are worthy of our attention and emulation. A pastoral evangelist is a pastor of a local church who is led to make evangelism the primary thrust of his ministry. While not neglecting the other purposes of the church—worship, ministry, fellowship, and discipleship[1]—the pastoral evangelist conscientiously accentuates evangelism. Why? Evangelism is the one area from which both pastor and parishioners will gravitate if not repeatedly emphasized.

The Lord Jesus gave us clear marching orders in the Great Commission. He did not recommend or suggest; he clearly commanded that we go and make disciples of all the nations (Matt. 28:19–20). The Great Commission is fundamental and straightforward and worthy of our greatest efforts.

The primary purpose of this chapter is to admonish and encourage the pastor to "do the work of an evangelist" (2 Tim. 4:5 NKJV). A dear pastor friend of mine asked me if this was going to be another effort to make the pastor feel guilty for not evangelizing. Absolutely not. The aim here is not guilt but stimulation to action. How do you stimulate the busiest guy on the planet to do what he knows he should be doing? By examining

147

the biblical basis for pastoral evangelism, as well as historical and contemporary models, today's pastoral evangelist is inspired to do the work.

Biblical Basis for Pastoral Evangelism

The apostle Paul wrote his epistles to Timothy around A.D. 67. Timothy was Paul's protégé, his son in the faith. Timothy worked with Paul during his second missionary journey, and he also served as the pastor of the church at Ephesus. As Paul penned his last words to Timothy, he told him with great urgency and passion: "But you be watchful in all things, endure afflictions, do the work of an evangelist, fulfill your ministry" (2 Tim. 4:5 NKJV). Paul used four quick, staccato-type imperatives as he addressed Timothy.[2]

As Paul spoke of pastoral evangelism, he used the word *ergon* which means "to toil, work, or labor." Paul knew from personal experience that evangelism takes work! Pastor, do you not agree? If you are to win others to Jesus Christ and lead your church to do the same, it will take much effort, labor, and energy. You must make a conscious, volitional effort to leave the church and go evangelize. Your personal example will speak volumes to your people.

Pastor, you are the key human personality in your local church.[3] Just as God looks upon the husband as the leader in the home, so he looks upon you as the leader in your church. It is a tremendous responsibility; do not neglect or abdicate it. Fulfill it! God has entrusted to you the most challenging and rewarding job. May our Lord energize you by his Holy Spirit as you fulfill your ministry by doing the work of an evangelist.

Historical Examples of Pastoral Evangelists

Church history is replete with men who exemplify pastoral evangelism. I have selected three men who faithfully executed their divine calling. Each one is in heaven today; however, they have left behind an inspirational legacy that encourages contemporary pastoral evangelists.

Richard Baxter (1615–1691)

Baxter was an English Puritan pastor who served at Kidderminster from 1641 to 1660.[4] His *Reformed Pastor* is must reading for all men who sense God has called them to serve as pastors. Baxter held firmly that every pastor should possess the assurance of salvation, a holiness of life, and a passion for personal soul-winning.

Assurance of salvation. Baxter, as did Gilbert Tennent in the eighteenth century, warned of the dangers of an unconverted ministry. He said: "Take heed to yourselves, lest you perish while you call upon others to take heed of perishing; and lest you famish yourselves while you prepare food for them. . . . Believe it, brethren, God never saved any man for being a preacher, nor because he was an able preacher; but because he was a justified, sanctified man, and consequently faithful in his Master's work."[5]

Holiness of life. Baxter admonished pastors to live godly lives. He advised ministers to preach their sermons to themselves before they preached them to others. He felt a pastor's example should always match his doctrine. "It is a palpable error of some ministers, who make such a disproportion between their preaching and their living—who study hard to preach exactly, and study little or not at all to live exactly."[6]

Consequently, Baxter cautioned ministers to beware of Satan's schemes; he felt preachers were tempted greater than other men. "He [Satan] beareth the greatest malice to those that are engaged to do him the greatest mischief."[7]

Personal soul-winning. Baxter said pastors must inexorably engage in what he called "personal catechizing," where pastors personally instruct each person in their congregation regarding salvation. He said:

> Now, in all our congregations, we have reason to fear the unconverted constitute by far the majority: their situation is peculiarly pitiable; their opportunities of salvation will soon be for ever over; their danger is not only very great, but very imminent; they are not secure from everlasting misery, even for a single moment.[8]

With great pathos and eloquence, Baxter tells the pastoral evangelist to give his greatest effort to win souls for Christ. As Paul told Timothy to do the work of an evangelist, Baxter likewise instructs every pastor:

> O, brethren, what a blow may we give to the kingdom of darkness, by faithful and skillful managing of this work. If, then, the saving of souls, of your neighbors' souls, of many souls, from everlasting misery, be worth your labor, up and be doing. If you would be the fathers of many that are born again, and would see the travail of your souls, and would be able to say at last, "Here am I, and the children whom thou hast given me," up and ply this blessed work. If it would do your heart good to see your converts among the saints in glory, and praising the Lamb before the throne; if you would rejoice to present them blameless and spotless to Christ, prosecute with diligence and ardor this singular opportunity that is offered you. . . . If, then, you are indeed fellow-workers with

Christ, set to his work, and neglect not the souls for whom he died.[9]

Jonathan Edwards (1703–1758)

Edwards was arguably the greatest mind colonial America produced. He entered Yale University when he was twelve years old and graduated valedictorian when he was seventeen. He served as pastor of the First Congregational Church of Northampton, Massachusetts, from 1729 until 1750. Edwards was the consummate pastoral evangelist. Notice the salient features of his pastoral evangelism.

Powerful sermons. Edwards faithfully prepared and delivered his messages to his parishioners at Northampton. Ola Winslow writes: "The making of sermons was to Jonathan Edwards one of the chief ends of his reading, his study, his thought. . . . It was on Sunday morning at the ringing of the meetinghouse bell that Northampton had its best chance to know Mr. Edwards."[10]

In the winter of 1734–35, Edwards preached a series of sermons entitled "Justification by Faith Alone." Soon thereafter, a revival broke out in Northampton. Edwards states:

> This work of God, as it was carried on, and the number of true saints multiplied, soon made a glorious alteration in the town; so that in the spring and summer falling, Anno 1735, the town seemed to be full of the presence of God; it was never so full of love, nor of joy, and yet so full of distress, as it was then. There were remarkable tokens of God's presence in almost every house.[11]

Two of Edwards's most noted sermons were "The Justice of God in the Damnation of Sinners" (1735) and

"Sinners in the Hands of an Angry God" (1741). An excerpt from the latter reads:

> The bow of God's wrath is bent, and the arrow made ready on the string, and justice bends the arrow at your heart, and strains the bow, and it is nothing but the mere pleasure of God, and that of an angry God, without promise or any obligation at all, that keeps the arrow one moment from being made drunk with your blood. Thus all you that never passed under a great change of heart, by the mighty power of the Spirit of God upon your souls; all you that were never born again, and made new creatures, and raised from being dead in sin, to a state of new, and before alltogether unexperienced, light and life, are in the hands of an angry God.[12]

Targeted youth with the gospel. Edwards emphasized to the young people in Northampton the benefits of salvation. He also warned them that if they neglected God's offer of eternal life, their later years would be filled with much bitterness.[13]

Disciplined work ethic. Edwards possessed an insatiable desire to read and study. He spent thirteen hours a day in sermon preparation! In the evenings after spending one hour with his family, he went back to his study. His prolific writings and theologically deep messages were a result of his commitment and discipline to work. Edwards was not slothful or lazy in carrying out his myriad duties as a pastoral evangelist.

Participated in and defended revivals. Edwards was instrumental in the First Great Awakening. His *Faithful Narrative* not only gave an accurate account of the revival, but it also plowed the New England soil for a subsequent, more powerful movement of God's Spirit. Edwards also defended and befriended the "Grand Itinerant" of the First Great Awakening, George Whitefield. As Whitefield preached throughout the

American colonies at the apex of the First Great Awakening in 1740, he also preached at Edwards's church on October 17–19. Edwards also traveled to other locations and preached; however, his greatest contribution to the revival was that of an apologist.[14]

Charles Haddon Spurgeon (1834–1892)

Spurgeon was the gifted "prince of preachers" who served as pastor of the Metropolitan Tabernacle from 1861 until 1891. Notice the characteristics of Spurgeon's pastoral evangelism.

Church growth. Spurgeon began his pastoral ministry when he was nineteen years old at New Park Street Church. The size of the congregation was approximately 200 members. The church moved to Metropolitan Tabernacle, which opened in 1861 and seated 5,600.[15] Under Spurgeon's ministry the church grew enormously. The primary form of growth was not biological or transfer but conversion growth. For example, in Tim McCoy's excellent treatment of Spurgeon's pastoral evangelism, he states that "of the 1,867 total additions recorded in the four year span 1863–1866, fully 1,489 (or 80.2%) were by baptism."[16]

Personal soul-winning. Spurgeon announced when he would be at the church to counsel with those who were recently converted or interested in becoming Christians. He also encouraged his congregation, as Charles Finney did in America, to look for those in the church services who appeared convicted and then go and witness to them before they left the building.[17]

Evangelistic preaching. Spurgeon persuasively preached the gospel of Jesus Christ to the unconverted. He said, "I take my text and make a bee line to the cross."[18] Lewis Drummond stated, "When it came to declaring the gospel in a relevant fashion to the common masses, Spurgeon was a master. He was a nineteenth-century reflection of George Whitefield."[19] He preached biblical sermons with great robust and authority. He gave the unconverted a clear, picturesque presentation of the gospel, and he exhorted them to repent and believe. In his sermon, "Compel Them to Come In," Spurgeon stated:

> Sinner, in God's name I *command* you to repent and believe. Do you ask me whence my authority? I am an ambassador of heaven. . . . O my brother, dost thou know what a loving Christ he is? Let me tell thee from my own soul what I know of him. . . . I thought he would smite me, but his hand was not clenched in anger but opened wide in mercy.[20]

Contemporary Examples of Pastoral Evangelists

There are literally thousands of faithful pastors today who are doing the work of an evangelist. I have selected only a few, but as you notice their effective ministries, learn from them and implement their principles into your own context.

Johnny Hunt

Dr. Hunt has served as pastor of First Baptist Church of Woodstock, Georgia, since December 1986. Hunt graduated from Gardner-Webb College (B.A.) and Southeastern Baptist Theological Seminary (M.Div.). On March 11, 1997, Southeastern Seminary named the chair of church growth in honor of Dr. Hunt. First Baptist Woodstock has experienced phenomenal growth under Dr. Hunt's leadership. The church's Sunday school attendance has increased from 275 people in 1986 to 3,200 (March 1997). Church membership has escalated from 1,027 in 1986 to over 7,800 (March 1997). The average attendance on Sunday morning is 4,400.[21]

Hunt exudes a deep passion for Jesus Christ and lost souls. Dr. Hunt was saved January 7, 1973, in Wilmington, North Carolina, and since his conversion to Christ, he has been telling others about the Savior.[22]

Dr. Hunt leads his church in evangelism from the pulpit and in personal soul-winning. He is a dynamic preacher of God's Word. People flock to First Baptist Woodstock to hear Hunt preach because they know they will hear a soul-stirring message from a man who is passionate for God and people. Hunt does not ask his parishioners to engage in something he does not engage in. He personally shares Christ in the following ways.

Evangelistic luncheons. Hunt states, "Most days that I am in my office, I attempt to have lunch with someone who is visiting our church, or someone that I met in the community."[23] During the luncheon Hunt asks his guest some diagnostic questions regarding his spiritual condition, and then he presents the gospel to him. Hunt has been a certified pastor-leader in Continuous Witness Training (CWT) for fifteen years.[24]

Race-track evangelism. Almost every Saturday night you can find Hunt at Dixie Speedway, a three-eighths mile oval dirt track. At the race track, he gives a brief devotion, and once a month he actually goes into the race pits and shares with the drivers and their crews. He also mingles in the crowds and hands out copies of *Out of the Poolroom* and gospel tracts First Baptist produced entitled, "How to Go to Heaven from Dixie Speedway." Hunt says, "God gives lots of opportunities to share the gospel in this particular setting."[25]

Personal travels. Hunt is in constant demand to preach both in the United States and abroad. As he travels, he constantly attempts to share Christ. He states, "I am of a deep conviction that my neighbor is whomever

I am with."[26] Armed with gospel tracts, he tells others about the life-changing message of Jesus Christ.

John Ed Mathison

Dr. Mathison is senior pastor of Frazer Memorial United Methodist Church in Montgomery, Alabama. He graduated from Huntingdon College (B.A.), Princeton University (Th.M.), and Candler School of Theology (D.Min.). Mathison has served as pastor at Frazer Memorial since 1972 and has led the church in consistent growth. Frazer Memorial has three Sunday morning services, with attendance over 4,500. The church has the largest Sunday school attendance, 2,600, of any United Methodist church in America. "In 1986 the Church Leadership Institute cited Frazer as the fastest growing church of any denomination in Alabama."[27]

Dr. Mathison and Frazer Memorial are committed to involving the laity in evangelism and ministry. Thirty-five percent of the church's total budget is allocated to missions.[28] Mathison says, "Evangelism is the number one priority of the church."[29] With regard to lay ministry, Frazer has 83 percent of the resident members involved in a specific type of ministry.[30] Mathison makes four statements regarding the church's need to mobilize the laypeople for effective evangelism.

1. Change the mind-set of those "who view the pastor as the one who does evangelism rather than the people."[31]

2. Remind each member that evangelistic ministry is not relegated to a committee but is the responsibility of every church member. "The whole church is the evangelism committee."[32]

3. Pastors must delegate, unleashing the laity for the ministry of evangelism.

4. There is a critical need for training laypeople to do evangelism.[33]

Gil Rugh

Dr. Gil Rugh has served as pastor of Indian Hills Community Church in Lincoln, Nebraska, since 1969. Dr. Rugh graduated from Grace Theological Seminary (B.A. and M.Div.) and the California Graduate School of Theology (Ph.D.). Rugh is a gifted expositor and teacher of God's Word. He is the radio Bible teacher of "Sound Words," and his sermons are heard in the United States and around the world. He has written over fifty books and study guides.[34]

Rugh has led Indian Hills in substantial growth. The church has grown from less than 100 to 1,250 members on Sunday mornings. (The average Sunday school attendance is 850.) Dr. Rugh has assisted his church in implementing the following evangelistic programs and efforts that have enabled Indian Hills to impact its community for Christ.

Evangelism training. Twice a year the church provides training for adults and teenagers. In three years they have trained "over 300 adults how to witness, 100 college men and women, not to mention the many high school and junior high students."[35]

Personal evangelism. The church has fifty adult teams that make evangelistic visits. The county in which the church is located has approximately one thousand new people each month. They are "putting together 10 teams to go visit these people and share the gospel."[36] They also have five teams who visit people who have quit coming to church and discover why they are not attending.

Off-campus Bible studies. The evangelistic training of young people is paying great spiritual dividends for Indian Hills. In each of the six public schools in their location, they have an ongoing Bible study led by the young people! Throughout their community they have thirty Bible studies that meet weekly.

Church planting. Indian Hills has planted five churches in the last six years. Their plans are to start other ones soon. Lincoln, Nebraska, is home to the University of Nebraska, which has 26,000 students. Indian Hills purchased a home on the campus and called a campus pastor, who will "preach the gospel on campus and grow a ministry there."[37]

Numerous other historical and contemporary pastoral evangelists have done and are doing the work of an evangelist. Those we have examined are excellent examples of how pastors are to lead their churches to fulfill the Great Commission. Pastor, learn from their ministries and ask for the Holy Spirit to empower you for the task to which you have been assigned.

Pastor, Do the Work of an Evangelist

Based on our study of 2 Timothy 4:5 and historical and contemporary models of pastoral evangelism, let us examine some practical ways in which you as the pastor of a local church can fulfill your biblical mandate to do the work of an evangelist.

1. *Share your passion for evangelism and discipleship.* May the Lord's passion be your passion. Share Christ daily during your normal traffic patterns. Also, set aside one night a week, preferably during your weekly church visitation, and go soul-winning! God will bless you. Robert Anderson says the pastor "will be called upon to do the work of the evangelist as a model for his people and as a means of equipping others for the task."[38]

Richard Jackson, former pastor of North Phoenix Baptist Church, personified evangelistic zeal before his congregation. Under Jackson's leadership, the church grew from 180 to 20,000 members. Jackson said, "I really didn't set out to grow a church. I just set out to do what God called all of us Christians to do—win souls."[39]

2. *Start new churches.* One of the great joys in ministry is to plant a church. Satan has convinced many pastors that starting new churches is detrimental to their church—it drains their church's financial resources and takes away their key leaders. While church planting does involve sacrifices, God richly repays! Pastor Rick Ferguson has led his church, Riverside Baptist Church in Denver, Colorado, in planting nineteen satellite churches or Bible study ministries in only four years. The satellite congregations have grown from 300 people in 1994 to 1,025 in 1997. Ferguson says: "I'm often asked if it is costly to start new churches. It's a little costly, but it's far more costly not to start churches. The only thing more costly than obedience to God is disobedience."[40]

Over the last five years, Riverside's attendance has increased by 1,100 members, and their Sunday school attendance has tripled. Their budget has burgeoned from $750,000 to $2.2 million.[41]

3. *Preach the Word.* If you are to be an effective pastoral evangelist, you must be faithful in the proclamation of the Word of God. Paul told Timothy, "Preach the word! Be ready in season and out of season. Convince, rebuke, exhort, with all longsuffering and teaching" (2 Tim. 4:2 NKJV). Strong New Testament churches are never grown without the faithful, consistent preaching of God's Word. The blessings of God have an affinity with the pastor who preaches the Bible and not his own philosophies.

Martin Thielen surveyed the five fastest-growing churches in middle Tennessee and discovered that engaging preaching was one of the key factors for growth. He stated, "The pastors at these five churches did not speak abstract theology, but dealt with real-life issues. Their sermons were Bible-based but relevant to daily living."[42] Pastors participate in extending the kingdom of God and in encouraging the saints when they diligently study, then faithfully communicate messages from God's Word.

4. *Develop a disciplined work ethic.* One of the great needs of the church is dedicated, disciplined pastors. The ubiquitous temptation for ministers of the gospel is to become slothful and lethargic in executing their duties. God expects ministers to possess a disciplined work ethic. Paul told Timothy, "Discipline yourself for the purpose of godliness" (1 Tim. 4:7).

Pastor, perhaps you desire to preach like John MacArthur or Charles Stanley or serve a large church like John Bisagno or D. James Kennedy. But are you willing to pay the price these men have paid? MacArthur and Stanley study hours for one message; Bisagno and Kennedy are where they are because of God's inspiration and their perspiration.

For example, while Bisagno served as pastor at First Baptist Church, Del City, Oklahoma, he visited prospects all Sunday afternoon, every Sunday afternoon. On Fridays, he visited from 4:30 P.M. until 9:00 P.M. and from 1:00 P.M. until 7:00 P.M. on Saturdays. He accurately states, "There is no substitute for hard work."[43]

Pastor, you may not study thirteen hours a day like Jonathan Edwards, pray three hours a day like Martin Luther, or visit twenty hours a week like John Bisagno, but you should roll up your sleeves and get busy!

It is humbling and convicting when those in the secular world consistently outwork those of us in the ministry. Mike Krzyzewski, head basketball coach at Duke University, is one who pursues excellence in his profession. When "Coach K" recruited the highly touted Elton

Brand, he was a man on a mission. For two hours the coach spoke with Brand in the home of his high school coach, Lou Panzanaro. Panzanaro was impressed with the coach. He said, "Coach K is very intense. He's very confident. He has the determination that once he makes up his mind that he wants somebody, he's going to get him."[44] Oh, that this type of intensity and passion characterized every pastor's zeal for lost souls.

Conclusion

The Word of God and the examples of past and present pastoral evangelists urge ministers of the gospel to do the work of an evangelist. God has called you and entrusted a congregation of people into your care. Your church will worship God, equip the saints, and evangelize the lost to the extent that you lead them. Lead them with determination and by example. Let your candle of devotion light the way for your parishioners. May your zeal for God, his Word, and the unconverted be exemplary before your people.

Chapter 9

Understanding Strategic
Evangelism
Harry L. Poe

DURING THE LAST QUARTER OF THE TWENTIETH
century, the evangelical community was entranced by
the business model of the church. Most of the plans for
having a vital congregation, developing a large church,
and seeing substantial numerical increase in membership
centered around this business or corporate model for the
church. The model called for running the church according to the business principles of American capitalism.

By the end of the century Americans had observed
the bankruptcy of this model for business. American
business practices had managed to destroy several
American industries. We lost our market share of the
manufacture of televisions, VCRs, and virtually the
entire consumer electronics industry. We saw the demise
of the American automobile industry, but we also lost
our edge in dozens of other areas that failed to attract
our attention.

At a number of levels one can see how the business
model failed business, as reflected in the huge trade
deficit, the collapse of the junk bond industry, the collapse of the real estate industry, and the failure of the
savings and loan industry.

American business lost confidence in its own
model and started looking elsewhere for a new way of

envisioning itself. At a time when the business model has fallen under suspicion for business, perhaps the church should look elsewhere for a more appropriate model. In the business model there tends to occur the promotion of the generic church, just like McDonald's restaurant. A person can go anywhere in the country and find a McDonald's where one will feel at home. These outlets have the feel of familiarity even when the seating arrangement is different. The menu looks the same, and the burgers taste the same regardless of who cooks them or in what part of the country they are served.

With the business model of the church, this cookie-cutter approach to church life and evangelism has flourished. Following this scheme, the pastor in Nashville who wants a vibrant, vital, growing church will do exactly what a vibrant, vital, growing church is doing in Chicago or Garden Grove or Dallas, without regard to the differences in the ministry settings and why God led a church to be the way it was in the first place.

In this way the generic McDonald's church has proliferated. These churches do not reflect their membership, their community, or the peculiar possibilities God has put together in that place. Instead, they attempt to duplicate something from somewhere else where, ironically, the ministry emerged by not doing it like anyone else.

Oddly enough, this business model is one of the few models specifically forbidden by Scripture: "We are not, like so many, peddlers of God's word" (2 Cor. 2:17a RSV). It would seem that a dynamic, growing church involves more than merely marketing merchandise or duplicating something someone is doing elsewhere.

Scripture contains a number of models for the church. Among these appear such metaphors as God's People, the Temple of the Holy Spirit, the Servant, the

Body of Christ, and the Bride of Christ. To these may be added another model, prominent in the early church though viewed with disfavor in more recent years due to some of its unfortunate connotations.

Beside the other metaphors stands the church as the Army of God. During the Crusades, and at other times in history, powerful forces have misused this metaphor for the church in its mission in order to marshall worldly armies to kill in the name of Christ. The Crusaders gathered from the Christian kingdoms of Europe to bring sword, lance, bow, and pike to massacre Saracens for the glory of God. Since then, the church as the Army of God has not seemed a particularly appropriate metaphor because of its association with conquest and death. Nonetheless, the military metaphor remains an important model for understanding the church's function in ministry and how the Lord intends to use his church in the world.

When the Lord described to Peter and the other disciples what the church would be and what it would accomplish, he used a military metaphor. In Matthew 16:18 following Peter's great confession, the Lord spoke of his church: "And I say also unto thee, That thou art Peter, and upon this rock I will build my church; and the gates of hell shall not prevail against it" (KJV).

In this passage the Lord mixed his metaphors. In modern English usage children learn in school that they should never mix their metaphors, but in theology mixed metaphors play a crucial role in understanding. No single metaphor can adequately carry the weight of divine revelation. In one respect the church is a temple into which all the parts are fitted together with Christ as the cornerstone. Christ emphasized two conspicuous matters of this metaphor. First, it is his church, and second, he does the building. So many plans in church life go awry because people forget whose church it is. The church cannot adequately be the church in terms of its internal vitality or its outreach to the world unless it constantly perceives itself as Christ's church.

The second part of the description shifts metaphors as Christ speaks of the gates of hell or the powers of death not prevailing against the church. Christians have tended to think of this model as the church standing like a mighty fortress built by God to protect Christians from the gates of hell when they attack. The gates of hell will not break down the fortress.

In the annals of military history, however, never has a gate attacked a fortress. Christ switched his metaphors. He intends for the church to attack hell, and the gates of hell will collapse at the onslaught of his church. In this world the church was never intended to seclude itself within the four walls of its building. We are to storm the gates of hell wherever we find it, however it may be manifest. Spiritual warfare is an assignment from Christ to the church.

What does this spiritual warfare mean? Paul discussed it in several places. In 2 Corinthians 10:3–4 Paul explained, "For though we live in the world we are not carrying on a worldly war, for the weapons of our warfare are not worldly but have divine power to destroy strongholds" (RSV).

He further elaborated in Ephesians 6:10–20 when he declared:

> Finally, be strong in the Lord and in the strength of his might. Put on the whole armor of God, that you may be able to stand against the wiles of the devil. For we are not contending against flesh and blood, but against the principalities, against the powers, against the world rulers of this present darkness, against the spiritual hosts of wickedness in the heavenly places. Therefore take the whole

armor of God, that you may be able to withstand in the evil day, and having done all, to stand. Stand therefore, having girded your loins with truth, and having put on the breastplate of righteousness, and having shod your feet with the equipment of the gospel of peace; besides these, all taking the shield of faith, with which you can quench all the flaming darts of the evil one. And take the helmet of salvation, and the sword of the Spirit, which is the word of God. Pray at all times in the Spirit, with all prayer and supplication. To that end keep alert with all perseverance, making supplication for all the saints, and also for me, that utterance may be given me in opening my mouth boldly to proclaim the mystery of the gospel, for which I am an ambassador in chains; that I may declare it boldly, as I ought to speak (RSV).

In these passages, military metaphors describe the struggle between the light of Christ and the darkness of wickedness all over the world. The word *strategy* takes on an entirely different meaning in the context of the military model for the church where the work of the church in ministry extends the kingdom of Christ. As agents of Christ, the church battles sin, wickedness, ignorance, darkness, bondage, oppression, and every other form the expression of sin may take.

People have spoken of strategy for ministry in recent years, but they have used the term in relation to the business model. The strategy for evangelism under this model revolves around techniques for "closing the sale." Unfortunately, with a good sales technique a minister may close the sale, add someone to the membership of a church, and experience numerical growth without the person ever being converted. A person may be attracted to a particular marketing plan for the church without ever coming to faith in Christ.

A clever marketing strategy may get increased membership, but have people been freed from the bondage of sin? Closing the sale fails as an apt metaphor to describe the ministry of evangelism and the proclamation of the gospel, because "we are not, like so many, peddlers of God's word" (2 Cor. 2:17a RSV).

Purpose

Strategy comes from the military vocabulary. Strategy describes the military approach to accomplishing its broad purpose in warfare. Something must precede a strategy. Strategy always has a context, and the first element of this context involves understanding one's mission for engaging in warfare.

During the Vietnam War, great unrest shook the United States. People took to the streets to protest the war. College campuses erupted in turmoil as students took over administration buildings to protest the war. While this great uproar spread across the country, morale sank lower and lower in the military. Those troops who fought in Vietnam were probably the least-supported troops in the history of modern warfare. It all seemed to revolve around the fact that the country had no commonly held consensus about why we fought in Vietnam. Whenever people enter into a conflict that will be costly, they need to be bound together by a compelling purpose that becomes the basis for judging and determining all that they will do for the cause.

The most recent experience that the United States had with war contrasts sharply with the Vietnam experience. In the fall of 1990, the debate about sending troops to the Persian Gulf revolved around this matter of mission. The President's most compelling problem at that point involved articulating a purpose for involvement which the American people agreed upon and would support. A sense of purpose had a crucial attraction for the American people when the risk of war seemed inevitable.

In the 1930s, Winston Churchill tried to be a leader and failed. Churchill recognized a danger that few in Britain perceived, but he could not communicate it successfully. After Hitler invaded Poland in 1939, Britain finally declared war, and the people of that island nation had to come to grips with why they had decided to fight.

At this point, Churchill rose to greatness as perhaps the most prominent political genius of the twentieth century. He rallied the nation to a cause and presented a clear purpose for which they would fight which held no possible alternatives. He could state it in a variety of ways: to defeat the Nazis, to liberate Europe, to save civilization. The purpose was simply stated but profound in its implications. It became the stackpole for organizing and integrating all the efforts that followed.

The average church has lost sight of its purpose. It has no concept of why it stands there on that corner, what it is supposed to do, or why it is supposed to do it. The beginning of vitality in an existing church comes when that congregation understands what God's purpose is for them. This understanding of God's purpose has particular significance for that church whose growth pattern has plateaued or has started to decline.

In those situations, the church has existed for a number of years, and it has lost its sense of purpose. Theologically speaking, they have lost their vision. Scripture warns, "Where there is no vision, the people perish" (Prov. 29:18 KJV). This proverb has literal application to churches. Churches all over the United States close their doors and sell their property every year because they have lost their vision and have no basis for continuing. They have lost all sense of God's purpose for them in that place.

The primary thesis presented here is that if God has a congregation in a specific location, he has some purpose for it to fulfill. Regardless of its size, it still has something God wants it to do. The fact that the neighborhood has changed is totally irrelevant. The number one priority for the church and its leadership rests in discerning God's purpose for that church in that place. The recognition of the uniqueness of location will determine how effectively a church uses appropriate methods to achieve its ministry. Unfortunately, many churches use means which they assume constitute a universal principle of ministry, simply because they worked somewhere else.

During the American Revolution, the British knew exactly how to fight, because it had worked well in Europe. They marched in neat rows, wore bright uniforms, and played loud music. The Americans hid behind trees, wore clothes that blended into the forest background, and crept up on the enemy unawares. The universal principle of a dynamic church corresponds to the military experience: do the appropriate thing in the unique location.

When Britain examined its purpose for entering into World War II, its purpose once the war started differed from what Churchill perceived as its purpose with respect to Germany prior to the war. Prior to the war, Churchill thought that Britain and the allies needed to prevent Germany from rearming. Britain needed to prevent Germany from reoccupying the Rhineland. Britain needed to prevent Germany from annexing Austria. Britain needed to prevent Germany from annexing Czechoslovakia.

At each point along the way in Germany's growing thirst for territory in the middle 1930s, Britain and her allies still had the capacity to do something about Hitler's ambitions. When matters deteriorated too far, however, the purpose changed. When Britain finally decided to do something about the situation, it had grown to an overwhelming problem. The greater part of central Europe had already fallen to Hitler.

In a church, the purpose changes with the situation, whether it be the situation within the church or in the community where the church meets. A church rarely has the same options in dealing with a problem that it would have had ten years before, if only it had the vision to deal with the matter then. As a situation deteriorates in a church or its surrounding community, it must reassess its purpose with respect to the situation. Survival does not constitute a worthy enough purpose for Christ's church.

As Churchill accepted the mandate to lead Britain as prime minister, survival never emerged as a viable option for the nation's purpose. Britain could have entered into a treaty with Hitler and war would not have ensued. Each church needs to see God's purpose for it as more glorious than survival.

Yet, for many churches the preoccupation rests not with the advancement of the kingdom of God, the salvation of those who do not know the liberating power of Christ, or the announcement of the word of life to those who are dying in sin. Rather, they see their purpose as assuring that the sanctuary will get a coat of paint next year, that the roof gets replaced in five years, and that no one steals any cups out of the kitchen cabinet.

A survival mentality is not a worthy purpose for the church. When this happens, a church has withdrawn from the Great Commission. Many of the churches in the United States find themselves in this very situation.

Growth does not supply an adequate purpose in many situations, because the underlying motivation is tinged by the survival mentality. Reaching people and incorporating them into the church merely provides a means of preserving the institution. In the Sermon on the Mount, Jesus took a rather dim view of motivations like this to do what might appear to be a pious work on the surface (Matt. 5:1–12).

To charity, prayer, and fasting might be added efforts to enlarge the church for the wrong reasons. People in the secular world already have the impression that the church only wants their money. Unfortunately, in many cases this impression proves true. The church has to be sure of its own motivation in ministry, and the solution to this problem comes in soberly considering God's purpose for a particular church in a particular place in a particular time. Growth then may become the worthy goal of an appropriate purpose. Britain did not grow as a result of World War II. Instead, it released dozens of colonies that became independent countries, but democracy spread.

Perhaps the greatest frustration for the leader of a church involves arriving at the mission for the church. The leader cannot impose a mission for the church in most situations. In most situations the mission must be a commonly agreed upon, consensus view.

In his studies Lyle Schaller identifies three situations in which a pastor may successfully define a church's purpose and receive a consensus following; large, relatively new and independent or sectarian churches in the South and West; downtown and inner-city churches; rapidly growing, new missions that revolve around the personality and gifts of the church planter.[1] In each of these exceptional situations, however, the leadership and relational dynamics which allow this style of decision making and consensus to work operate in different ways.

Many pastors have attempted to bring about change by basing their leadership style on the model of a pastor in an entirely different kind of ministry setting and church size—and this has brought disastrous results. In most situations, the purpose must be arrived at jointly through major involvement by the congregation.

It took a number of years for Winston Churchill to build a consensus for the purpose of Britain with respect to Germany. Because of the British parliamentary system, Churchill knew he finally had the consensus when he was asked to lead the country as prime minister. His years of consensus building while a back bencher in parliament finally paid off.

Unfortunately, most pastors believe that going to a church as pastor means that the people will follow their lead. For the average church on plateau or decline, the pastor is viewed as a sojourner stopping off along the way to his next church. Consensus building takes a little time. Discovering what God wants a church to do is essentially a spiritual matter. The lack of purpose is a spiritual problem. Cavalier solutions copied from other churches will not work.

It is possible to present an idea to the elders, deacons, vestry, business meeting, or other body in a church charged with making a decision which results in a unanimous vote to adopt the pastor's plan, yet nothing ever comes of it. It never was their plan. They will allow the pastor to do it, but they will not do it. They have to believe the purpose is what God wants them to do. They may agree to build a family life center at a business meeting, but they do not really vote until the collection plate is passed.

Reconnaissance

A mission always has a context or environment. In World War II and the days leading up to it, Winston Churchill was preoccupied with facts and figures about Britain, Germany, the Empire and its Commonwealth,

France, the United States, and a host of other matters. Here was a tiny island nation with limited resources cut off from the rest of the world except through the sea lanes.

On the other hand, Germany sat securely in the middle of Europe as the most powerful nation on the continent and rich in resources, except for oil. Germany had a huge population, and Hitler had been at work rearming since coming to power. Britain and her allies, on the other hand, began disarming in the 1920s. In the mid 1930s, Britain and Germany passed one another as Britain declined in vitality and Germany grew in its ability to commit aggression.

During the prewar years, Winston Churchill spouted statistics to anyone who would listen. Whether in his newspaper column, on the floor of the House of Commons, or at borough political meetings, Churchill recited his litany of statistics in a futile effort to wake Britain up to the danger the nation faced from Hitler. Britain did not wake up until the bombs began to fall. By then, an entirely different set of circumstances existed which would demand a different course of action from what Britain could have done a few years earlier.

By 1939 Britain faced a much larger problem with smaller resources to meet the challenge and fewer allies to help. Rather than give up when he realized that Britain did not have the resources to carry on its struggle, Churchill found creative ways to gather the resources. One of these emerged as the lend-lease agreement with the United States—at that time a neutral, isolationist nation.

Most churches do not face the challenge of their real ministry until survival needs force them to deal with reality. In this regard, comfort tends to be the greatest obstacle to a church engaging the spiritual battle it is uniquely suited to fight. A comfortable church does not have to deal with how hell manifests itself in the community or how people may suffer as a consequence of sin. A church will never come to the aid of a dying world if it will not open its eyes to the signs of death that must be confronted. For the comfortable church that does not face imminent extinction, the primary challenge of leadership is to rally the church to do something when survival is not an issue.

Since most churches in the United States sit on a membership plateau or have entered a decline, recognizing their environment is a crucial issue. Churches on plateau often wait until they have slipped into decline before they try to do anything, and then they tend to operate desperately out of a survival mode.

This phenomenon illustrates the basic problem of ministry. The ministry is always the Lord's ministry. Any church that does the Lord's ministry will successfully attack the gates of hell. The church that sees its purpose as survival will die, because it has no faith in the One who calls and establishes the ministry. For this reason, facing one's ministry context is essentially a spiritual matter, though it may involve statistics, sociology, and administrative concerns.

When I left the pastorate to serve in the evangelism department of the Kentucky Baptist Convention, Mary Anne and I decided to join a church where we could make a difference. We settled in a one-hundred-year-old church in the inner-city with a bivocational pastor. When Jerry Summerfield went to the church ten years earlier, he preached his first sermon to seven people in a sanctuary that seats eight hundred.

The church never did very well at surviving. When it finally realized that since it had not died God must still have something for it to do, it began to grow again. It looked at itself and saw only old people. Then it looked at its neighborhood and found two thousand senior citizens in a two-block radius. It started an outreach Bible study in a nearby retirement home, and the church began to grow with senior citizens! The church soon had a ministry to forty inner-city children which it has developed through a "lend-lease" plan with a more comfortable church.

After that the church began a Hispanic ministry that involved over fifty Spanish-speaking adults whose English-speaking children became part of the English-speaking youth ministry. Because of the transient nature of the inner city and the death rate of people more than seventy-five years old, the form of ministry and evangelism constantly changes at Fourth Avenue Baptist Church in Louisville.

Reconnaissance provides a basis for matching needs and resources. It recognizes limitations and makes realistic judgments of priorities. It is a spiritual exercise that calls upon people to see that the fields are ready for harvest, and it calls upon people to pray that the Lord of the harvest will supply the resources to reap the harvest. It is a spiritual exercise that calls upon the entire church to count the cost before entering the battle.

Objectives

Eisenhower said that he had one objective: to take Berlin. Objectives should be simply stated and should be obvious in their simplicity. A church cannot have too many objectives or it will weaken itself through too much diversification. A church should always be looking to new objectives, however, when old ones are met. By focusing on a few objectives a church can maintain an integrated ministry that makes sense. The pieces of church life seem to fit together.

The major objectives of a church will usually fall within five basic categories that may be described as worship, education, fellowship, ministry, and administration. These categories represent functional areas of church life in which major objectives arise. In the early passages of Acts these different functions blend together harmoniously so that one would struggle to draw too sharp a line of distinction between them. After Pentecost the description of the church reflects these categories:

> And they devoted themselves to the apostles' teaching and fellowship, to the breaking of bread and the prayers. And fear came upon every soul; and many wonders and signs were done through the apostles. And all who believed were together and had all things in common; and they sold their possessions and goods and distributed them to all, as any had need. And day by day, attending the temple together and breaking bread in their homes, they partook of food with glad and generous hearts, praising God and having favor with all the people. And the Lord added to their number day by day those who were being saved (Acts 2:42–47 RSV).

The worship elements included attending the temple, prayer, and praise. The education element focused on the apostles' teaching. The fellowship element is specifically mentioned, but also implied by gathering together for meals in homes.

Finally, this passage speaks of the ministry of the church expressed through the miracles of healing done through the apostles. The functional area not mentioned in this passage, not surprisingly, represented the area in which the first church conflict arose. When the problem of food distribution for the widows arose, the church found an administrative solution to the problem by appointing seven men to see that the distribution took place properly (Acts 6:1–6). In the context of all these dimensions of church life, the "Lord added to their number day by day those who were being saved" (Acts 2:47b RSV).

In some churches, the evangelism centers around worship. In others it expresses itself in education, fellowship, or ministry. In some churches a successful evangelism program revolves around administration, where an organized visitation program depends upon administrative skill. In the most vibrant churches, evangelism expresses itself in every functional category of church life, because each of these areas has a dimension of "Good News" to it which becomes a context for verbalizing the gospel.

Each church must come to grips with those areas of its life that require attention. In a situation in which someone walks in off the street to a worship service, the church has a problem with what to do with that person if he or she is converted. How will they be integrated into the fellowship of the church? How will they grow in the nurture and admonition of the Lord? How will they become equipped for the work of ministry?

All of the teaching cannot be done from the pulpit on Sunday morning. That is not the purpose of worship. Unfortunately, too many pastors try to accomplish everything from the pulpit, including recruitment and promotion which are administrative functions. If the church does not adequately attend to these five functional areas, it becomes too weak internally to do anything externally.

On the basis of a sound understanding of a church's environment, including demography of the community and areas of strength and weakness, a church may then set some solid objectives. A worship objective might be to develop a worship style more appropriate to the changing community. An education objective might be to make Bible study more applicable to the lives of church members. A ministry objective might be to relieve the drug abuse problem of teenagers in the community. The church must identify the spiritual battles that must be fought and the functional dimension of church life best suited to lead the charge.

Strategy

The crucial area of strategy development grows out of clearly described objectives. *Strategy* is a military term that has to do with the integration of an effort in its broad dimension to achieve a specific result. In the European theater of World War II, the allied strategy involved united operations of multinational forces that included naval, army, and army air corps services.

Each of these branches of the military, in turn, had particular groups that attended to different operations. The air corps, the navy, and the army did entirely different things, but within the army, the cavalry did something entirely different from the engineers, the infantry, the artillery, or the quartermaster corps.

In a church, the different functional areas seem to do entirely different things. The morning worship service is entirely different from the women's mission group, which is entirely different from Sunday school, which is entirely different from that nebulous thing called the "youth group."

The average church has all of this activity going on, but it all happens in pigeon holes so that no connection ever occurs between them. The different ministries go off in opposite directions, busily attending to themselves as though their purpose under God is merely to exist. It is little wonder that most laypeople do not see any purpose or direction for the church.

In most cases, the ministers do not know how things fit together or where they are going either. Most pastors of plateaued or declining churches function more like jugglers than as strategists. They are trying to keep all the balls in the air at the same time. Strategy is the process for drawing all the pieces together toward some common purpose.

Robert E. Lee was one of the most brilliant military strategists who ever lived. With limited troops and resources, he won battles and kept a vastly superior Union Army occupied for four years. He wore out one general after another as Lincoln sought to find anyone who could meet him in the field. Lincoln finally found Ulysses S. Grant, another great strategist. Grant was finally able to defeat Lee with an army three times as large as Lee's.

In that great American struggle, Lee's strategy was greatly handicapped by the purpose dictated by President Jefferson Davis, who ordered Lee to defend Richmond. The purpose was unworthy of a military engagement. Lee could never take the initiative. He could only fight increasingly desperate battles until his troops could fight no more.

If a church sees its primary purpose as survival, no strategy can be developed to help it do that. The existence of the institution can be prolonged, but strategy is not intended for survival. Strategy is for victory. The church that has a glorious purpose can find a strategy that will help it realize its purpose.

In World War II, allied strategy involved destroying the axis power in North Africa and the Middle East, the source of German oil. Then it involved disrupting the sea lanes that supplied Germany with resources. Next, it involved attacking Germany from the south, up the Italian Peninsula, from the west through France, and from the east where the Russians kept the Germans tied down.

In the invasions, the navy transported troops and provided bombardment support, the corps of engineers
cleared the beaches of mines, the air corps bombed supply
lines and dropped paratroopers behind enemy lines to dis-
rupt communication systems. Each element of the military
did something entirely different, but for a single unified
purpose.

If churches could begin to think of operating in their
different functions toward a common purpose, then even
the most feeble of congregations would experience victory in their purpose under God. The people will begin
to see how all the parts fit together. Then, instead of
church programs competing with one another, they will
support one another.

The average church has two, three, or four youth
"programs" going on at the same time. A youth minister
may run the youth group, but have nothing to do with
the youth choir which is often seen as competition for
time and space on the church calendar. Neither of these
have any connection with youth Sunday school or, in
some churches, the youth mission group.

What if the people who relate to youth in different
ways got together and developed a youth strategy for
ministry that gave a sense of direction to the way the
church treated its youth? Perhaps youth would not feel
they had graduated from church when they graduate
from high school.

Goals

With a clear strategy in mind of how all the parts
will work together to accomplish the common purpose,
a church can set appropriate goals to map out its
progress. In World War II, the allies needed X number
of troops in England ready to embark by June 1, 1944.
In order to accomplish that goal, however, they had to

have X number of troop carriers prepared to carry the troops by May 31, 1944. In order to operate the carriers, however, they had to have on hand X barrels of fuel by May 30, 1944. Goal setting involves thinking ahead.

In the church, goal setting involves the simple planning needed to make things happen. It answers the simple questions of who, what, when, where, and how much. Purpose and strategy answer the questions of why and how. Goal setting helps to ensure that our efforts will succeed. Goal setting helps to protect the church from looking like a collection of bumbling oafs.

So often a church sabotages its own ministry by not having realistic goals stated and planned in advance. Surprises will always happen, but goal setting helps to keep the devastating surprises to a minimum. With established goals, things will more likely happen. A church can set a goal for the number of visitors it expects at the Christmas cantata. Then it will be in a position to set a goal for the number of cookies needed for the reception and how many contacts must take place to achieve the desired number of visitors.

One of the greatest military disasters in history took place as a result of unrealistic goal setting. Napoleon Bonapart invaded Russia in the summer with the expectation of conquering the nation before the winter. Because his goal was unrealistic, he did not make adequate provision for winter uniforms, food, and other supplies. Realistic goal setting helps anticipate what must happen in order for an effort to succeed.

Staff Support

Established goals enable the support staff to formulate the plans necessary to accomplish the goals. The army has an old joke about young officers. In his training, a young officer candidate is asked to explain the correct course of action in a case study. He is charged with erecting a twenty-foot flag pole. He has a shovel, a ten-foot piece of rope, a sergeant, and three enlisted men. What should he do? The correct answer is that he should tell the sergeant, "Sergeant, erect the pole." Then he should leave.

In the church, a number of people have responsible jobs and much more experience in making things happen than the average seminary-trained minister. For some reason, however, ministers want to be in the middle of every decision when they should spend more of their time making sure the right person is in each position of responsibility.

This problem usually boils down to an administrative matter of how people are chosen for positions of responsibility in a church. If the pastor or other responsible ministry leader feels they cannot leave the designated person alone to make week-to-week plans for programs and events, then the whole process of leadership selection (administration) and leadership development (education) has broken down.

For a church to operate in a vital way, the laity need to express themselves. The apostles recognized this when they set aside seven people to take care of the food distribution for needy widows. They did not tell them how to do it. They simply set for them the goal of making sure everyone got fed. The role of the "ministers" was to make sure the right people were matched up with that particular task.

Deciding on the purpose of the church requires the involvement of all the church in reaching consensus. A smaller group can do the work of environmental reconnaissance and objective setting. Strategy development and goal setting can operate at the supervisory committee level, but when it comes to planning the pizza blast for the youth, the ones who work with youth must be let loose.

Before D-Day, Eisenhower and the general staff briefed their officers on the established goals and objectives of the invasion force. The officers then developed detailed action plans for achieving those goals and objectives. Eisenhower would not be on the beach at Normandy when the fighting started. Similarly, most pastors should not be involved in every little detail of church life. They cannot be. Rather, the laity should feel the freedom and have confidence in their ability to plan and carry out the ministry of the church.

Tactics

The last level of this strategic planning process involves the particular programs, events, processes, or structures devised to accomplish the specific goals and objectives the church has set for itself. In the average church, this is the only part of the process that ever takes place. It usually involves filling up dates on the calendar without any consideration given to the impact these activities will have on one another and the church as a whole. Each activity has a life of its own without any relationship to the other activities of the church. Each activity becomes its own purpose, objective, and goal.

In the Vietnam War the military had a lot of tactics. The troops took a village, then left the village to take a hill. From the hill they went to take a bridge, before finally returning to take the same village again. Each engagement was fought in isolation as though nothing had preceded it and nothing would come after it.

The troops played their part well. They carried out the tactics, but nothing tied the tactics together to give an overall guiding direction. Tactics could not move toward the accomplishment of the governing purpose, because those who planned, financed, and debated the war gave it no purpose.

Planned activities are not enough to give a church a vital, growing life. Not even goals and objectives are enough to help this happen. A church can have a well-planned schedule of goals and objectives, yet remain in a maintenance pattern. Many planning processes only help reinforce the maintenance attitude. Packard Motor Company had goals and objectives. These matters degenerate into irrelevancy when not tied to a vision which integrates them and gives direction to the whole enterprise.

A church can calendar Vacation Bible School. Very few churches have plans for follow-up to Vacation Bible School. Still fewer have integrated VBS into the education program of the church which would involve new children in Sunday school. Even fewer churches have plans for what to do with the parents of children who come to Vacation Bible School. Strategy develops as other parts of the church impact and are impacted by Vacation Bible School.

The youth group may have a pizza blast after the football game in the fall. Does this event fit into the total strategy of youth ministry? Does the adult leadership team that works with youth take the time to get to know visitors at these events? Are events like this designed to encourage youth to bring their friends? At some time during the party, does someone say something about why they gather together? For some reason these events seem to gravitate toward either saying nothing about Christ or preaching a sermon.

Discovering the appropriate way to introduce Christ in different settings forms part of the overall strategy. How to follow up a pizza blast and determining what activity would follow a pizza blast represent questions that a strategy must answer. All of these issues come into play when deciding when to calendar events, what kinds of events to calendar, and the sequence in which events should take place.

Bringing a coherent picture of what the church is trying to do probably represents the primary challenge of leadership in the church today. Church leaders need to make sense of a church program that grinds workers into grist without the church ever going anywhere. Strategic thinking will help the ministers move away from the kind of maintenance ministry in which they oil the machinery, only to see the church accomplish less and less every year. Strategic thinking can help turn the situation around so that the church recognizes its purpose, and realizes that its purpose is God's purpose.

Conclusion

The military model for the church is only one of many ways the Bible describes the church. Like all models, it cannot be pressed too far or it will collapse. It could be, and has been, seriously abused. Nonetheless, it has about it the urgency and seriousness of our mission that the business model lacks. The church faces a relentless struggle against all the wickedness of hell that would destroy humanity and all creation. The church cannot settle for business as usual.

Each congregation and each Christian must come to grips with the part God intends they should play in the redemption of the world. The ministry is a matter of life and death for those who do not know Jesus Christ. The church does not win the victory of this battle. Only Christ can win that victory, but we bring the message and the fruit of that victory.

Chapter 10

Creating a Culture for World Evangelism: How Are We Doing?
Phil Roberts

EVANGELISM AND MISSIONS FORM THE LIFEBLOOD OF Baptist churches as well as that of their respective associations and conventions. It is generally recognized in Baptist circles that the only avenue to God's blessings on them and their fellowship is to be fully obedient to the assignment given by the Lord Jesus Christ himself:

> All authority has been given to Me in heaven and on earth. Go therefore and make disciples of all the nations, baptizing them in the name of the Father and of the Son and of the Holy Spirit, teaching them to observe all things that I have commanded you; and lo, I am with you always, even to the end of the age (Matt. 28:18–20 NKJV).

To fulfill this task will require the infilling of the Holy Spirit so that his pentecostal empowering will energize the people of God to complete the pentecostal task—the evangelization of the world. And from the human perspective, the church must focus its resources, both financial and personnel, on the aim of finishing this assignment. In order to focus resources, however, a Great Commission culture must be created and sustained so that all of God's people may know from the new birth onwards what part they can play in this most important of all tasks.

Building a Great Commission culture, a culture for world evangelism, must therefore be the priority of the followers of Jesus Christ. Hence, the purpose of this chapter is to raise the question: "How are we doing?" How are we doing in framing a climate conducive for universal and total world evangelism mobilization?

Rival Gospels: How Are They Doing?

Let's go a step further: How are we doing compared to rival gospels, and those who propagate them? Here we are referring to new religions, movements, or cults, which in large part are finding much success and growth on mission fields inside and outside the United States. But the hot news for "cult watchers" and those who observe new religious movements is their growing success as world mission forces.

It is the experience of U.S. travelers and tourists wherever they go—Asia, Africa, Latin America, or Europe—that they often encounter Jehovah's Witnesses publishers or missionaries from the Church of Jesus Christ of Latter-day Saints aggressively proselytizing in foreign countries. Church growth rates and numbers of converts overseas from such groups are impressive.

As recently as 1942 Jehovah's Witnesses had only 100,000 adherents. When their numbers increased to more than 144,000 shortly thereafter—and with failed prophecies regarding Armageddon and the end of the world—Jehovah's Witnesses theology was changed. "Earthly paradise" was designated as a place of eternal bliss for those who were deemed worthy while continuing to maintain that only the worthiest 144,000 would join Jehovah in heaven. Worldwide membership rolls have continued to swell. There are now five million members of kingdom halls around the globe, four million of whom reside outside the United States.[1]

In some ways more impressively, the Latter-day Saints have grown from less than a million members in 1950—most of whom resided in the inter-mountain west—to a worldwide count of over ten million today.[2] That computes to a 1,000 percent increase in forty years. In February 1996 the Church of Jesus Christ of Latter-day Saints announced that for the first time in its history, it had more members outside the United States than it had resident in the fifty states. Approximately 4.8 million Latter-day Saints of a 9.5 million membership were non-U.S. residents.

Our main purpose in the remainder of this chapter is to examine in greater detail the mission strategy and program of the Church of Jesus Christ of Latter-day Saints in order to ask how such growth is possible. We will initially consider some of their general proselytizing principles and then review their approach to developing a missions culture for mobilizing Mormon people for missionary work. The question will then be considered as to whether Southern Baptists and evangelicals generally have, pound for pound, established as fruitful a missions culture as Mormons.

Latter-day Saints—A Missions Sending Culture?

What are the tactics utilized by Mormons in their proselytization efforts? There are several.

First, they have generally followed the Christian missions movement and have sought to win converts from among its nominal members. The Church of Jesus Christ of Latter-day Saints market themselves as the genuine and complete form of Christianity. It is the conviction of the church that genuine "Christian truth" is Mormonism. The early church in their view was Mormon. The practice and belief system of the New

Testament church was Mormonism. Mormon temple rituals, including baptism for the dead, eternal marriages, and endowment ceremonies, are identical to those practiced in the early church.

Latter-day Saints (LDS) authorities claim that when the apostles of Jesus passed from the scene the church was corrupted and Jesus and his beliefs, doctrines, authority, the priesthood, and rituals were then lost. The church was hellenized, pagan elements corrupted the pristine order of Mormon faith and practice, and subsequently what Mormons call the "great apostasy" fell upon the world. One LDS source explains this phenomenon: "It was lost—the gospel with its powers and blessings—sometime after the Savior's crucifixion and the loss of his apostles. The laws were changed, the ordinances were changed, and the everlasting covenant was broken that the Lord gave to his people . . . There was a long period of centuries when the gospel was not available to people on their earth."[3]

Mormons still hold tenaciously to this skewed and inaccurate view of church history—one which denies the promise of Jesus that his church, though oft embattled, would not disappear from the earth (cf. Matt. 16:13–20) and that the nature of the Bible as God's totally accurate source book for the Gospel would not be lost (cf. 2 Tim. 3).

Their interpretation of the "apostasy" also provides the rationale for their own name "Latter-day Saints," which attempts to bond them with "early-day saints" of the New Testament and distance themselves from all other denominations. In their view, all other denominations are "wrong," their "confessions are admonitions," and their "professors" (or members) "are corrupt."[4]

In following the Christian movement, Mormonism touts itself as a friendly but unique church; in fact, the only true church. It siphons off members from Christian churches who become convinced of Mormonism's superiority as well as church members who have become disillusioned by difficulties or problems in their own fellowship.[5]

Second, Mormons use the media extensively. In airing public service announcements and media buys that advocate moral values and Mormon scripture, Mormons seek both legitimization and profile for their movement. As a result, a positive reception may be engendered for Mormon missionaries. Who has not seen these attractive, appealing and often family-oriented ads? And who would not perhaps be more inclined to discuss with Mormon missionaries their views on religious and spiritual concerns? Reluctance to talk with Mormon missionaries is lessened by media solicitation.

Missionary referrals are also generated through television and radio advertising. Often a *Book of Mormon,* or more recently a Bible, is offered as a free gift for those calling the LDS 800 number. What is often not known is that both the Bible and the *Book of Mormon* as offered on television are generally hand-delivered by Mormon missionaries. Consequently, LDS missionaries often have access to not only the general populace but to people in restricted housing areas where open solicitation is not allowed.

The media, therefore, creates opportunities and an atmosphere in which traditional missionary canvassing can work more effectively. The Church of Jesus Christ of Latter-day Saints is projected through the media as a user-friendly, moral, upright, and thoroughly attractive organization—the kind of group that many people would want to belong to.

Third, Mormonism maintains an aggressive public relations campaign in order to generate goodwill for the church. In this regard, a delicate balance is sought. Mormonism is presented as a mainstream Christian church while not compromising their basic conviction that the LDS church is the one true church. Mormonism is particularly eager to shed the albatross of "cult" and to establish itself as "Christian." The strategy used to achieve this goal is to emphasize the name of Jesus Christ as much as possible. In 1993 the church logo was changed so that the lettering in the name of Jesus Christ was tripled in size. The effect, of course, is to lessen resistance on the part of mainstream Protestants and evangelicals.

And in responding to theological criticism that Mormonism is a Christian cult, Mormon leaders answer that the LDS Church uses the name of Jesus profusely:

> We obey the commandment "Whatsoever ye shall
> do, ye shall do it in my name." Every prayer we offer
> is in His name. Every ordinance performed is in His
> name. Every baptism, confirmation, blessing, ordina-
> tion, every sermon, every testimony is concluded with
> the invocation of this sacred name.[6]

Mormon leaders obviously feel that their frequent use of the name of Jesus justifies their claim to be Christian. But it does not. Every major heretical movement in history, including the Arians, Nestorians, Sabellians, and others, also invoked the name of Jesus. Mormonism, like them, has defined the person of Jesus Christ. For them he is the literal first-born child of God and his heavenly wife in the "premortal" estate. He was sired by God heavenly father, a god in a body of flesh and bones, in consort with the virgin Mary and thus came to earth. He is a procreated being with a limited past.

Obviously, the protest of LDS thinkers that they are Christian flies in the face of all biblical and historical teaching regarding Christ. While a person may confess that he is Evander Holyfield and perhaps even change his name to Evander Holyfield, this does not mean that the person is *the* Evander Holyfield, heavyweight boxing champion of the world. Similarly, just because the Mormons say they believe in "Jesus," this is not the same as believing in the biblical person of Jesus Christ.

In spite of the Mormons' obvious heresies regarding Jesus, the Gospel and God—whom they believe was once a mortal man and achieved exaltation to godhood—the Latter-day Saints have made progress in being accepted as thoroughly Christian within some circles. An occasional ministerial alliance or pastor's fellowship has received them into membership and has allowed their full participation in its organization.

Such notice has generally come through the efforts of people like Darrell Anderson of Mesa, Arizona. He has produced materials and in fact written a book entitled *Soft Answers to Hard Questions* in which he encourages Latter-day Saints to be circumspect in their relations with non-LDS church leaders. Polite and appealing responses to tough questions regarding secret temple rituals, racist attitudes of the Mormon god, and the possibility of Mormons becoming gods are suggested and taught.[7]

All of these tactics are designed to build an image of the Mormon church as an acceptable and vital Christian movement. Public relations, however, are used only to supplement the most vital and traditional part of the LDS mission strategy—the use of missionaries.

The most vital element in the progress and growth of the LDS church is their proselytization efforts led by a growing corps of traditional Mormon missionaries. What is the traditional profile of a Mormon missionary? He is generally a male student of college age, although increasingly women are being used. These missionaries may come from a longstanding Mormon family or may, in fact, be recent converts to the church. Their goal is to convert families to the church.

These missionaries generally give a two-year period of service which is preceded by a two- to three-month training period in a Mormon training center for proselytization. Here they learn how to iron their clothes, cook their food, and speak the language of the country where they are going—if it is an overseas assignment. They also learn to share their testimonies and to proselytize non-Mormons effectively.

Remarkably, missionaries and their families generally have saved enough money to pay their own way. Once on the field, they exist in spartan conditions. During their two-year stint of service, they may not return home even in the case of a death of a parent. And they are allowed to call home only twice a year—at Christmas and on Mother's Day.

How is the LDS church doing in the recruitment and deployment of missionaries? We might think that it would be hard to recruit young people to work under such strict requirements. In fact, since World War II when there were only a few thousand missionaries, they have grown to number over fifty thousand. These missionaries now produce three hundred thousand converts to the Mormon church each year. This does not mean that they produce converts from Mormon children. Mormon children are automatically baptized at age eight and are not included in annual convert baptismal statistics. The 317,000-plus baptisms recorded by the church in 1997 were converts from non-Mormon movements. That means that each missionary produces about six converts per year.

What is the church's plan to increase their baptisms? It is to raise the per-missionary convert output slightly. From about six per annum, they hope over the next few years to raise it to seven or eight converts per year per missionary and perhaps even more. They know they cannot hope for a great increase. So their second strategy includes increasing the number of missionaries dramatically. Their goal is to have one hundred thousand missionaries out proselytizing by the year 2005.

If they are able to do that, Mormons will look toward baptizing seven hundred thousand converts to the church, maybe more, by the middle of the next decade. At this rate of growth, sociologist Rodney Stark estimates that the Mormons could number at least 280,000,000 by the year 2085. This raises the possibility that Mormonism will become the next great world religion.

How is it possible that such growth in missionaries is expected? If it is possible, it will happen because Mormonism has learned to create a mission culture—a culture where the exceptions are those who stay home and not the ones who go. It seems to me that in much of Southern Baptist and evangelical life, we have basically achieved the reverse. Those who go are the exceptions. They are the unusual types. They are the people who pay the ultimate price as the vast majority of the body of Christ stays behind and supports them, but evangelical missionaries are generally viewed as the few and the brave who are the point people for world missions.

How is Mormonism able to generate this concept— that everyone, every young person, has a part to play and everyone can make a critical contribution to the flow of Mormon missions and the production of converts? The answer can be attributed to the fact that they have produced a missions culture. The first way this dynamic is created by educating their children that missions is to be expected of them. They sing about it as children and they sing missionary choruses with a definite view of being a missionary themselves and making a personal contribution to missions. The Mormons clearly expect that of their children and they have taken over the children's missionary chorus industry. Here are two examples:

> I hope they call me on a mission. I hope they call me on a mission. When I have grown a foot or two, I hope by then I will be ready to teach and preach and work as missionaries do. I hope that I can share the gospel with those who want to know the truth. I want to be a missionary and serve and help the Lord while I am in my youth.
>
> I want to be a missionary now. I want to be a missionary now. I don't want to wait until I am grown. I want to share the gospel while I am young for I have a testimony of my own. I want to let my friends know about our church and the happiness it brings to me. I'll let them know the gospel was restored, tell them how *The Book of Mormon* came to be. Then I can be a missionary now. I don't have to wait until I am grown. I'll live each day the best that I know how and they'll know that I have a testimony.

Mormons educate their children to expect to be involved in their missionary enterprise.

Secondly, they condition their children. They begin by making it a part of every child's upbringing. When a baby is born, the parents will often go to the Deseret bookstore and buy a little plastic label that they attach to the baby's clothes. It says, "Future Mormon Missionary."

Every week Mormon families gather in what they call the "family home evening." It is expected that the parents will remind their youth that when they're about twenty years old, they will have the privilege of giving two years of their lives to the cause of Mormon missions.

Returned missionaries circulate regularly among Mormon youth groups, repeating their testimonies that the two years they spent as Mormon missionaries were the best years of their lives. Many indicate when they are older, they hope to return to give more time to the cause of Mormon missions. The Mormons have made missions their church motto: "Every member a missionary."

Not only do Mormons educate and condition their youth to be involved in missions; they plan for it. The author asked Sandra Tanner, a fifth-generation descendent of Brigham Young, who is now a convert to Christianity and authority on Mormon history, "How is it possible that a movement of five million U.S. members is able to produce fifty thousand Mormon missionaries?" She replied, "They plan for it."

When a child turns six years of age, the Mormon parents open a bank account on his or her behalf. This is not a bank account to save for their college or university education. It is not a bank account to save for their first car. It is a bank account for their Mormon mission. Why? Because each Mormon missionary who goes pays his or her own expense. They pay their airfare to the place where they are going. They support themselves while they are there. This includes all of their living expenses. The one benefit a missionary has from the church is a ticket home once he or she has finished his or her assignment.

As they plan for it, the Mormon church includes their educational system. Brigham Young University, which is an outstanding educational institution and the largest private religious undergraduate school in the United States, charges less than two thousand dollars for a semester's tuition. Why? Because they want the missionaries to have the money saved and available to help them to go on their mission. So it is not surprising to learn that of BYU's

27,000 undergraduates, 17,000 have either been missionaries or will be missionaries before they graduate.

Mormons have succeeded in creating a missionary culture by making missions a personal expectation and a priority for the lives of its youth.

Their success has generated the single largest overseas missionary force of a single church or denomination and one that far exceeds the number of missionaries of Southern Baptists.[8] The aggressive confrontational proselytization efforts of the church present a major challenge to the evangelical mission movement. Mormonism has been particularly successful at the task of recruiting and mobilizing students to do direct church recruitment and to offer lessons and principles that evangelicals ought to take note of in doing missions themselves.

Serious Evaluation

What can be learned from Mormon missionary efforts?

First of all, evangelical denominational mission agencies and churches must learn not only to encourage in a vague sort of way, but to challenge and recruit people directly to become a part of a growing evangelistic corps for world missions. Passivity and vagueness are inappropriate, as the cause of world evangelism becomes increasingly urgent in this late hour of world history. If appropriate opportunities and structures were established for student evangelism, whether or not people feel called to full-time career missions, they could still be challenged to spend months or several years of their lives sharing the gospel in a missionary context.

Second, youth should be recruited and challenged, under the leadership of the Spirit of God, to be involved in direct evangelism. Among Mormon missionaries, there are approximately five thousand doing what they call "service missions"—school teaching, charitable work, community involvement, health services, etc. But their main efforts are focused on producing fifty thousand full-time personal recruiters (i.e., personal and small-group evangelists or proselytizers). It seems that evangelical missions has been distracted. Could it be that the service and administrative element in world missions has been emphasized over the direct evangelism element? Shouldn't our energies be spent primarily at doing not just church work but the work of the church—and that is direct evangelism and discipleship?

Why is it that an organization like Campus Crusade can recruit tens of thousands of volunteers who pay their own way, who give their lives and their time and energies and involvement with that organization? Could it be that these youth are challenged by the notion of being involved in direct evangelism? This certainly results in a person's knowledge that he or she is part of God's mission enterprise to the fullest and ultimate degree? This is not to belittle service assignments, but it is to say that if we spend too much energy and effort doing "church work," we could miss the main focus of doing the work of the church.

Third, we should make available to our young people missionary experiences from three months up to two years. Structures would have to be created to facilitate these opportunities. But to do so would be a very wise investment.

Fourth, we should raise expectations. We should teach and expect and pray that the exceptions for the years ahead would be those who do not get involved in volunteer missions and not those who do. Is it too much to expect that every evangelical student give several months to doing direct evangelism, no matter what their career path or plans?

Fifth, we should bring missions involvement into the children and youth groups, and even into the families of the evangelical world. Missions education must be the responsibility of everyone, including children's workers, youth pastors, and parents. It is the author's opinion that in no way will emphasis on short-term volunteers involving young people and college-age students detract from full-time vocational mission assignments.

In fact, I predict three positive side effects would be seen. One is that more full-time responses to career missions would be produced. Once many of these young people have been on the field and have seen people's lives changed by Jesus Christ, they will sense the call of God on their life to full-time service. Second, we'll discover more trained, energized and effective soul-winners back in local churches who spent that time abroad or somewhere in the United States sharing the gospel directly with people. And third, believers will be more open to contributing to missions efforts as they see firsthand the needs and the impact that the gospel is making around our world.

Sixth, we must see the cults as a mission people. We must realize that the best response to cult proselytization is a good offense and not just a good defense. The Great Commission knows no limits or restrictions. If Jesus commanded us to take the gospel to all people everywhere, then the kingdoms of the cults—including Jehovah's Witnesses and Latter-day Saints—must be seen as part of the Christian world's mission field.

Conclusion

During the first two weeks of June 1998, the Southern Baptist Convention undertook the most intensive evangelistic effort in the history of the Salt Lake Valley. Door-to-door canvassing, television spots including the offer of a free copy of the "Jesus Video" as well as extensive distribution by mail of an evangelistic tabloid resulted in almost two thousand decisions for Christ. Such efforts must be increased. Individual Christians must see that when Mormon missionaries and other similar proselytizers knock on our doors, it is an opportunity for evangelism. The evangelical world's commitment must be that all the world, including the world of the cults, must know that the biblical Jesus Christ came to this earth and was crucified for all of the sins of the world so that by faith in him they may be saved!

PART III

TELLING THE GOSPEL

Chapter 11

Telling the Gospel One on One
G. William Schweer

PERSONAL ONE-ON-ONE OUTREACH IS FOUNDATIONAL TO all evangelism. It is evangelism in its most powerful form. In fact, when there is no one-on-one activity, evangelism is profoundly stunted.

Mass crusades and nationally televised programs led by outstanding personalities are more spectacular, and, of course, have their place. People are intrigued with the massive and the glamorous. Yet it is still the quiet, one-on-one, lovingly confrontational encounter that is most effective in bringing about life-changing decisions.

Such evangelism is never the path of least resistance. There are other valuable things to be done in the life of a church. Many would prefer teaching a class or leading a cell group. Not a few would choose committee work, cooking, moving furniture, or laying linoleum. Those are all good things that need doing, but the weightier matter of personal witness is light years ahead in importance. When churches neglect this activity, they soon plateau, decline, or even die.

Delos Miles's definition of evangelism is a classic statement containing both essential truth and positive teaching.[1] When he stated that we have majored on telling, minored on doing, and made an elective of being, he was of course patently correct. The latter two dimensions do suffer neglect, even indifference. Yet, he did not suggest less telling. Telling is an absolutely essential element of witness. In a world of lost persons, we dare not have less. We must have more, and it must be of the most competent kind.

There are voices today which insist that in-home personal evangelism can no longer be done. Some suggest that personal danger, the inclination toward cocooning, resentment of intrusion, and fear of door knocking strangers all militate against it. Granted, there are places today where it may be difficult or even impossible. Yet two things should keep us from yielding too quickly to these obstacles.

One is that Jesus never promised that his work would be easy. We should never expect that his work will be unencumbered without certain hindrances. Second, the fastest growing cult groups, Jehovah's Witnesses and Mormons, are knocking on more doors than ever before. While I am not suggesting that we follow their precise patterns, it is more than possible that some have surrendered this method of discovering and winning prospects all too quickly. (At-the-door confrontational witness is their primary method.) There are, of course, other ways to tell the message one on one.

It seems to me that there are at least five compelling reasons why telling one on one must remain the major priority of the churches. Any one of these contentions would be enough to make this activity essential. The force of the five together make it absolutely imperative.

It Is Commanded

Almost before he did anything else in public ministry, Jesus began to call his disciples. He addressed two fishermen saying, "Follow me and I will make you become fishers of men" (Mark 1:17 RSV). Although the word translated "follow" is actually an adverb meaning "hither" or "come hither," when it is used with the adverb that follows, it serves as a kind of imperative meaning "come with me." They were to come with him as disciples and learn to fish for men. Jesus was quite up-front. He made it clear that they were to learn to win persons.

It is crucial to see that this was more than an event of historical interest. It was the inauguration of a strategy. It was his method for multiplying disciples then and now. It means that in any generation, following Jesus involves fishing for persons.

The evangelism thrust of the five commissions in the post-resurrection ministry of Jesus is powerful indeed (Matt. 28:18–20; Mark 16:15; Luke 24:27–49; John 20:21; and Acts 1:8). The composite focus of all five might look something like this: Following the example of Jesus, every believer has the responsibility of making, baptizing and growing disciples in the power of the Holy Spirit, in all the world. The very fact that each of the evangelists has his own version of the commission suggest strongly that this was a major emphasis of Jesus during the forty days. Not a few have pointed out that Jesus began his ministry by calling disciples to be "fishers of men" (Mark 1:17), and he ended it with a comprehensive command to bear witness (Acts 1:8).

A brief passage in Acts reveals just how seriously early believers took the content of the commissions. Due to Stephen's courageous defense, a persecution broke out, compelling many believers to leave Jerusalem. Those who fled became spiritual refugees, uprooted from their homes, livelihoods, families, and friends. Many of them had no assurance of shelter nor a certain source for their next meal. Despite those considerable concerns, "those who were scattered went about preaching the word" (Acts 8:4 RSV). They had taken their responsibility of verbal witness so seriously that not even persecution and insecurity could silence them.

One cannot leave this passage without comment on the nature of their preaching. We must not forget that these were new believers. They were hardly the sort who could have rented public halls for the purpose of speaking to large crowds. These fledgling disciples simply "overflowed" one on one, or one on two in the casual, everyday contacts of life. It was just the sort of preaching that any believer can do and should do today.

Jesus' early venture into the country of the Gerasenes produced a marvelous incident of healing and salvation. He encountered a man possessed by an unclean spirit who could not be held even with chains and fetters. He was completely out of control, doing destructive things to himself. Furthermore, he dwelt among the tombs, apparently unable to relate normally to society. His appeal to Jesus for help resulted in a marvelous transformation which brought forth amazement and fear on the part of area residents. This well-known burden on society was now "clothed and in his right mind" (Mark 5:15 RSV).

As Jesus prepared to leave the area, the man implored him that he might go with him. That was quite understandable. So momentous was the transformation that he was quite ready to follow wherever Jesus might lead. The Lord's response, however, was most noteworthy. He said, "Go home to your friends, and tell them how much the Lord has done for you, and how he has had mercy on you" (Mark 5:19 RSV). The proper response to the man's marvelous experience was to verbally share it with his known acquaintances. The next verse tells us that he did exactly that, so much so that "all men marveled."

Believers today have the same charge. Once transformed by Jesus, the believer takes on the immediate responsibility for witness. Telling what happened one on one is the most natural and logical way to share the life-changing news with one's friends.

While numerous other passages lend firm biblical support to telling one on one, one in particular demands our attention. It is often called the *locus classicus* of lay ministry. Few passages state more clearly the task of believers in the present age.

After using careful Old Testament language to indicate that what Israel failed to do has now been assigned to the individual members of the church, Peter revealed the task. It was that believers have been chosen to "declare the wonderful deeds of him who called [them] out of darkness into his marvelous light" (1 Pet. 2:9 RSV; cf. Exod. 19:4–6). Every believer is a priest, a member of a royal priesthood, given the task of witness proclamation. There is simply no way of escaping this responsibility. It is clearly what believers are called to do.

It Is Modeled

The New Testament models are almost as powerful as the commands. They are also almost as numerous.

Jesus' model is ably discussed elsewhere in this book. I do not want to duplicate that, but I want to refer to it briefly as it touches upon telling one on one.

John's commission teaches clearly that believers are to follow Jesus' model. That is a large order, but his words are transparent and succinct. "As the Father has sent me, even so I send you" (John 20:21 RSV).

Jesus was the evangelist *par excellence*. There is simply no doubt that he engaged in much one-on-one activity. It was Leighton Ford who pointed out many years ago that the Gospels record thirty-five encounters with Jesus that may be regarded as evangelistic.[2] Some of these, such as the encounter with Nicodemus, the woman at the well, the Gerasene demoniac, the adulterous woman and the inquisitive Zacchaeus, come immediately to mind. Jesus was a master of the personal encounter.

Mark tells us that on at least one occasion, he was so thronged by crowds that he did not even have time to eat. The implication is that while he spoke to the crowds, he also had time for many individual cases of which we are not told. Elsewhere we see Jesus spending a great deal of time with individuals. Many of them were those whom the other religious leaders would have scorned.

We cannot help but be impressed by Jesus' method and style. He dealt with no two persons in the same way. He dealt with all sorts of persons: fishermen, tax collectors, lepers, cripples, people with seizures, adulterers, prostitutes, thieves, the demon-possessed, religious leaders, the poor and the well-to-do, and always in accordance with their needs. Every person was important. He treated them with respect, dignity, and sympathy. He was always tender and compassionate with sinners. At the same time, he made clear demands upon their lives. Harsh words were reserved for the prideful and the religious establishment. Jesus' model deserves careful prayer and meditation. Clearly, however, to follow his model means much one-on-one telling to individuals.

It seems to me that many interpreters miss the personal witness implications of Pentecost. There is much emphasis on Peter's sermon and the heartfelt response of the 3000. There is much less on the crucial preliminary activity of the 120.

After their baptism by the Holy Spirit, the apostles witnessed powerfully to the crowds gathered to celebrate Pentecost. An amazing thing took place. "Each one heard them speaking in his own language" (Acts 2:6 RSV). The 120 disciples were sharing their experience and knowledge out among the crowds. While the Scriptures do not tell us specifically, it is extremely doubtful that these spoke to large gatherings at once. What is more logical is that they were telling their story one on one, one on two, or one on a small group. It was this spontaneous, spirit-filled overflow to many individuals that became the talk of Jerusalem (Acts 2:6, 12). It prepared many hearts to respond to Peter's sermon. It is my contention that, had it not been for this fervent one-on-one telling of the story, Peter would not have been so productive in drawing the net.

There is more to the story of Pentecost. The Holy Spirit was poured out on all believing flesh. All were empowered to prophesy, meaning to "tell forth" the gospel story. This included Gentiles as well as Jews, women as well as men, young men as well as old, servants as well as masters (Acts 2:17–18). There would be no exceptions. This is in contrast to the Old Testament era where the Holy Spirit seemed to come upon certain individuals to enable them to accomplish specific tasks. Now every believer was to be a living temple of the Holy Spirit, and thus empowered to witness. According to Joel's prophecy, this would usher in a new day of evangelism in which "whoever calls on the name of the Lord shall be saved" (Acts 2:21 RSV). And the great thrust of that evangelism would be telling the story one on one.

Philip was one of those scattered by the post-Stephen persecution. He had been one of the seven chosen by the church to solve the widows' alms-sharing problem. Compelled to scatter, he first went to Samaria and reaped a significant harvest. Then the Spirit led him to a desert place on the road going down to Gaza. There he met the Ethiopian eunuch, a dignitary returning from Jerusalem. Since he possessed a manuscript of Isaiah, he was probably a Gentile God-fearer—a Gentile attracted to the religion of Judaism but who had not yet become a full proselyte. Philip joined him and began at the place where he was reading and "told him the good news of Jesus" (Acts 8:35 RSV).

Perhaps the important point here is that God had sent Philip there to deal personally with this one hungry soul. Our world is full of similarly confused persons lacking in understanding. Most of them, like the eunuch, will not be able to understand unless someone helps them. There are all too few Philips, sensitive to the Spirit's leading, who will inconvenience themselves to guide lost persons to Jesus.

We have already seen the remarkable sharing of the other disciples who fled the Jerusalem persecution (Acts 8:1–4). There are many churches mentioned in Acts for which we have no record of their founding; this fact strongly indicates a continuous, spontaneous, personal witness on their part.

Aside from Jesus himself, the apostle Paul is the premier witness model in the New Testament. He was a master of telling the story one on one. When he said good-bye to the Ephesian elders, he reminded them that he had taught both publicly and from house to house (Acts 20:20). The latter phrase implies much telling one on one. So diligent had he been in Ephesus that he declared himself to be innocent of the blood of all persons (Acts 20:26).

Paul seemed to tell the story one on one wherever he was. He did so while making tents, in the marketplace, in prison, on shipboard to the crew and to his guards, to kings, governors, proconsuls, to individuals who carried the message into the emperor's household, and to many other persons.

It Is Necessary

It is equally important to see the indispensable nature of one-on-one verbal witness. The fact that so many people today want to witness "just by the way they live" makes this understanding essential. This is not to denigrate being and doing in any way. It is important to say, however, that without a verbalization of the gospel, the witness is, at best, incomplete.

There are many aspects of the gospel that require telling with words. There is simply no way to demonstrate the virgin birth of Jesus, his sinless life, his crucifixion and resurrection by the way a person lives. These matters require verbal explanation.

Some say they will leave that verbal explanation to the public ministry of the church, that is, to public preaching. It is clear, however, that many lost persons will not go to a church under any circumstances. Even if they did, there is no assurance today that they would hear a clear message of salvation. In their case, only a personal one-on-one witness will do.

Even the best demonstrations require words. In the days before movies had sound tracks, there were silent movies. The actors who played in them were superb. They were masters of pantomime and the expressive arts. Names like Charlie Chaplin and Buster Keaton are still recognizable even though it has been several decades since the "talkies" came on the scene. Interestingly enough, even with the best of thespians acting out the stories, those movies required subtitles. There was no way to get the whole story across without the aid of words. Such is the case with the gospel. Indeed, it must be acted out with increasing skill, but it will still require words.

A word from Peter adds further confirmation of verbal responsibility. He addressed scattered believers by saying that each individual believer must "declare the wonderful deeds of him" who called them "out of darkness into his marvelous light" (1 Pet. 2:9 RSV). It is interesting that the word translated "declare" reflects a Greek verb that includes the idea of verbal witness. It is to "tell forth," or "proclaim." "The words 'show Forth' . . . refer to a spoken message."[3] Only a verbal witness can fulfill the meaning of that verb, although it does not exclude, of course, what one is or does. Thus, a one-on-one verbalization of the gospel message, preferably on the turf of the prospect, is the normal ful-fillment of this command.

It Is Effective

Many people feel that preaching, especially the mass crusade variety or that which comes over television, is the means of great masses of people coming to Christ. The fact is that preaching to large audiences is a very poor way to bring about the radical changes of mind and alterations of life involved in conversion. Communication specialists have known this and taught it for a long time. Charles Kraft, in his book, *Communication Theory for Witnesses,* makes this clear. "Monologue preaching," he says, "though useful for certain purposes, is too frail a vehicle to adequately carry life-changing messages."[4]

There are a number of reasons why this is so. In varying degrees, such a situation is always largely impersonal. The preacher is shouting from a distance. He is not vulnerable, and it is usually one-way commu-nication that reaches a largely Christian audience. In the case of television preaching, it has the further limita-tions of being largely "non-prophetic," and being thought of as an entertainment medium. Mass commu-nication of whatever variety is not, by itself, a very effective way of bringing people to Christ, though it may be very useful as part of a media-mix.

In these areas where mass evangelism is weak, however, personal, one-on-one evangelism is strong. This method can be used of God to bring about radical changes of thought and behavior. There are several reasons why it is effective in contrast to mass evangelism.

For one thing, it affords an opportunity for the personal witness to listen to the prospect. In this way the evangelist can discover just where the prospect is spiritually.

Evangelism owes a large debt to Dr. James Engel, who, with his students, produced "The Engel Scale."[5] This scale shows that prospects are at varying spiritual distances from the point of conversion. The witness must begin where the prospects are, and not where one might wish them to be. Deductive witnessing methods have been used quite effectively with many people, and doubtless will continue to be. However, with the secularization and pluralization of society, there is an increasing need to use an inductive approach and to deal with the prospect in his current spiritual situation.

Listening helps develop the level of trust often necessary for effective communication. To listen carefully to another person is a kind of silent compliment. It says, "I am interested in you. What you have to say is important to me. You are a person of value and I care about what you are saying." Listening is one of the most effective ways of building bridges of confidence across which productive witness can flow.

Careful listening also earns the witness the right to be heard. For many people, it is only after they have been heard that they are willing to listen.

Telling one on one lends itself to two-way communication. It is in dialogue that questions can be answered, objections countered, and doubts resolved.

Here a person's beliefs and presuppositions can be examined and altered in the light of Scripture.

Dialogue also provides prospects an opportunity to understand and communicate with themselves. People can understand their own thoughts best by expressing them to another person.[6] Careful listening draws them out and provides further opportunity for discussion.

Not least, in dialogue, the matter of loving concern can best manifest itself. Few things are more essential in winning other persons to Christ.

In recent years, a great deal of research has been done concerning how people adopt innovations. Accepting Christ for a non-believer would indeed qualify as an innovation. According to Engel,[7] things such as mass media can influence a limited number of persons to adopt a new idea.

These persons would be classified by Rogers[8] as innovators (about 2 percent) and early adopters (about 13 percent). Later adopters are also influenced by mass media, but, "in addition they have the chance both to observe and interact with innovators and early adopters. More often than not, this informal face-to-face interaction is the dominant factor in adoption decision." His conclusion is that these innovators and early adopters (representing 16 percent, but varying depending on what the innovation is) serve as "influentials" or "opinion leaders" who play a significant role in the decisions of others.[9]

Elsewhere Engel affirms that diffusion research has shown that "mass media can trigger initial awareness and interest both with opinion leaders and nonopinion leaders," but "word of mouth . . . is usually a more decisive influence."[10] Communication theory has much more to say concerning evangelism, but what has been written serves to emphasize the superior power of telling one on one. The fact is that most persons come to Christ because someone speaks to them personally and lovingly urges them to trust him as Savior and Lord.

It Is Productive

As the years have passed, I have been amazed at the number of persons who have come to Christ after listening to what I consider a rather incomplete one-on-one presentation of the gospel. Sometimes their decision came months, even years later. Paul wrote, "It pleased God through the folly of what we preach to save those who believe" (1 Cor. 1:21b RSV). "What we preach" is a powerful message in the hands of the Holy Spirit. Often conviction lingers or deepens long after we have shared it. People also may have other spiritual encounters and experiences which add to their concern.

Several years after I moved to California, I received a phone call from a man in another state. I had called in his home some years before and shared the gospel with him one on one, I supposed, without success. The Holy Spirit had been at work in his heart ever since then, and when he made his decision, he felt he should call me and tell me about it. What joy!

On another occasion, I received an early morning phone call from a man I hardly remembered. He wanted to take me to breakfast and talk a bit. While we ate, he explained that when I had shared Christ with him years before, he was having a great deal of conflict with his wife. He said, "You don't know how much I wanted to accept Christ and know his forgiveness. To have done that then, however, would have meant that my wife would have won our battle. I just couldn't do it at the time." He had finally gotten his marital life straightened out as best he could, and he had made the great decision.

He wanted to tell me about it and thank me for the witness I had shared.

I am convinced that if we are faithful in telling one on one, we will one day be surprised at some of the converts with whom we felt we did not succeed. It is far and away the most effective means of evangelism. Sincere followers of Christ can hardly spend their time more profitably.

Chapter 12

Proclaiming Christ to American Religious Groups
George W. Braswell Jr.

PROFESSOR DELOS MILES HAS BEEN A COLLEAGUE AND friend for some twenty years. We have served together in the teaching of missions and evangelism. Professor Miles has advocated a wholesome and intelligent evangelism in his ministry, in his teaching, and in his writing. It is a distinct honor and a joyful opportunity to write this chapter in this book dedicated to him.

Context

Religious pluralism is wide and deep among the continents and peoples of the globe. The ancient religions of Hinduism and Buddhism which preceded Christianity are strong in their native land of India. They also have become missionary religions spreading not only in the East but into Europe and the Americas. In the United States, gurus and swamis and yoga masters whose antecedents are in Hinduism have established transcendental meditation centers and Hare Krishna temples. Buddhism has Zen centers in key American cities, and the Nichiren Shoshu of America is a zealous Buddhist missionary movement. Buddhist churches of America appeal to Asian immigrants.

Islam became a highly missionary and mobile religion once it was established in the Arabian Peninsula in the seventh century A.D. Following its prophet Muhammad and his successors, Muslims carried their religion to Africa, Europe, Asia, and the United States.

Mosques and Islamic associations are widespread in the United States. Both immigrant Muslims, African-American Muslims, and the indigenous Nation of Islam represent millions. Islam is purported to have over one billion adherents worldwide with some six to eight million in the United States. It is forecast that Muslims will supplant Jews in the near future as the second largest religion in America.

Alongside tens of millions of world religion followers in the United States, there are also native religions which have emerged out of discontent and disagreement with Christianity. Notable are the Church of Jesus Christ of Latter-day Saints and the Jehovah's Witnesses which together number some fourteen million. These two religious communities have targeted all peoples—and Christians in particular—as possible converts.

Other religious communities which have emerged out of Christianity include Christian Science, Unity School of Christianity, Unification Church, and The Way International. Also there is the New Age with its worldview and values, an eclectic of many philosophies and theologies of other religions. Too, there are astrology and witchcraft and Church of Satan.[1]

The context for proclamation to American religious groups is one of great religious diversity and ferment. The Constitution and Bill of Rights guarantee religious liberty and freedom and the separation of church and state. Religions may thrive in the marketplace of free enterprise with properties, investments, buildings, human resources, and political involvements. Religions may compete for peoples and resources against and alongside one another. Mass media may be utilized in conveying religious messengers and their messages.

Thus, the context for proclamation of the gospel is one of growing competition and of expanding religious communities. In the workplace, schools, and among the professions, people of various religions meet. Muslim children sit beside Christian children in classes. Muslim and Hindu medical doctors treat Christian patients. A Muslim leader offers the prayer to begin a session of the United States Senate. Mormon and Muslim chaplains serve in the armed services. At the beginning of the twenty-first century, the context for encountering and living among peoples of diverse religions in the United States has become more prevalent and challenging.

The term "American religious groups" will refer to those religious institutions and peoples who significantly deviate in theology and practice from orthodox Christianity. For this particular writing the American religious groups which are emphasized are Hinduism, Islam, The Church of Jesus Christ of Latter-day Saints (Mormons), and Jehovah's Witnesses. The deviations of these groups from orthodox Christianity will include their views of God and humanity, of Jesus Christ, of salvation, and the institutions of church and state.

Christian Proclamation

The apostle Paul in the nascent days of the first-century church journeyed from Palestine to Athens. In the midst of the marketplace of idols and ideologies, he observed that the people were very religious. He did not flee the marketplace or the people, but he affirmed them in their quest for God and then proclaimed to them the God of the resurrection of Jesus Christ (Acts 17).

Proclamation has its source and inspiration in God the Father of Jesus Christ. Its message is in the Good

News of the Lord Jesus Christ and his life, death, and resurrection. The Bible is the sourcebook for the revelatory teachings of God through the prophets, through Jesus Christ, and through the church. It has its purpose in reaching the minds and hearts of people to change their lives in salvation in Jesus—the author and finisher of faith.

The messengers of the proclamation have the globe as their habitat, the peoples of the world as their recipients, and the commission to share the Good News of salvation in Jesus Christ as their message. Their commission for proclamation is not only to be apologists for their faith, but also to be active witnesses in initiating contacts and relationships with peoples in order to share their faith. That commission includes Hindus, Muslims, Mormons, and Jehovah's Witnesses.

Proclamation and Hinduism

Hinduism is an ancient religion of India, preceding the Christian church by several thousand years.[2] It is the major religious tradition in India today with perhaps over 800 million Hindus. America was introduced to Hindu thought especially through the writings of the nineteenth-century American authors, Henry David Thoreau and Ralph Waldo Emerson. However, various forms of Hinduism entered America after World War II. They include Vedanta societies, transcendental meditation, and Hare Khrisna.

Hinduism may emphasize metaphysics, mysticism, and meditation. Its teachers are individuals of wisdom called swamis and gurus. Its wisdom literature includes the Vedas, the Upanishads, and the Bhagavad-Gita. Its institutions include temples where priests perform ceremonies before the statues of deities, meditation classes led by swamis or their designates, and lecture halls where gurus provide philosophical addresses on Hindu teachings.

Key concepts are the unity of all beings and things, ignorance based on dualistic thinking, and freedom and salvation gained through various practices, rituals, devotions, and meditations. Popular Hinduism emphasizes making gifts to and asking help from named deities like Krishna, Rama, Vishnu, and Shiva. Intellectual Hinduism philosophizes about the world reality of Brahman and ways to attain complete freedom and unity in Brahman by shedding ignorance and gaining knowledge and enlightenment.

In Christian proclamation to Hindus, it is important to understand that Hinduism is so eclectic and inclusive that it tends to be accepting of many religions in beliefs and practices. One needs to know that whereas one Hindu may desire a personal deity and a life lived that is fit for eternal rewards, another Hindu may believe in an impersonal being into which one is united at death like a drop of water from a river flows into the larger ocean.

Deity for the Hindu may be an impersonal being called Brahman or it may be that Brahman is the spirit force in a statue like Krishna. Deity is like a large soul or being. Humanity is a part of that spirit or being and has lost its way because of ignorance and erroneous knowledge and thinking. Humanity needs to learn from the wisdom writings as interpreted by swamis in order to be freed up to be unified with supreme being or soul. That is ultimate freedom.

When one gains this understanding, one becomes a part of Brahman. Humanity's "sin" is really ignorance. Humanity's "salvation" is really unity in oneness with reality or the universe or the over-soul or the supreme being or soul. One gains this unity and freedom through works and devotion, although it may take several life-times in transmigrations and reincarnations of the soul.

Christian proclamation takes into account the background of the Hindu in order to clarify to the Hindu its own words and meanings.[3] God is a personal Creator who created all things and humanity. God is distinct from the creation and is in relationship to it. God loves, judges, and offers salvation and reconciliation to all humanity.

Humanity, though created good and in the image of God, has rebelled and sinned against God through the temptation of Satan. Humanity's sin is more than ignorance and lack of knowledge. It resides in the will, in desire, in decision making against the will of God. Thus, Christianity diverges from Hinduism in its concept of God and humanity.

Hinduism views Jesus Christ as another avatar or incarnation or expression of deity like other Hindu such deities as Krishna and Rama. Jesus Christ brought good teachings and examples to the people of his culture and time. He continues to be a great exemplar of truth. However, Hinduism subsumes the truths and teachings of Jesus under the larger truths of its own treasures of wisdom literature and interpretations by swamis and gurus.

Christian proclamation does not include numbers of incarnations of God like Hinduism or any kind of gradations or degrees of deity. The doctrine of the Trinity speaks of the oneness of God expressed in three personal ways: God the Father, God the Son, and God the Holy Spirit.

Jesus Christ is the Word made flesh, full of truth and grace (John 1:14). There is no other name under heaven by which a person is saved than that of Jesus Christ. Jesus Christ was crucified for the sins of humanity. He was resurrected from the grave that all humanity might have that hope. Thus, Christian proclamation calls the Hindu from rituals and devotions and works expressed to a multiplicity of deities and Brahman. It calls the Hindu to Jesus Christ alone.

The church is the fellowship of Christians where worship and ministry are experienced. The church is separate from the state. It prepares itself through worship, study, and fellowship to extend the teachings of Jesus Christ to humanity. Hinduism has its temples concentrated on individualistic offerings to deities and the preservation of the wisdom and ways of Hinduism. Christianity has its churches as frontiers for engaging the world in its ministries and missions.

Various forms of Hinduism are appealing to Americans. Behind the forms the concepts are consistent. Perhaps the eclectic and inclusive nature of Hinduism is attractive to many. The transcendental meditation of Swami Maharishi Mahesh Yogi has reached hundreds of thousands of Americans. It has promised them peace of mind and soul. The Hare Krishna have reached a few Americans with its disciplined, ascetic lifestyle. Hinduism has come to America and is making an impact on its culture. Christians must be aware of it. But more so, they must be prepared to proclaim the Good News to it.

Proclamation and Islam

The religion Islam was birthed in Saudi Arabia in the seventh century A.D.[4] Religious wars were swirling around the Arabian peninsula between the Byzantine Christians centered in Constantinople and the Zoroastrians of Persia. Prior to Islam the Byzantine Christians, known as the Eastern Orthodox, had doctrinal infighting with the Roman Catholic Church of Rome. The Eastern Orthodox was declared a heretical group, especially because of its teachings on the nature of God and of Jesus. Into this maelstrom came Islam.

Muhammad was the founder of Islam, the religion of submission to Allah (the God). He was born in the city of Mecca, Saudi Arabia, to a prominent tribal group with economic ties to trade. He married Khadija, a wealthy merchant, who traded as far away as Damascus. By the year 610 A.D., Muhammad was having visions (Muslims call them revelations) from the angel Gabriel. The angel revealed the Quran to Muhammad and told him to recite it or preach it to the tribesmen of Mecca. The Quran is the sacred book of Islam. The words in it came directly from heaven where the book is located with Allah.

Muhammad preached that God is one, that he was the last prophet of God, that God wanted all people to submit to him, and that all people would go either to heaven or to hell. This message infuriated the Meccan tribes, many of whom were Muhammad's kinsmen. The message attacked the polytheism and paganism of Arabian society.

Muhammad gathered his few followers, fled from Mecca to Medina in 622 A.D., and became the prophet and leader of the tribes of Medina. By his death in 632 A.D., he had captured Mecca and made it the center of his religion. Within a hundred years, Islam had spread over the Middle East and North Africa as far away as Spain to the east, and westward to Persia and India and the fringes of China. Today, there are some one billion Muslims throughout the world. It is a religion of great significance and challenge.

Muslims entered America in numbers in the late nineteenth century from the Middle East. Native African-Americans became Muslims with the beginning of the Nation of Islam under Elijah Muhammad in the

1930s. With the oil wealth of Muslim nations after World War II, these nations sent their children to study in America. Mosques and Islamic associations were established across the land. Currently, there are some six to eight million Muslims in America. Shortly after the beginning of the twenty-first century, Islam will become the second largest religion of America, displacing Judaism.[5]

Many in the church consider Islam to be one of the greatest challenges to Christianity. It has its origin in the history and theology of Christianity. It has a mission to the world rooted in a theocratic vision to subsume all peoples and nations under the banner of Islam.

The common beliefs of Islam include monotheism, angels, prophets, scriptures, and a judgment day. The uniform and universal practices of Islam are a confession that "there is one God, and Muhammad is the apostle of God," prayer, giving, fasting, pilgrimage to Mecca, and jihad (holy efforts for Allah).

Christian understanding for proclamation to Muslims needs to include knowledge that Islam arose out of Jewish and Christian backgrounds. Muhammad preached a strict monotheism. Muslims believe that Christians are polytheists in that they say Christians worship three gods: God, Jesus, and the virgin Mary. They do not understand the doctrine of the Trinity, and they interpret it as polytheism.

Not only do Muslims misinterpret and misrepresent the Christian doctrine of God; they also view Jesus as only a man. Jesus is a prophet alongside other prophets, including Abraham and Moses and Muhammad. But Muhammad is the final prophet. Jesus brought the truth in the gospel (Injil) to his people like Moses brought the truth (Torah) to the Jews. But Jesus did not die on the cross. Someone took his place. Jesus was not resurrected. Jesus was not the Son of God, the Word become flesh.

The sacred book for Muslims is the Quran. It has stories about Abraham and Moses and Jesus and many other stories located in the Old and New Testaments. However, the Quran is the final revelation for all peoples, and it supercedes all other sacred writings. Thus, when it says that Jesus did not die on the cross, that is the truth for over one billion Muslims. Islam denies the central biblical truths and the heart of Christianity in its understanding of Jesus. Jesus does not save, according to Islam. Salvation in Islam is correct belief and practice. One submits to Allah. One practices the "pillars" from confession to jihad. One believes that the Quran is the inerrant and infallible teaching of Allah, and the original and mother book is in heaven. Whatever is in the Bible that the Quran reports and affirms is believed by Muslims. All else must be believed from the Quran.

Religion and governance are integrated in the Islamic view. There is no separation of "church" and state. The world is divided into two realms under the rule of Allah through his agencies: namely, the world of Islam or submission to Allah and the world of war or disobedience or nonsubmission to Allah. The world of Islam must be victorious and must rule. It rules through the vice regents of Allah: namely, ayatollahs or caliphs or Islamic governments. Christianity and other religions may be tolerated by the rule of Islam and assigned status as minorities.

Christian proclamation to Muslims must be sensitive to Islamic views of God, humanity, Jesus Christ, salvation, and community.[6] For fourteen centuries Christianity and Islam have either ignored each other, fought each other militarily or theologically, feared each other, remained at some distance from each other, or minimally engaged one another in missions and dialogue. Both are global religions and face each other among most of the world's peoples.

Christian proclamation can pursue with Muslims the meanings of monotheism, the tradition of sacred scripture, the place of Abraham and Moses and the virgin Mary, revelation, the place of prophets, Jesus Christ (as Word of God, Son of God, Messiah, Spirit of God), and the meaning of church and mosque in relation to government.

Islam is growing in America not only in numbers but in influence. A Muslim leader gave the prayer to open the session of the United States Senate. The armed forces has named a Muslim as chaplain. Louis Farrakhan, the leader of the Nation of Islam, planned and administered the million-man march in Washington. Muslims are building their own schools and colleges. Muslim organizations are becoming politically active.

Toward the twenty-first century, Christianity must take Islam seriously not only internationally but also in America. Two key issues between the two communities have been and continue to be (1) who Jesus and Muhammad are and (2) religion and governance and the freedom of religion.

Christian proclamation tells the salvific story of Jesus the Savior of the world and the Lord of life. It also counsels to render unto Caesar what is Caesar's and unto God what is God's. The challenge for Christianity is that throughout its fourteen centuries of existence with Islam, it has done little communication and little witness to the Islamic world in general and to Muslims in particular.

Proclamation and Mormonism

The Church of Jesus Christ of Latter-day Saints (Mormonism) was founded in New York state by Joseph Smith in 1830.[7] Smith had a series of visions in which both God and Jesus and the angel Moroni appeared to him. The basic message was that all churches and clergy were corrupt since the early days of the church of the first century.

Smith was told that he was to restore the true gospel, the true church, and the true priesthood. *The Book of Mormon, Doctrine and Covenants,* and *Pearl of Great Price* contain the truths by which Mormons live. Mormons accept these as historically accurate documents that are inspired by God.

Early Mormonism faced persecution as it migrated from New York to the far west. It settled in Salt Lake City in the 1870s led by Brigham Young, built its famous temple, and continued to grow in numbers and influence. Today, The Church of Jesus Christ of Latter-day Saints has over nine million members and over fifty thousand missionaries around the world.

Joseph Smith was the first prophet-president of the church. All revelations contained in their books came to him except for two. In the 1890s a revelation came to prophet-president Woodruff that the church should cease its practice of polygamy. In the 1970s a revelation came to prophet-president Kimball that black males would be eligible for the Mormon priesthood.

Mormons claim that they are a Christian church. They point out that the name of Jesus Christ is in their title. They seek recognition and acceptance from other denominations of their Christian status. Mormons are an aggressive missionary church seeking members from all denominations.

Christian proclamation to Mormons needs to take account of their foundational belief that they consider themselves the true church with the true gospel and the true priesthood. All other churches with their clergy have been corrupt. One needs to know that Mormons refer to the Bible as "another testament" to Jesus Christ; the *Book of Mormon* is the other testament. The major teachings of Mormonism are found in *Doctrine and Covenants* and *Pearl of Great Price*.

Distinctive Mormon beliefs include the claims that God is a God of flesh and bone; that Jesus' name is Jehovah and that his spirit brother was Lucifer; that there is universal salvation but only a temple Mormon may achieve exaltation; and that their church is the true church. Authority resides with the prophet-president and his close male counselors.[8]

Christian proclamation states that God is Spirit and not flesh and bone. Humanity is distinct from God in creation and is not divine. Mormonism claims that as God became man, so man may become divine. There are many gods in Mormonism, for any temple Mormon who qualifies may become a god and rule with his family in the celestial heaven for eternity. The Jesus of Mormonism was a spirit son of his Father God who came to earth. He lived, died on the cross, was resurrected, and ascended to heaven. His name is Jehovah. Jesus' death was an atonement for all peoples. Thus, all peoples, depending on their merits, may live in the telestial or terrestrial heavens.

However, only Mormons who have earned the right to attend one of the fifty temples may qualify to become a god and enter the celestial heaven. In the temple the Mormon may be married for eternity and may baptize for the dead to help the dead gain merit in the afterlife. Mormons believe that Jesus was married, had a family, and will reign with his family in the heavens.

Mormon beliefs about the nature of God, the nature and mission of Jesus Christ, and the doctrine of salvation differ radically from those of orthodox Christianity. God is Spirit. Jesus is the Son of God, the Word who became flesh. He came to save sinners. His death on the cross was an atonement for those who in faith would accept the grace and love of God through Jesus.

Humanity is not generally saved or individually exalted. Man does not earn exaltation to godhood through either good living or performing rituals in a temple. Christian proclamation states that a person is saved by grace through faith. There is no exclusive temple practice in Christianity which enables a person to merit goodness for oneself or for anyone deceased in baptismal rites for the dead.

Mormonism has several important institutions. The office of the prophet-president presides over levels of men divided into groups of twelve and seventy who compose the priesthood. Mormonism is a layperson movement. The relief society is composed of women who meet for study and for home affairs. The ward is the local fellowship for worship and study. The stake is an association of several wards. The temple is the building where qualified Mormons go to perform the rituals of marriage for eternity and baptism for the dead. Entry to the temple is gained through good works of tithing, no consumption of alcoholic beverages, no caffeine products, and wholesome family living. It is estimated that less than one-half of Mormons qualify for temple privileges.

Christian proclamation needs to note that Mormonism uses the vocabulary of the Bible and of Christianity, yet brings entirely different meanings and expressions to these ideas. Mormons emphasize family, clean living, and wholesome communities. Mormons are one of the most active groups with Scouts. They send out their missionaries two by two for two-year assignments to proselytize all peoples, including pagans and Muslims and Methodists and Baptists.

Christian proclamation must understand where Mormons are coming from in their beliefs and practices. Biblical terms and meanings must be presented with clarity and conviction. The biblical revelation of God and Jesus and salvation and church must be communicated to Mormons. Mormons often say that their church stands or falls on one's belief that Joseph Smith was a prophet. Christian proclamation neither considers Smith a prophet nor does it find validity in the *Book of Mormon* or *Doctrine and Covenants*.

Christian proclamation respects Mormons and loves Mormons. It invites Mormons to reconsider the biblical revelation.

Proclamation and Jehovah's Witnesses

In the 1870s Charles Taze Russell founded the Jehovah's Witnesses, known in those days as the Watchtower Bible and Tract Society.[10] Russell had become dissatisfied with the churches of his experience and their Bible teaching. Among his dislikes were their belief in hell and their lack of interest in prophecy and last things. In his *Studies in the Scriptures* he set out to give correct teachings.

Russell contended there was no hell, only annihilation. He taught that only 144,000 witnesses would attain heaven and live forever with Jehovah and King Jesus. Other worthy witnesses would inherit the cleansed earth and live forever. Russell claimed through an elaborate chronological table, based on his biblical analysis, that Jesus returned near the earth in 1914 and the countdown began for the coming of Armageddon.

There have been five presidents of Jehovah's Witnesses who have presided over their theocratic organization located in Bethel headquarters in Brooklyn, New York. The male governing board at Bethel supervises the writing and publication of all Witness materials world-wide. They rely on the New World Translation of the Holy Scriptures, their interpretation of the Bible. They disseminate two magazines, *Watchtower* and *Awake,* and have many other publications.

Witnesses meet in kingdom halls, built through the voluntary efforts of members. Several hundred will gather over a long weekend and complete the facility for dedication by Sunday. They gather in kingdom halls for study and training to go door to door to spread their message and materials. They refuse blood transfusions, military service, and the salute and oath to the American flag. Their membership is open to any race, and attendance at the kingdom halls is exemplary of races working together. Witnesses are all laypersons who share their faith. They number some five million, and they send missionaries around the world.

Christian proclamation needs to know the deviations of Jehovah's Witnesses' teachings and practices from orthodox Christianity. Witnesses view Christianity and the churches as "whores of Babylon." Therefore, they have the correct truth and others do not.

They emphasize that the correct name for God is Jehovah. Jesus is the mighty spirit son of God sent into the world to die on the stake and to offer salvation. In the first chapter of the Gospel of John, they translate and interpret, "In the beginning the Word was, and the Word was with God, and the Word was a god"[10] (John 1:1). Thus, they view Jesus as a god separate from Jehovah God. They detest the doctrine of the Trinity and think it was Satan-inspired.

Jesus' work was to defeat Satan and to bring salvation. However, Witnesses teach that there is a heaven, a cleansed earth, and annihilation. The select 144,000 have been chosen by Jehovah to be in heaven and to rule with King Jesus over the cleansed earth. Some of the select are still living and are the only ones to partake of the Lord's Supper during the annual meetings of the kingdom halls.

Witnesses who are faithful and honor Jehovah and King Jesus will inherit the cleansed earth. They will be ruled over by the 144,000 and King Jesus. Non-Witnesses will be annihilated during the judgment. During the end times Witnesses will offer non-Witnesses another chance. If accepted, they will avoid annihilation and claim the cleansed earth.

Since Jehovah's Witnesses began, many dates have been set in their literature and teachings of the coming of Armageddon, judgment day, and rewards and punishments. Each date has passed, often to the chagrin of the Witnesses and sometimes to the departure of Witnesses from the kingdom hall. A crisis may loom soon if Armageddon is delayed, because it has been promised that it will come during the lifetime of the select Witnesses.

Christian proclamation must be aware that Jehovah's Witnesses view Christians and churches as apostates. Christians are targeted by the Witnesses through door-to-door efforts to join the kingdom halls and avoid annihilation.

The Witnesses' concept of God and of Jesus Christ and of the Holy Spirit denies the doctrine of the Trinity. Christian proclamation is based on a trinitarian understanding of the nature and meaning of God. There is God the Father, God the Son, and God the Holy Spirit. For Witnesses, God is the almighty God; Jesus is the mighty god, the spirit Son; and there is no personal Holy Spirit but only an impersonal force of Jehovah in the world.

Witnesses teach that salvation was brought by the god Jesus who died on a stake, not a cross. However, they divide the elect into two groups: those who merit heaven and those who gain the cleansed earth. Witnesses know which of the elect they are, and those who inherit the cleansed earth have no desire or regret that they will not be with Jehovah and King Jesus forever.

Salvation for the Christian is not based on any merit and is not divided between a heaven and a cleansed earth.

Christian proclamation does not set specific dates for the return of Jesus Christ and for Armageddon as Witnesses do. Blood transfusions, allegiance to the flag, and military service are not vital issues with Christians as they are with Witnesses.

Jehovah's Witnesses belong to a theocratic organization. The male elders think, write, publish, and speak on behalf of Jehovah from Bethel headquarters in Brooklyn. They pass their knowledge and teachings down to the kingdom halls in publications and exhortations. They use the Bible as it has been interpreted by their elders in the New World Translation of the Holy Scriptures. The Christian churches represent a variety of forms of worship, teaching methodologies, and ministries. The churches are not a theocratic organization.

Faithful Jehovah's Witnesses know their Bibles and have been well trained in the way of the elders. Christians need to be sensitive to them and to be patient with them. Christian proclamation will have to deal forthrightly and meaningfully with the doctrine of the Trinity which the Witnesses not only deny but despise. Perhaps the Christian can emphasize Jesus Christ as the Son of God and the Savior of the world in the context of the personal view that he is a friend of sinners, not a mighty god in contrast to the almighty Jehovah.

Conclusion

America is a marketplace of religious ideas and practices. Religious pluralism has always been a feature of its culture. Especially since World War II, Hinduism, Buddhism, and Islam have migrated and found new homes. They have appealed to tens of millions of Americans. Likewise, American nativistic religions have awakened and grown dramatically, especially Mormons and Jehovah's Witnesses.

There is a religious appetite among Americans. Often, they seek simplicity in beliefs, clarity in ideas, devotion in commitment, strong authority in leadership, what makes sense in expectations, acceptance in warm community, and positive feelings about the present and the future. American religious groups appeal to many of these desires. As the twenty-first century approaches, these groups are growing and impacting individuals, communities, and the body politic.

Christianity has tended to ignore these groups either out of ignorance, fear, superiority feelings, or lack of concern. They must be taken seriously as individuals and as communities. Agape love must be at the core of Christian proclamation. Knowledge of the beliefs and practices of these groups must inform Christian proclamation. And Christian proclamation must voice and live the Good News of Jesus Christ rooted in the biblical revelation and expressed in the servant ministry of Jesus Christ. As Hindus, Muslims, Mormons, and Jehovah's Witnesses boldly spread their religions, so Christians must positively and persuasively go out to their neighbors as messengers with the life-saving message.

Chapter 13

Inductive Versus Deductive Methods of Telling the Gospel
Bill Mackey

THE CHURCH IS MADE UP OF MANY VARIETIES OF PEOPLE. Some worship in English in Great Britain, Canada, or the United States. Others worship in French in France and in much of Africa. Still others worship in Spanish in Spain and throughout Central and South America. There are men and women in the church. The church includes senior adults and children. Some people in the church own their own businesses and others are unemployed. Some are gregarious and others are introverted. Surely the church includes tremendous social diversity.

On top of this social diversity comes the sovereign work of the Holy Spirit dispersing spiritual gifts as he pleases. With this spiritual diversity, the church becomes a wide blend of hues and tones. With this rich blend of persons and giftedness, it almost naturally follows that the Great Commission will take on many colors corresponding to the wide variety of personalities and giftedness found within the church. Likewise, the task of evangelism is not left to one variety or method. The Bible encourages this rich assortment of people called "the church" to reach out to the lost in their own unique way. This approach may perhaps be called *diversity evangelism.*

This chapter will note how Delos Miles came to develop his differentiation of inductive and deductive evangelism. It will look at two Scripture passages that explain the need for different approaches of evangelism for different people. Then it will delve into contemporary examples of inductive and deductive evangelism. Finally, it will provide some guiding principles for inductive and deductive evangelism.

Defining Inductive and Deductive Evangelism

Early in his ministry Delos Miles did not differentiate between inductive and deductive evangelism. In fact, there was a time when he thought that inductive evangelism was an escape from real evangelism. He explains, "I confess that I once thought of most inductive evangelizing as a cop-out and a subterfuge. Study, personal experience, and observation have changed my mind."[1] There was a turning point in the ministry of Delos Miles when he began to see the need for and the importance of inductive evangelism. Miles began to see a clear differentiation in two methodologies of evangelism: inductive and deductive.

Deductive evangelism is best understood in relation to the three "P's" of the church growth movement: presence, proclamation, and persuasion. The order of these "P's" is important to distinguish deductive from inductive evangelism. "Deductive methodology accentuates proclamation, persuasion and presence in that order."[2] It emphasizes the proclamation of the gospel with the purpose of persuading the unreconciled to receive Christ as Savior. Likewise, it may have less emphasis on living out the presence of Christ before the nonbeliever. On the other hand, inductive evangelism focuses on presence, then persuasion, and then proclamation—in that order. Of utmost importance in the inductive approach is presence. "Establishing credibility is crucial for those who prefer the inductive approach. Much of their persuading is done before the gospel is verbally proclaimed."[3] Thus, Miles concludes that "we definitely have two contrasting styles in the two approaches."

To further explain the differences between inductive and deductive evangelism, Miles has provided a helpful diagram that he calls "a taxonomy of personal evangelism." In this diagram, he differentiates the intentionality of each of the two approaches to evangelism:[4]

Deductive	Inductive
Receptivity (high)	Receptivity (low)
Monological (telling)	Dialogical (listening)
Short-term gains	Long-term gains
Canned	Spontaneous
Instant	Incarnational
Religious persons	Secular persons
Proclamation	Affirmation (Petersen)
Propositional	Point-of-Need (Hunter)
Stereotyped	Service (Armstrong)
Contact	Conversational (Pippert)
Functional	Friendship (McPhee)
Rational	Relational (McGill)
Traditional	Target-Group (Neighbour)
Individual	Household (Green, et al)
Lips	Lifestyle (Aldrich)
One day	Every day (McIntosh)
Hook	Hospitality (Rowlison)

Miles explains that his "concern has not been to put down those who use deductive methods."[5] Rather, he wants Christians to be aware of both the content and context of opportunities to share the gospel.

With these definitions in mind, let us move to look at two Bible passages which exhibit the need for different approaches in the evangelization of different people.

A Biblical Look at Inductive and Deductive Evangelism

Two passages will be used to show how the Bible teaches the need for *diversity evangelism*. First Corinthians 9 explains the apostle Paul's differing methodology with four different groups of people. In Mark 4 the parable of the sower teaches that different people will respond differently to the gospel message. Our evangelism style should be shaped by the persons we are seeking to reach and the context in which we will have contact with them.

First Corinthians 9:19–23. The apostle Paul makes it clear in several key passages that evangelism will need to be different to reach different people with the gospel. Perhaps the best expression of this concept is found in 1 Corinthians 9:19–23. It is in this context that the apostle distinguishes between ministry to those under the law and those not under the law.

Martin Luther in his commentary on 1 Corinthians explains that the Christian has the most freedom of all people, as he is under obligation to nobody. But he adds that the Christian is the most duty-bound of all, for he is under obligation to all people. This explains the thrust of the apostle Paul in this passage. Paul uses the word "all" in referring to the duty of the believer in verses 19 and 22 of this passage, as well as in 10:33. In Colossians 1:28, the apostle uses the words "every man" (NASB) three times to explain the breadth of his ministry. Surely the apostle had a heart for every person in the world. It is in this context that he addresses the need for diversity evangelism.

The apostle Paul understood the diverse varieties of people in the world. He knew that different persons needed to hear the gospel in different ways. He offers four groups of people as examples: the Jew, those under

the law, those without law, and the weak. The apostle
Paul's methodology with each group was determined
by their set of beliefs. To those with the law, he
approached them from the standpoint of having a law.
To those without the law, he approached as without the
law. Paul is quick to provide the necessary disclaimers
lest he be misunderstood. For example, he tells his
readers that he is not without law, but under the law of
Christ (1 Cor. 9:21).

Christians cannot expect one method or approach to
evangelism to reach all people. God uses diverse methods
to bring people into his kingdom.

The parable of the sower. The parable of the sower
has a place of prominence in each of the first three
Gospels. In this important parable, Jesus teaches us
that the gospel is to be shared with all persons regardless of their receptivity. Only God can know the heart
of a person. "For God sees not as man sees, for man
looks at the outward appearance, but the LORD looks at
the heart" (1 Sam. 16:7). Due to the persecution of
Christians, Saul of Tarsus may have been viewed as
hard soil by Christians in his day. Likewise, the
Philippian jailer would have been feared by the
Christian. Yet Barnabas and Paul respectively reached
out to these men.

Again, the parable of the sower helps us understand
the relationship between method and receptivity. If a
person is resistant to the gospel, an inductive approach
may be more effective. If a person is fertile soil, why
wait? Share the Good News, give a clear invitation to
receive Christ and follow him in baptism, church membership, and discipleship.

A person who is good soil is sensitive to God and the
conviction of the Holy Spirit. This person sees his need

for Christ and needs a friend to help him understand trust and commitment.

The rocky soil is the person who is a seeker. This person has keen interest, but may not understand the nature of grace. Patience will be required along with other inductive approaches. Philip taught the Ethiopian eunuch from the Scriptures. Paul met with God-fearers for prayer and taught them about Jesus. Among them were Priscilla and Aquila.

The thorny soil represents the skeptical person who has questions. It turns out that his interest in the faith focuses primarily on how it can help him achieve his secular goals. He will need inductive evangelism. Successful Christians will need to help him understand his need for trusting Jesus.

The hard soil represents the secular person. This secular person may have had disappointing experiences with the church or may have had no experience with it at all. Inductive approaches, friendship, and loving care will be needed to reach this person.[6]

We have learned from the Scriptures that there are varieties of methods, differences in spiritual gifts, and various levels of receptivity. All of these influence the blend of inductive and deductive evangelism necessary to reach the unsaved for Christ.

Practically speaking, the methods are different, and the receptivity is different, but the goal remains the same. "I have become all things to all men, that I may by all means save some" (1 Cor. 9:22). What are examples of diversity evangelism? The next section will explore current examples of inductive and deductive evangelism.

Inductive and Deductive Methods and Approaches of Evangelism

Inductive and deductive evangelism methods are being used across the world. As the church is faithful to meeting people where they are and proclaiming the gospel in a relevant way, it is seeing the fruits of conversion growth. This section highlights examples of inductive and deductive evangelism. It is not exhaustive; in fact, the reader will certainly have further examples to add to this list. The following are exemples of ways in which Christians are reaching out effectively through inductive and deductive evangelism.

Servant evangelism. Servant evangelism[7] and ministry evangelism[8] are primary examples of inductive evangelism at work. Sjogren emphasizes the use of "low risk" and "high grace" methods of getting into the lives of others to prepare them for hearing the gospel. He calls this approach "servant evangelism." It includes sponsoring free car washes in the name of Jesus, giving a warm cup of hot chocolate during a cold winter night in the name of Jesus, and handing out free matches at bars with church information in the name of Jesus.

Atkinson and Roesel emphasize the need for a holistic approach to evangelism in the life of the local church. They see the church as both salt and light in the community. As the church meets people at their point of pain, they can then minister the gospel to them in a credible way. Both servant evangelism and ministry evangelism have opened the minds of evangelical Christians across the United States to a need for using inductive evangelism. The result is a healthy church with a greater impact for Christ.

Spiritual gifts. Larry Gilbert is one of several who advocate the use of spiritual gifts in evangelism.[9] His approach includes primarily the deductive aspects of evangelism. As a follow-up to Gilbert's spiritual gifts inventory, the reader or the conferencee is encouraged to use whatever gifts he has for furthering the work of evangelism through the local church. *How To Reach Your Loved Ones* teaches about the nine "church growth gifts," from Romans 12 and Ephesians 4. It shows how every believer can be used in the evangelism process in the lives of others. In his materials Gilbert includes a helpful booklet to pray for and watch the progress of unsaved contacts for the purpose of bringing them to Christ.

Network is a program developed by Willow Creek Community Church to test the spiritual gifts of its members and maintain a database of these records. This tool is very helpful to the mid-size or larger church desiring to help its members use their gifts effectively to further the ministry of the church. In Acts 20:28, Paul exhorts the Ephesian elders to "shepherd the church of God." Network is a tool developed to help churches properly shepherd the spiritual gifts of those people whom God has sent their way.[10]

Friendship evangelism. In *Becoming a Contagious Christian,*[11] Bill Hybels and Mark Mittelberg encourage the believer to reach out to those in their sphere of influence with the gospel. Hybels and Mittelberg encourage a lifestyle of evangelism through the acronym: HP + CP + CC = MI. The letters mean: High Potency + Close Proximity + Clear Communication = Maximum Impact. In their portion on clear communication, they explain the importance of verbally sharing Jesus in order to have a maximum impact.

The friendship style of evangelism relies on an accurate knowledge of the target group the believer desires to reach. In his book *Inside the Mind of the Unreached Harry and Mary,* Lee Strobel has written an analysis of the unchurched, and he offers strategies to reach them for Christ.[12] Perhaps the most prolific author in this area in recent years has been George Barna. His *Evangelism that Works* begins with results from extensive sociological analysis of the church and culture and provides recommendations on how to reach the unsaved more effectively.[13]

William Fay explains the socratic approach to personal evangelism in *Share Jesus Without Fear.*[14] After getting acquainted with an individual, at an appropriate time, Fay asks the person to read a Scripture verse and tell him what it means. He moves sequentially through the Roman Road with the individual. If they do not ask him a question, then he does not offer an opinion. Fay tells his readers that it is hard for the unsaved to argue with their own responses.

Evangelism Explosion, IV[15] also emphasizes the need for friendship evangelism. Evangelism Explosion has assisted churches through providing them with a vibrant evangelism program for over three decades. Now it has enhanced the friendship factor to encourage all believers to share their faith. Chapter 2 of this resource is titled "Witnessing as a Way of Life." It explains the importance of relational evangelism. This latest version of EE promises to breathe new life into the evangelism programs of local churches.

Building Witnessing Relationships, developed by Jack Smith of the North American Mission Board, provides a thorough process for identifying your circle of influence.[16] Once these people are identified, Smith develops an intentional strategy for sharing Christ at the appropriate time, empowered by the Holy Spirit.

Worship evangelism. Since the rise of the contemporary worship style and seeker church ministries, worship evangelism has become a tool to reach the lost. In her book *Worship Evangelism: Inviting Unbelievers into the Presence of God,* Sally Morgenthaler writes, "Worship evangelism is really happening."[17] *Worship Evangelism* contains extensive information which includes biblical foundations for worship evangelism, as well as practical principles for shaping a worship service for an evangelistic impact. This is an inductive approach which prepares participants for the deductive.

Jack Hayford and John Wimber have provided leadership in the area of contemporary Christian worship through their examples. The worship and praise of God's people lifts the name of Jesus and provides an avenue in which the love and greatness of God is proclaimed.

A parallel to worship evangelism is the seeker church philosophy of ministry. While Bill Hybels at Willow Creek Community Church popularized this philosophy of ministry, George Hunter III in his book *Church for the Unchurched*[18] helps his readers understand the why and how of developing a seeker-oriented church. Sometimes the "seeker service" is a more subtle style of worship evangelism.

Prayer Evangelism. Ed Silvoso, founder of Harvest Evangelism, teaches the importance of prayer evangelism.[19] This style of evangelism seeks out cities that have been spiritual strongholds for the Evil One. By empowering local churches through united prayer, Silvoso has developed a six-year strategy for prayer evangelism in which believers pray for each home in a city. This prayer evangelism is said to begin to produce results after six months to a year of concerted and individual prayer.

Likewise, Tony Campolo, speaking to a regional Baptist Student Union conference in Athens, Georgia, invited students to participate in prayer ministry for a semester. Students were to go door to door in cities, offering to pray for special needs. Following a time of prayer, they then returned to the houses and offered church ministries to meet the needs that were expressed, such as need for a job or help for a son on drugs. Prayer evangelism focuses on the spiritual, but it also brings the practical into evangelism.

One of the great evangelism challenges in our present day is for people in the marketplace to network and reach people through prayer in their corporation or building. Ted DeMoss, president of Christian Business Men's Committee of USA, explains the importance of prayer in the marketplace in his book *The Gospel and the Briefcase.*[20] In a chapter entitled "Talking to God about Men," he explains the need for the convicting ministry of the Holy Spirit in a heart to ripen it for the gospel.

Prayer walking is another significant prayer evangelism strategy that is inductive in nature. Rev. Tom Swilley, Antioch Baptist Church, Hartsville, South Carolina, has experienced a fresh anointing in worship and a dramatic increase in baptisms following Sunday morning prayer walks around the church facilities by ten to fifteen people. Prayer walking has become the only evangelism strategy in some countries where witnessing is illegal.

Henry Blackaby's *Experiencing God* has been used to teach people how to look for places where God is at work and to join him in his work. The North American Mission Board has established a department of prayer evangelism and church renewal with Chris Scofield as manager. He will lead the Southern Baptist Convention in prayer evangelism.

A mapping center for evangelism has been developed in Kansas City, Missouri, to assist churches and individual Christians in praying for those in their neighborhoods.[21] This center can provide a list of names related to your neighborhood. This is a way that technology and prayer evangelism combine for effective out-reach ministry.

Technology. Technology is being used by the church for both inductive and deductive evangelism. Numerous groups are seeking to evangelize the unsaved on the Internet. For example, www.christiananswers.net provides an effective apologetic ministry. Browsers on their site have multiple choices for answers to questions about the faith. This site is also home to Dawson McAllister Live's "Hope Line."

The Web-site www.lovelines.org offers an excellent telephone counseling ministry which reaches a broad segment of U.S. society.[22] Since 1996 it has been on the Internet, providing answers to hurting people. Recently it has been publicized through its "1–888-NEED-HIM" radio advertising campaign.

The Billy Graham Evangelistic Association[23] has used technology in a variety of ways to reach the world's populations. It maintains several websites,[24] offers Billy Graham telephone ministry during its quarterly telecasts, and has utilized simultaneous digital links in several of its crusades.

Another important use of technology in deductive evangelism is the use of the *Jesus* film across the world. The *Jesus* film contains word-for-word quotes from the Book of Luke and is followed by a brief presentation of the gospel. This technological tool has been used in numerous countries to introduce the unsaved to Christ.

Musical outreach. Music plays an important role in preparing people for the ministry of the Word in deductive evangelism. As an example, Christian music festivals have sprouted up all over the country throughout several decades. At these festivals, church youth groups attend for fellowship and also for outreach. Typically, certain bands are designated to share the gospel and to give an invitation. Counselors are then available for prayer, and the churches that brought the kids are encouraged to follow up on those who make professions of faith.

This same approach is used in the youth portions of Billy Graham crusades. Since the first youth special in Detroit in 1995, music has played an important role in Billy Graham's outreach to youth. Musical groups who have taken part in youth specials include Michael W. Smith and DC Talk. In a fashion similar to all the Graham crusades, counselors are trained to minister to those who come forward during an invitation. Often the response is overwhelming, as 20 to 30 percent or more of the audiences come forward.

In his book called *Rock Priest,*[25] David Pierce tells of his opportunities to share Christ in music clubs throughout Europe, Russia, Australia, and New Zealand.[26] He is both biblical and theologically conservative, yet his methodology is aggressive. He seeks to work with local churches and pastors wherever he goes.

Creative outreach. For the church to remain relevant and effective in its evangelism, it will need to continue to nurture creativity. There are numerous other creative approaches to reach the unsaved through both inductive and deductive evangelism. Street drama continues to open doors for the gospel around the world. Reign Ministries[27] is one of several ministries focusing on this method. They train and send youth for street evangelism to Europe and the Far East. They use mime and drama to portray the gospel and follow up with one-on-one conversations about Christ.

Some churches use coffee houses as gathering places for youth to provide venues for evangelism. For example, Shandon Baptist Church runs an effective coffee-house outreach to students at the University of South Carolina. Bill Jones of "Cross-Over Ministries" makes good use of this method at Columbia International University. This method is inductive in its approach as participants enjoy the comfortable atmosphere of the coffee house. Christian students are encouraged to share their faith with the unsaved in relational ways through the coffee-house method.

Many other methods are used to proclaim the gospel both inductively and deductively. Not mentioned are affinity group evangelism, crusade evangelism, evangelistic camps or conferences, and small-group or cell-group evangelism. The list continues as methods are developed which relate to the variety of the world's cultures and interests, as well as the many personalities of Christians. Inductive and deductive methodologies encourage *diversity evangelism,* as the church seeks to reach the diverse communities of the world.

Guiding Principles

The guiding principles for developing effective inductive and deductive evangelism ministries in the local church fall into three areas: those that relate to the witness, the situation, and the prospect. The witness must have a strong and growing relationship with Jesus—or nothing else matters. In John 15:5, Jesus said "apart from Me you can do nothing." But with Jesus, the call is clear (cf. John 15:16).

Having moved to a new level in my relationship with Jesus, I get uncomfortable when his name is not mentioned in conversation. I begin looking for creative ways to talk about Jesus to people around me. The Holy Spirit works in the life of the witness and the life of the prospect. He convicts the person of his or her need for Jesus (John 16:8), convinces the person that Jesus is who he said he was (John 4:26), and brings conversion (2 Cor. 5:17).

The second major area relates to the situation. The witness must be sensitive to the life situation of the prospect. What are the evident life needs, transitions, challenges or successes for this person? How does the gospel relate to the point of need or hurt? What is the receptivity of the person? Open-ended questions help the witness to know how God is at work in the life of the prospect—"Do you ever think much about spiritual things? I would love to hear about it." The witness must listen carefully to the prospect to discover his or her receptivity to the gospel. Use of the acrostic FIRE is an excellent way to determine receptivity and to help the witness understand the nature of the response:

F—Family
I—Interests
R—Religious background
E—Explanation of the gospel

If the prospect will listen to explanations of the gospel, that is an indication that receptivity is high. But if the prospect will only let you talk about family or other interests, this is an indication of low receptivity.

During a witnessing training seminar in Camden, South Carolina, I visited a home where the mother, daughter, and father prayed to receive Christ. When I asked who would want to know about their commitment, the mother replied, "Oh, my mother, because she has been praying that this would happen for six years."

When there is immediate receptivity to the gospel, it usually means that someone else has prayed and sowed the seed. The principle of sowing and cultivating usually precedes harvest, especially in a secular culture. Due to a lack of Christian memory or awareness, multiple explanations of the gospel may be necessary. Formal studies may prove effective in explaining the gospel so that the person can make an authentic commitment to Christ. Patience and persistence are required.

A third major area relates to the nature of the prospect. Personality and cognitive style will influence how a prospect will respond to a different personality and how a person prefers to think and learn.

The outgoing person can express how he or she feels about the witness and the gospel easily and readily. However, the internal and intuitive person may require time to reflect and process the gospel internally. The person who is logical may prefer a linear presentation, but a visual and feeling person will prefer word pictures and real stories. Both will probably enjoy personal testimonies. The deductive approach may work best with the outgoing person. But feeling and visual people will prefer an inductive approach.

Think about an unsaved friend, relative, or coworker. Review that person's life situation, needs, opportunities, and transitions. What is the person's personality and preferred style of thinking and learning? Now think about your personality and preferred style of relating and communicating. Work at starting where the person is rather than where you are. Start with who the other person is rather than who you are. I think the apostle Paul had this in mind in 1 Corinthians 9:22, "I have become all things to all men, that I may by all means save some."

Conclusion

Paul had a passion to see people come to Christ, "For I could wish that I myself were accursed, separated from Christ for the sake of my brethren, my kinsmen according to the flesh" (Rom. 9:3). Paul utilized both inductive and deductive methods, depending on how God was at work, the situation, and the prospect. He kept in mind the diversity of people to whom he was ministering. Paul was always looking for a way to tell the story of how Jesus had changed his life on the road to Damascus. Should we not tell our Jesus story as often?

Chapter 14

Christian Apologetics And Intentional Evangelism

L. Russ Bush

NOT ONLY DID DELOS MILES STAND AS A BEACON OF LIGHT for a generation of students, but he also demonstrated his faith in both praxis and principle. In this essay, I want to elaborate on a principle without forgetting the importance of practical application. It is a great honor to be permitted to contribute to this series of essays dedicated to Professor Miles. His attention to detail models for us the importance of principle as the best means of assuring effective praxis.

Historical Excursus

Apologetics is an old word from the Greek legal system. To make an "apology" today is to make a humble excuse for some acknowledged error, but the ancient meaning of the term was to make a defense against some accusation. Before the ancient court, a person would attempt to defend himself or herself against a charge by making a strong apology, claiming innocence from a false accusation and providing a reasoned case for the defense.[1]

Early Christians found themselves facing persecution that was associated with specific accusations against them. For example, Christians were accused of being cannibals since they "ate the body" and "drank the blood" of their Lord. Christians were accused of being "atheists" because they worshiped at no temple and honored no idol. Christians were accused of "immorality" because they met at night, men and women together, for secret "love feasts." Thus, some Christian scholars found it necessary to take on the role of apologists, not so much in court but in the culture generally.[2]

Apologists, such as Athenagoras,[3] defended the Christians against these false accusations, but they often went beyond these charges and also offered positive arguments for the truth of Christianity as well. For example, Irenaus argued that the commonly accepted pagan belief in the idea of multiple gods led to all kinds of absurdities,[4] and Athanasius set forth in some detail how the fulfillment of prophecy provided convincing reasons to believe that Jesus was in fact God's identified Messiah.[5]

In the late Middle Ages when Thomas Aquinas began his extensive writing, he directed some of his early material toward an effort to assist the missionaries, especially in Spain, to present persuasively the claims of Christian faith.[6] When he later attempted to review and summarize the entire body of theological knowledge, he found it important to begin by providing some preliminary arguments from nature in favor of basic principles that must be accepted as foundational to Christian faith. His "five ways" of establishing the existence of God are the best known example of this apologetic technique.[7]

Though a more extensive historical review of all types of apologetic writing would be helpful, it can be found in other places easily enough.[8] Suffice it to say that a complete review would need to be more comprehensive than one might suspect. Descartes believed he had discovered an ontological argument that was sufficiently compelling to justify his Christian beliefs, as did

John Locke (with a cosmological argument), as did Kant (with his moral defense of theism).

We may have wished that many of these thinkers had understood some things more clearly or that they had made better cases, but it has been common through the centuries for Christian thinkers of various philosophical persuasions to suggest reasons and evidences for their belief.[9]

Unfortunately those who, like Hume, doubted the validity of these reasons and evidences often turned against the church altogether. As Darwin's alternative to Paley's teleology took root in nineteenth-century Europe, the credibility of faith seemed weaker. As twentieth-century human medicine "healed" the previously incurable and as human technology performed "miracles" greater in scope and impact than those recorded in the Bible, the basis for faith seemed weaker still.

Many Christians, unable to answer their modern critics, yet touched in their hearts by the Holy Spirit, fell back on anti-intellectual faith as their only hope. In the Baptist world in America, the antimission forces grew alongside the antieducation sentiment,[10] and even today Baptists do not require theological education, much less a seminary degree, as a qualification for ordination to the gospel ministry. Only educated theologians are liberal, so the reasoning went, and the best defense against the loss of faith was the avoidance of higher education.

In so brief an essay as this one, I cannot respond to all the issues raised above. I do wish to suggest a direction, however, that I hope others will be able to pursue in future research. While I do not know if this direction is sufficient to establish all that I might hope, it does seem to me to be a fruitful line of inquiry, and it speaks directly to the issue of evangelistic methods.

Apologetical Reasoning and Evangelism

The conclusion I have reached is that apologetic reasoning is an aid to evangelism though it is not essential. There is a specific reason why it is technically nonessential, but there is also an important reason why it is an appropriate aid to faith, and thus an important reason why apologetic presentations are useful for evangelism as well as for spiritual growth and discipleship among believers.

First, a word about reasoning as a mental process. The human mind communicates with other minds through grammatical language, that is, through a rationally structured language. We also use sounds and hand motions and body language in general, and we do not consider the speechless individual to be less than human. But if someone did not think rationally or if he or she could not form discreet and ordered thoughts, we might consider him or her mentally deficient.

It is the genetic structure of the biological cells rather than mental performance that is properly used to define the *homo sapiens* species, but we consider a rational mind to be normal in this species. Nevertheless, I have concluded that even "normal" rationality has a dual nature.

Next a word about apologetic reasoning. By this we mean the ability of the mind to question, challenge, and analyze ideas. We also mean the capacity of the mind to distinguish between viewpoints, and the seemingly inherent assumption of the mind that considers truth to be that which is in fact the case, and the further persuasion that truth is better than non-truth. Moreover, the rational mind is capable of being persuaded by truth claims though not always without mistake. Apologetic reasoning, therefore, is that presentation of a set of reasons representing the basis for some truth claim and that set of reasons offered to dispute incorrect truth claims.

In terms of Christian truth claims, apologetic reasoning is that set of rationally connected ideas and statements that are considered to be supportive of the conclusion that what the Bible affirms and teaches is in fact the case in history and in eternity, especially those things said about Jesus Christ. These things include his fulfillment of messianic prophecy, his virgin birth, his deity, his sinless life, his miracle-working teaching ministry, his sacrificial and righteously acceptable death, his unique third-day resurrection from among the dead according to the prophetic Scriptures, and the identifiable existence of his organized followers through the ages.

But the Scripture also sets the stage for Christian truth by affirming a theistic reality (a world created by a personal God) and a providentially directed prophetic history with a verifiability sufficient for rational persuasion.

Apologetic reasoning, then, in this sense is the evidence from natural science for intelligent design and the corresponding evidence against theories of random naturalistic development. It is that set of persuasive concepts that lead to the conclusion that the universe had a beginning rather than being composed of an infinite regression of caused events.

Moreover, it is that set of knowable facts corresponding to biblical claims about nature and about history. It is that set of rational concepts which appropriately define biblical Christianity and thus defends the faith from false accusations or challenges from other truth claims. Apologetic reasoning also includes the challenges that can be legitimately offered against all rival truth claims.

Persuasion Versus Manipulation

Given the description above, it seems obvious that if in fact there is such a set of reasons, it would be important to know them and to share them with those we would hope to persuade. We should speak the truth even if we do not succeed in the goal of persuasion. To persuade someone on some other basis, even if the truth is finally embraced, is manipulation.

But why is manipulation wrong if the end result is the acceptance of truth? The reason is simple. The human mind is not respected by a manipulator. The persuader who manipulates is not an evangelist who is making disciples of Christ but is one making disciples of himself. We manipulate in order to make others conform to our conclusions. We evangelize, however, to proclaim the Good News from God about sin and salvation. We provide every bit of information we can regarding the truth context in which this good news comes.

However, we do not perform the spiritual transaction. God alone justifies. God alone elects, regenerates, and sanctifies. To step into God's place and talk another person into verbalizing some words consistent with the truth is not truly to evangelize. People are not saved merely because they verbalize the truth. They must also believe in their heart (Rom. 10:9–10); that is, they must truly find an internal conviction in their soul regarding these matters.

Apologetical Reasoning: A Nonessential Aid to Evangelism

This leads to the final part of this discussion. Why do two people hear the same apologetic and yet only one believes? Why do we state the truth clearly and persuasively and yet some are not persuaded? And why are others persuaded with such a small amount of apologetic reasoning? Not everyone comes to Christ at the end of a logical argument. For some people, belief is easy; and for others doubts continually arise.

The answer lies in a basic philosophical truth about the rational human mind. It is this truth that makes the apologetic reasoning nonessential (though it does not overcome the lack of all knowledge about gospel truths). No one can believe if he or she has never heard (Rom. 10:14), but someone can believe even if he or she did not hear the full apology. On the other hand, someone can hear the full case against all rival claims and the full defense of the truth and still not receive it as that which "converts" the soul.

In brief, the answer lies in the study of epistemology, that branch of philosophy that asks and analyzes proposed answers to the question, "How do we know?" The question is, *How do we know anything?* not only, *How do we know spiritual truths?* I contend that we do not know various truths in essentially different ways, though we do have different kinds of evidences and different patterns of persuasion.

Perhaps the simplest way to introduce the concept proposed in this essay is to ask a few questions. Let's begin with some very basic ones.

What would convince you that you do not exist? Could anything convince you of that? Why or why not?

Did you answer by proposing "self-evidence" as an indisputable given? Did you suggest "intuition"? Did you respond by saying that non-self-existence is a rational contradiction, an empirical impossibility, or that this was simply an inane question unworthy of consideration?

Would you have answered differently if the question had been, "What would convince you that I do not exist?" Is the fact of my existence, if it is a fact, as obvious to you as it is to me? If not, why not? And even if the assurance level were in some sense less, are you justified in refusing to believe that I exist?

What would convince you that God does not exist? *Oh wait,* you say, *that's different!*

Why? I respond. . . . Your answer here moves the discussion significantly forward, but not necessarily to a quick resolution.

God is not visible, you say. But do you only accept the reality of visible things? Visible to the naked eye only? Are radio waves visible?

God is not tangible, you say. Not only do I want to know how you know this supposed fact, but what does it mean to suggest tangibility as an essential of existence? Is gravity tangible?

Without extending this hypothetical dialogue to include all possible areas of discussion, I must now conclude this essay and leave the elaboration of the argument to a later essay and/or to others. In summary, however, a discussion such as this does not end. Many people think the theistic responses are compelling and clever and easily persuasive. But others will consider them as sophistry and remain unconvinced of theistic conclusions.

It seems that the following points are very likely true.

1. The same evidence and the same rational arguments produce varied conclusions in different human minds.

2. The very existence of contingent reality leads some people to conclude that it is necessary for a noncontingent reality to exist which is the ultimate and/or immediate ground of the contingent reality. Others simply suppose that infinite regress is equally or more likely to be the case. The one readily adopts theism; the other does not. Neither seems easily to comprehend how the other arrives at his or her conclusion.

3. Thus, it seems that "the human mind" is a misnomer, and there are at least two species of mind. They have many similarities, and both may be fully rational, but they also have essential differences.

(a) One is a natural mind, the product of a natural developmental process that increasingly grows skeptical of biblical truth;

(b) One is a spiritual mind, the original state of the mind before it is affected by sin, which produces guilt, which leads to the skepticism of the "natural" mind.

4. God's Spirit may regenerate a natural mind and restore it to its spiritual status. Apart from this regeneration, the human mind progressively hardens against persuasion of Christian truths. This is a process of self-defense on the part of the mind, resisting the self-condemnation arising from an innocent conscience. Guilt for sin is not a feeling only, for even a dog might show some emotional response if caught disobeying the rules of the house. True guilt, however, is characterized by a recognition of the standard, the judge, and the consequences of some act that violates the standard. It transcends the moment. It is unique to the rational mind.

5. By implication, the original state of a normal, new mind is the spiritual state. God is the creator of the mind, and it is originally in harmony with him. The child nurtured in a loving and secure family environment is trusting, open, and accepting. Children do not question the existence of their environment or attempt to distinguish between noumena and phenomena. They do not question causality or think that religious belief is irrational. And some of these are touched by God's Spirit early so that their disposition of mind does not harden against spiritual truth or distort the spiritual realities.

Others, however, receive not that spiritual renewal and thus progress along the path of increasing resistance to spiritual truth. This resistance may manifest itself by rejecting spiritual reality or by distorting spiritual reality. The one clings to nature and denies God; the other merges nature with God.

6. Apologetic reasoning is our attack against this non-Christian, natural mind. It is also our defense against allowing ourselves to be influenced by false doctrine. It is thus an important part of spiritual growth and evangelistic persuasion.

7. The spiritual mind will degenerate due to the effect of sin, but a regenerate mind, the tender heart produced thereby, and the conviction and recognition of the consequences of sin that come from God's Spirit are the true essentials for evangelistic persuasion. The spiritual mind will believe a simple gospel tract and will rejoice at the abundance of apologetic evidence and reason. The natural mind, on the other hand, always finds "reasons" to remain skeptical and unbelieving.

Apologetics is not the essential core of evangelistic witness, but it is nevertheless a valuable and viable tool for witness both to the lost and the saved. My conclusion does not imply that this distinction is exclusively intellectual, only that the rational component is an essential aspect of what it means to be saved or lost.

Chapter 15

Evangelistic Preaching in the Twenty-First Century
Wayne McDill

THE TWENTIETH CENTURY WAS ONE OF RAPID AND significant change. In 1970 Alvin Toffler wrote in *Future Shock* that society was experiencing "a stream of change so accelerated that it influences our sense of time, revolutionizes the tempo of daily life, and affects the way we 'feel' the world around us."[1] He said that this speedup of change in every area of modern life was causing us to think of everything as temporary. All our thoughts were being colored by this impermanence. Our relationships with people, values, things, and our whole world were affected.

More than thirty years later we can see that Toffler's assessment was accurate, only now the pace of change has increased. Marshall McLuhan, another prophet of three decades ago, also saw unprecedented changes coming. McLuhan wrote that the entire pattern of thinking for modern man had changed, that he has been "massaged" by modern communications media which brought the world in upon him like a "global village."[2] His assessment has also proved to be accurate.

If these two prophets were correct thirty years ago, can the prophets of today be correct as well? Do current trends point to a very different world we will face in the new century? If so, can we be prepared to adapt to the new situation in our proclamation of the gospel of Christ?

The secular and religious prophets of the 1990s said that all of Western culture is in the throes of a major shift in the way we see ourselves and our world. The old way of thinking has been called *modernism* and the new way, *postmodernism*. Some of the changes on the horizon are so profound and basic that they affect every aspect of life. As these changes come, how will they affect our preaching of the gospel? Will there be any place for evangelistic preaching? If so, what form should it take?

The difficulty we face in communicating the gospel is that we must explain how the death of a Jew two thousand years ago is significant for the life of people today. We must make the abstract theological meaning of the atonement of Christ concrete and understandable for modern man. We must make clear and specific the often misunderstood connection between the cross of Christ and the conversion of a sinner.

This essay will offer some comments on these questions. First we will consider the changed nature of the audience we will face. Then we will attempt to clarify the essentials of the evangelistic message. Finally, I want to present the need for evangelistic preaching in the new century, for unbeliever and believer alike.

Understanding the Audience

Vital to effective communication is a clear understanding of the audience. John Stott wrote that the preacher stands between two worlds, the ancient world of the Bible and the contemporary world of his audience.[3] The preacher of the Bible first seeks to discern from the text the intended message of the original writer. Out of that particularized message he draws the theological truths that transcend the time and place of the original writing. Then he must place those truths back into a particular context as he declares them within the framework of contemporary thinking and in terms of the life experience of his hearers.

In this process of interpretation and proclamation, the preacher must study the text carefully and thoroughly. He must also study his own time, his own generation, his culture, and his particular audience. This kind of careful audience analysis is necessary if he is to present the timeless message in terms his audience can understand. Audience *analysis* is naturally followed by audience *adaptation*. The preacher does not adapt the content to the extent that he changes the message. Rather, he adapts the presentation of those universal principles to the cultural framework of his hearers.

In *A Primer on Postmodernism,* Stanley Grenz has identified the key features of this changing outlook and suggested their significance for gospel preaching.[4] Evangelicals, he writes, are closely tied to the worldview of *modernism,* with its emphasis on reason, science, and secularism. This kind of thinking has served as the opposing view in the debate over the Christian message. Evangelical preaching has responded with rational appeals for the existence of God, the trustworthiness of the Bible, and the fact of Jesus' resurrection. But now the rules have changed. A new generation doesn't raise the same objections to the gospel any more.

Postmodernism denies the reality of universal truth, asserting that truth is a matter for local community interpretation. Anyone's idea of truth is as good as another's. There is no unifying center of universal truth. The Christian knows, however, that there is a grand design to all of reality, an interpretation by which all claims to truth may be judged. It is the truth personified in Jesus of Nazareth, the eternal Word of God made flesh and dwelling among us. Christianity can never be just one more faith among the many in the world. It is God's truth for all people, to the ends of the earth.

Grenz suggests that the presentation of the gospel in a postmodern world will require several important changes in emphasis.[5] (1) Postmodernism rejects modernist individualism in favor of community. This emphasis is consistent with the biblical idea of God's intention to create a new community of all people in Christ. (2) The preaching of the gospel in a postmodern world can also reject the supremacy of reason in favor of a more biblical view of Christian truth. The reality of God is beyond the powers of reason. Becoming a Christian is not a matter of embracing a set of religious propositions. It is coming into a new and life-changing relationship with God through Jesus Christ. (3) Postmodernism rejects the modernist dualism that sees reality as mind and matter. The preaching of the gospel can also avoid the concern for souls while disregarding the body. Man, in the biblical view, is a unified whole, a person best understood in relationship with his world, with himself, with others, and with God. So, instead of rejecting either modernism or postmodernism, or affirming either one, the preacher of the new century will need to seek a biblical way to speak to the needs of the whole person.

Of course, all of the audience will not be buying into the postmodern mind-set. Modernist thinking will not just disappear with the turn of the century. Most people will go on with the same worldview as their parents. But they will also be propagandized daily with these changing ideas and attitudes. As in any other generation, the church must provide a clear alternative voice to both the old secular ideas and the new ones.

Much has been made in recent years of the various *generations* alive today and the differences in their outlook and preferences. Michael Sack has described generations as they should be seen by the contemporary preacher. Look at a summary of his interpretation:[6]

Generation X: born between 1970 and 1985, they tend to suffer low self-esteem, the "Feed me" generation, like to retreat into small groups.

Busters: born between 1960 and 1970, they don't like crowds or mingling with other generations, are skeptical of guarantees.

Boomers: born between 1945 and 1960, they are faddish and intellectually lazy, the "entertain me and earn me" generation, looking for spiritual direction.

Older Adults: born before 1945, they have skills and money and want to do something worthwhile, the "Need me and show me" generation.

George Barna offers a somewhat different interpretation.[7] The differences in these two categorizations suggest that generational analysis is something less than an exact science. Barna points out that as we approach the beginning of the new century, there are four generations still alive. *The Seniors* are those born before 1927, now 27 million strong in the U.S. *The Builders* were born from 1927 to 1945 and number 43 million today. Thirdly, *The Boomers,* the largest group, were born between 1946 and 1964, including 78 million. The fourth group, *The Baby Busters,* are the nation's second largest generation ever, with more than 70 million born between 1965 and 1983.

Barna's point is that 60 percent of the population is now 50 or younger. If the congregation on a given Sunday follows that pattern, the sermon will be addressed to a new majority of younger hearers who have ways of thinking and listening different from those over 50. He also points out that more than half the audience is likely to be female. As we enter the first decade of the new century, the younger generations will age and the older ones will shrink. The preacher will face a very different audience.[8]

This new audience will differ from earlier generations in the way they receive and interpret information. Barna suggests several specifics. (1) They are accustomed to receiving information at a faster rate. The preacher's pacing in his sermon will affect their interest. (2) Their attention span is much shorter. They will lose interest sooner than their parents and grandparents. (3) They are especially sensitive to the language and style of the preacher. If he seems judgmental, theological, or condescending, he will lose them.[9]

The implications of these tendencies are clear for the preacher. If he seems to drag and stray from the subject, their attention will likely be lost. After twenty minutes, a sermon will reap diminishing returns. The preacher should think of his sermon in brief segments and keep something new coming every few minutes. Though his message may be biblical and thus authoritative, his attitude must not be authoritarian. Barna also insists that these new hearers are less interested in a smooth presentation than preaching that is genuine, authentic, and relevant. They want the preacher to talk *with* them instead of talking *at* them.[10]

The cultural shift currently taking place will dramatically change the preacher's audience in the way they see themselves and their world. This current period of transition may well stretch far into the new century, with the discussion among academics continuing as to the nature and validity of the ideas swirling around postmodernism. All the while, the ordinary person is largely unaware of the debate, even while he is unknowingly affected by the changes. His own interpretation of reality is shifting with the culture around him.

The preacher of the gospel of Christ must not be so caught up in this culture that he misses the significance of these changes. He must preach the unchanging gospel in the midst of the changes.

Clarifying the Message

What exactly is the gospel? From the time of the New Testament this question has been crucial. Paul confidently preached the gospel of Jesus Christ, declaring it to be "the power of God for the salvation of everyone who believes" (Rom. 1:16 NIV). But he also referred to "a different gospel—which is really no gospel at all" (Gal. 1:6–7 and 2 Cor. 11:4 NIV). This "other gospel" was a gospel of error which sought to add the work of man to the finished work of Christ.

In 1 Corinthians 15 Paul spells out as clearly as anywhere else in the New Testament the simple gospel of Jesus Christ. He urges his readers to hold firmly to this gospel which brought salvation to them:

> That Christ died for our sins according to the Scriptures, that he was buried, that he was raised on the third day according to the Scriptures, and that he appeared to Peter, and then to the Twelve. After that, he appeared to more than five hundred of the brothers at the same time, most of whom are still living, though some have fallen asleep (1 Cor. 15:3–6 NIV).

The gospel Paul spelled out in this passage is the story of Jesus' experience here on earth. It speaks of his death on the cross for our sins, his burial in the earth, his resurrection on the third day, and the fact that he was seen risen by a great host of people. This is the gospel of Jesus Christ. Even at the time of the writing many were alive who could testify to these facts. It is actually but a simple narrative of significant, prophecy-fulfilling events in the life of Jesus of Nazareth. It is told as a matter of historical record.

Notice what is not in Paul's definition of the gospel. The gospel is not about what happened to the followers of Jesus except that they were eyewitnesses to the resurrection. It is not about the experiences of the church. It is not about the morality of the church. The gospel is not even about the philosophy and teachings of Jesus. It is not about his healing ministry. It is not about the miracles he worked. The gospel is about those eternally significant events in the life of Jesus by which he made atonement for our sins and was victorious over death in our behalf.

The Bible assumes man's need for some atoning actions if he is to be right with God. It is understood that he is cut off from fellowship with God. He is totally at fault in the problem, for it is his refusal of God's will that has alienated him from God. This alienation must be dealt with first if he is to be restored to a right relationship with God. The sin barrier must be removed. The New Testament declares plainly God's hatred of sin. He refuses to remove the terrible consequences he has determined will come from sin. But God's attitude is not a distant and uncaring contempt for the sinner.

The supreme gesture of God's love and mercy is seen in Christ, particularly in his atoning death on the cross. Jesus came "to give his life as a ransom for many" (Mark 10:45 NIV). Paul wrote that "we were reconciled to him through the death of his Son" (Rom. 5:10 NIV), for "while we were still sinners, Christ died for us" (Rom. 5:8 NIV). We "have been brought near through the blood of Christ" (Eph. 2:13 NIV), for "God presented him as a sacrifice of atonement, through faith in his blood" (Rom. 3:25 NIV).

Peter wrote that "he himself bore our sins in his body on the tree" (1 Pet. 2:24 NIV). In Hebrews we read that "Christ was sacrificed once to take away the sins of many people" (Heb. 9:28 NIV). It is clear that God does not forgive sin by lovingly overlooking it. He forgives sin because atonement for sin has been made in the cross of Christ.

The New Testament does not explain precisely how Christ was able to overcome the effects of man's sin and restore him to fellowship with God. But with a number of graphic metaphors it does clearly affirm the truth of what he did. Some of the pictures describing how Jesus removed the sin barrier are these: he was the "sacrifice" for our sins; he was the Lamb of God; he gave his life as a ransom; he was able to satisfy the demands of God's justice; he "bought" our salvation.

The atoning death of Jesus is beyond our experience and understanding. Since the fact of Jesus' death is absolutely unique, these metaphors are but illustrations and must not be expected to explain every detail. For our examination, we will group the metaphors into three portraits of how Jesus' death on the cross deals with the sin barrier.

A Timeless Sacrifice

The Bible pictures Jesus as sacrificing his life to bring us to "at-one-ment" with God. This striking picture comes from the sacrificial practices of Judaism where atonement was connected to the slaying of an animal as a sacrifice for sin. Since the Hebrews believed the life was "in the blood" (Lev. 17:11), the blood of the animals had to be shed in the sacrifice. So the blood of Christ is often mentioned as of great importance.

This does not mean the physical blood only, but the timeless benefit of that blood as Jesus yielded his life to God in complete obedience to his will. His death is called a "sacrifice for sins" (Heb. 10:12 NIV) and "a fragrant offering and sacrifice to God" (Eph. 5:2 NIV).

The power of Christ's death is associated with his perfect obedience to the Father's will (Heb. 10:7–9). He was "obedient to death—even death on a cross!" (Phil. 2:8 NIV). This obedient willingness made the effect of his sacrifice complete. It is a sacrifice which did what the Old Testament sacrifices could never do (Heb. 10:4). It was a permanent sacrifice, for when Jesus "had offered for all time one sacrifice for sins, he sat down at the right hand of God" (Heb. 10:12 NIV). So in willingly sacrificing his life, he canceled out the effect of sin. Not only did Jesus act as the officiating priest who offered the sacrifice; he was himself that sacrifice.

The connection between the cross of Christ and the sin problem of man is pictured in this metaphor in terms of a timeless sacrifice that Jesus made for man's sin. Does this communicate to contemporary man? That is difficult to say.

A child is drowning. A brother leaps into the water and rushes to his aid. In the process of saving his little brother, the rescuer loses his life. We understand the meaning of a sacrifice like that. A soldier on the battlefield throws himself over a live enemy grenade to shield his companions from the blast with his own body. We know what sacrifice means here. The swimmer gave his life accidentally while saving his brother. The soldier threw himself over the grenade out of instinct and training. But Jesus chose deliberately to offer his life.

Jesus planned his submission to the cross as the climax of his purpose in this life. In the cross the sinless Christ gathered all the sin of mankind to himself and there "God made him who had no sin to be sin for us, so that in him we might become the righteousness of God" (2 Cor. 5:21 NIV). How can we explain the timeless relationship between Jesus Christ and all mankind? It is beyond us. The verbal pictures are only helpful to a limited degree. We can nonetheless try to communicate this great truth in the images of contemporary man so that he can begin to grasp it.

A Costly Ransom

Another biblical picture helping us see the connection between the cross and our condition is the portrayal of Jesus' death as a ransom paid for man's release from bondage to sin. Jesus said, "For even the Son of Man did not come to be served, but to serve, and to give his life as a ransom for many" (Mark 10:45 NIV). The ransom Jesus paid for mankind was his own life. He placed himself in the hands of the enemy as a substitute for the captives of sin. Therefore, Paul writes to Christians, "You are not your own; you were bought at a price" (1 Cor. 6:19–20 NIV). He charges further, "You were bought at a price; do not become slaves of men" (1 Cor. 7:23 NIV).

Being set free from the captivity of sin, the believer must allow no force to take him captive again. He was released from the clutches of the enemy into the hands of a loving but sovereign heavenly Father so that now he belongs fully to him.

Can modern man understand this picture of Jesus' death as a ransom and substitute that breaks the bonds of our sin? Again, we cannot tell. A Japanese airliner is highjacked by extremists. The passengers and crew are threatened with death unless demands are met by the officials. After some discussion three airline executives offer themselves as hostages if the passengers and crew are released. Irish extremists capture a British businessman and his wife. Their demands are presented to police with the threat of death for their captives. A police official offers himself as a substitute hostage for the woman. This kind of ransom as a personal substitute is clear to modern man. It helps somewhat to clarify the meaning of Jesus' death in our behalf.

Peter declared in his Pentecost sermon, "This man was handed over to you by God's set purpose and fore-knowledge; and you, with the help of wicked men, put him to death by nailing him to the cross" (Acts 2:23 NIV). It was, in fact, his death that broke the hold of the enemy on man. Paul declares, "And having disarmed the powers and authorities, he made a public spectacle of them, triumphing over them by the cross" (Col. 2:15 NIV).

Satisfying the Demands of Justice

Another portrait of Jesus' death is the picture of Jesus accepting the punishment due for man's sin. God has made known to mankind the law which reflects his righteous character. Paul wrote that even if men do not have the written law they are responsible for their sin because "the requirements of the law are written on their hearts" (Rom. 2:15 NIV). After making clear that Jew and Gentile alike have broken God's law, he wrote that "no one will be declared righteous in his sight by observing the law; rather, through the law we become conscious of sin" (Rom. 3:20 NIV). Then, "when we were still powerless, Christ died for the ungodly" (Rom. 5:6 NIV). Just as Adam's one act of disobedience allowed sin to capture every person, so also through the obedience of Christ many will be made righteous.

In Jesus' perfect obedience even to death, he satisfied the righteous demands of God. He overcame the power of sin by his perfect life. He overcame death by embracing it and breaking its grip on man as the dread result of sin. He overcame hell by the resurrection. He accepted the wrath of God against sin for all mankind and so took the atoning action that blotted out sin. Isaiah wrote centuries earlier of Jesus' perfect obedience in taking our sins upon himself:

He was pierced through for our transgressions, He was crushed for our iniquities; The chastening for our well-being fell upon Him, And by His scourging we are healed. All of us like sheep have gone astray, Each of us has turned to his own way; But the LORD has caused the iniquity of us all To fall on Him (Isa. 53:5–6).

Will this picture of the perfectly obedient Son accepting the penalty for sin in our behalf communicate to modern man? That is not clear. We do know man normally believes that the lawbreaker should be punished. He thinks of this as fair and necessary for an orderly society. He also knows that the innocent often suffer for the sins of the guilty. Paul wrote, "Very rarely will anyone die for a righteous man, though for a good man someone might possibly dare to die. But God demonstrates his own love for us in this: While we were still sinners, Christ died for us" (Rom. 5:7–8 NIV).

I'll never forget hearing a dramatic parable illustrating these ideas in a sermon several years ago. The story was about a rebellious young prince who ran away from home. His father, the king, was heartbroken. The elder son saw his father wasting away in sorrow over the loss of the younger man. To ease his grief he offered to begin a personal search in an effort to find the young prince. The father protested at first but then approved the plan. Month after month the elder son searched, hoping in every crowd, down every street, to see the familiar face of his erring brother.

Finally one day, as he entered a strange village, he found everyone rushing toward the town square. Arriving there with the crowd, he discovered that an execution was about to take place. He overheard people in the crowd tell of a young man who had killed another in a drunken fight. Then the executioner mounted the platform with the prisoner. The elder son was shocked to see it was his brother. After all this time, all this grief, was it to end like this?

Then, to his surprise an official on the platform made an appeal to the gathered crowd. "Be it known that any man may now step forward to accept in his behalf the punishment about to be executed upon the prisoner." The elder brother quickly learned from those around him that this was a law in the town which allowed any person to accept punishment in behalf of another. But certainly none would have any concern for this stranger.

The elder brother pushed his way forward toward the platform. "I will do it, sir," he shouted. A murmur of astonishment swept through the crowd. On the platform the younger man recognized him. "Go home," the elder brother said. "Tell our father I have found you and sent you to him." The rebellious young man's heart was broken over his sins. He returned home a free man because of the one who honored his father and loved him enough to die for him.

Will a parable such as this speak to today's audience? Who can say? Nevertheless, it captures our imagination with a portion of the truth of Jesus' death for our sins. Communicating theological truth has never been easy. Neither is it easy today to describe how Jesus removed the barrier between man and God and what that means for us now. Nevertheless, we can know that God does not leave us without a way of describing what it means to be a Christian. The ancient pictures given us in Scripture can be repainted in such a way that modern man may see what God has done in Christ. Again, let us be able to say about our witness what Paul did about his: "Before your very eyes Jesus Christ was clearly portrayed as crucified" (Gal. 3:1 NIV).

The Need for Evangelistic Preaching

We have seen briefly that the preacher's audience in this new century will be quite different from the one faced during most of the twentieth century. We have also considered how the timeless message of the atonement of Christ can be communicated effectively to that new audience. Now let me briefly suggest why evangelistic preaching has such great importance for this new century.

The first and most obvious need for evangelistic preaching in America is the fact that so many have not yet heard. With a long tradition of gospel preaching, near saturation by radio, television, and print media, and (as a Russian student recently pointed out to me) a church on every corner, we would think that Americans have heard the gospel by now. The truth is, however, that there are hundreds of thousands, even millions, of Americans who must respond as did a Seattle man recently, "I have heard of Jesus, but I have no idea who he is."

One of the major problems in all the preaching in the broadcast media and in the pulpits across the country is that much of it is not the gospel at all. The atoning work of Christ for our sins is not an appealing subject to many of the preachers of our day. I recently attended a Christmas Eve communion service at a Baptist church in which the preacher said the juice represented the joy of the Spirit and the bread that Jesus was the Bread of Life. This is not the gospel. Christians must not ask whether the preaching of the cross will be accepted. We must be faithful to preach Christ and him crucified within the thought patterns of the contemporary audience, but not to compromise or abandon that message.

The problem for most contemporary evangelistic preaching is getting a hearing. Seeker services and seeker-friendly services are being offered by an increasing number of churches. The basic idea is to distinguish between what the believers need in preaching and what the unbelieving seekers need. Believer services are planned for taking the Christian deeper in his faith, for discipling from the pulpit. The seeker services, on the other hand, are designed to present the gospel clearly and simply to those who have not yet put their faith in Christ.

The writer of Hebrews advocated leaving the discussion of the elementary principles of Christ, and said, let us "go on to maturity" (Heb. 6:1 NIV). Evangelistic preaching can do both. Making the gospel clear to seekers does not mean it must be boring to believers. There is a depth to be explored that most believers have not yet seen. This brings me to the second need.

Evangelistic preaching is needed to strengthen believers in their faith. Christians need to be taught the depth of meaning in the atonement of Christ. They need to see the many biblical pictures of the transformation the cross makes possible in the life of the believer. We can preach on regeneration, reconciliation, salvation, justification, adoption, and redemption. These graphic biblical themes can be presented in terms of the life of postmodern man with illustrations and analogies he can understand. As these ancient pictures are repainted, the believer's faith will be increased and the seeker will be presented with the gospel at the same time.

The believer needs to hear effective evangelistic preaching to equip him for witnessing in his normal traffic pattern. As his pastor presents the gospel of Christ in clearly biblical and imaginatively contemporary ways, the witnessing Christian will gain better insight into the simple and profound message that brings salvation.

The key may well be for the pastor to recognize that there can be responses to the message other than an immediate profession of faith. When he presses for that response alone, he may give the rest of the congregation reason for tuning out. Each of the biblical themes for salvation has clear implications for the Christian life. There are faith responses "that accompany salvation" (Heb. 6:9 NIV). Paul writes to believers, "As you therefore have received Christ Jesus the Lord, so walk in Him" (Col. 2:6).

The new international opportunity for evangelistic preaching offers another reason for its importance in the new century. Never before have so many pastors and laypersons traveled abroad in direct missions activities. Baptists and other Christians have numerous opportunities every year to join these mission trips. Often they include medical or dental ministry, building projects, children's programs, and other efforts to minister at the point of need. The hope is usually to help establish new churches on these mission fields. Inevitably, however, there is gospel preaching and witnessing. Many short-term missionaries are engaging in street preaching for the first time.

Americans find that they are themselves something of an oddity and an attraction. People in Eastern Europe, Africa, and Asian countries will gather in the town square or come to meetings to hear Americans. Very often they have never heard the gospel before. The celebrity status of any American can open doors to a witness in schools, businesses, government offices, even military installations. In most cases the host countries will graciously welcome their testimony and preaching. Preachers in the United States who seldom preach evangelistic sermons find that they have to prepare them for these trips. They usually return with a new vision for missions and a new zeal for evangelism.

The twenty-first century will indeed bring challenges for the believer as he seeks to communicate the gospel to a new audience. As in every generation, there will be new obstacles and new opportunities. If we are convinced that Jesus is the way and that "no one comes to the Father except through [him]" (John 14:6 NIV), we have no choice but to proclaim the good news that is "the power of God for salvation to everyone who believes" (Rom. 1:16). We can preach it in its simplicity so that even the children may understand, and in its depth so that the academic is challenged, and in its dramatic imagery so that postmodern man can grasp its meaning.

Chapter 16

Jesus Christ: Our Master Model
For Sharing the Gospel

Jack Stanton

THROUGH THE MANY YEARS THAT I HAVE KNOWN
Dr. Delos Miles, he has lived a life of evangelism that
can be characterized by the words of Galatians 2:20: "I
am crucified with Christ: nevertheless I live; yet not I, but
Christ liveth in me: and the life which I now live in the
flesh I live by the faith of the Son of God, who loved me,
and gave himself for me" (KJV). In his ministry of evangelism Delos Miles has always sought to know the mind
of Christ, obey the will of Christ, radiate the love of
Christ, and live and witness in the strength of Christ.

Dr. Miles's "life of evangelism" challenges us to
excellence in our evangelistic endeavors. This "life of
evangelism" Miles learned from walking with Jesus,
whom he calls the Master Evangelist. Thus, according to
Dr. Miles, Jesus is the perfect model for all of life, especially for sharing the gospel.

In Revelation 1:5 Jesus Christ is called "the faithful
witness" (KJV). In 1 Peter 2:21, believers are told that
Christ is our example: "For even hereunto were ye
called: because Christ also suffered for us, leaving us an
example, that ye should follow his steps" (KJV).

In John 17:13–20 Jesus prays for all believers and
reminds us that he is sending us, as the Father sent him:

And now come I to thee; and these things I speak in the world, that they might have my joy fulfilled in themselves. I have given them thy word; and the world hath hated them, because they are not of the world, even as I am not of the world. I pray not that thou shouldest take them out of the world, but that thou shouldest keep them from the evil. They are not of the world, even as I am not of the world. Sanctify them through thy truth: thy word is truth. *As thou hast sent me into the world,* even so *have I also sent them into the world.* And for their sakes I sanctify myself, that they also might be sanctified through the truth. *Neither pray I for these alone, but for them also which shall believe on me through their word* (KJV, emphasis added).

In Luke 19:10, we are told Jesus came "to seek and to save that which was lost" (KJV). As obedient followers of Jesus we must seek people, that they, through Jesus, might be saved. Christians are to have the same purpose that Jesus had. The gospel is not so much something to "come and hear," as it is something to "go and tell." It is the Good News of the redemptive acts of God in Christ. All the people of God are called to go into the world, with all the gospel, all the time.

In my preaching I urge people to go into all the world, sharing Jesus Christ. I have been asked a time or two by sincere people, "What right do we have, as Americans, to go into all the world, and impose Western culture and religion upon people who already have a culture and a religion."

My answer is that we are not trying to extend Western culture or Western religion; we are simply following the example of Jesus Christ by telling the story of a God who is the God of the universe. We are following the example of God's Son, the Lord Jesus Christ.

As his children, and at his command, we are to share the Good News of the Father wherever we go, and in every way possible. Jesus spoke to individuals, small groups, and large crowds. As his followers we should do likewise.

All of us have feelings of inadequacy at times. We feel that we do not have the ability to carry out the task assigned to us. When Jesus left the glory of heaven, he put off the robes of glory and came to earth as a man, yet without sin. He was conceived by the Holy Spirit and born of the virgin Mary. When Jesus was tempted by the devil, he could have said to the devil, "I am Jesus," and the devil would have fled from him; but he used weapons to defeat the devil that are available to every believer in Jesus Christ. The Bible says that Jesus was filled with the Spirit of God without measure and so he lived in the power of the Holy Spirit. As believers we are commanded of God in Ephesians 5:18 to "be filled [literally translated as "continually overflowing"] with the Spirit."

Therefore, as Christians it should not be our practice to walk in weakness and be devastated by fear when we are filled and controlled by the Holy Spirit. Jesus quoted Scripture to every question raised by the devil. We, too, have the Word of God which is the power of God unto salvation. Hence, Jesus left us spiritual weapons of warfare that enable us to live a full and meaningful life, defeat the devil, and be effective in our witnessing.

This effectiveness in witnessing is exemplified in Christ's encounter with the woman at the well (John 4). From this passage a number of salient features surface, demonstrating the "Master's" way of effective witness. This example of effective witness is worthy of emulation.

Jesus Sought Her

Jesus sought her; that is, he positioned himself so they would meet. In John 4:4 we read, "And he must needs go through Samaria" (KJV). Most of the Jews went around Samaria; they did not want to be contaminated by what they would find there. Why then, does the Spirit of God have John use this double emphasis on going through Samaria? The words *must needs* almost tumble over each other. Why this note of urgency? There are three good reasons.

First, a lost person was there, in Samaria, and every lost person has a need to hear about Jesus. Only those who know the Father can share the Good News of the gospel of Jesus Christ; therefore, as children of the Father, we need to take advantage of every method available to share the Good News about Jesus with those who need to know him as their Lord and Savior. Some of the greatest churches in America use the bus ministry to reach, not only children, but also adults for the Lord Jesus Christ.

Dr. E. V. Hill, a pastor in the Watts area of Los Angeles, seeks to have a Christian family in every block in that neighborhood. He and his church then equip that family to reach out to meet the needs of the people living in their block, to lead them to know Jesus Christ as Lord and Savior, and to encourage them to be baptized and become active members in the church.

Dr. Cho, pastor of the largest church in the world, has divided Seoul, Korea, into a number of sections. He has installed in each section of the city a group of workers whose main task is to meet the people who live there, minister to their needs, lead them to faith in Jesus Christ, and then to baptism, church membership, and active Christian witness and ministry.

In addition, many pastors are experiencing tremendous numerical and spiritual growth in their churches as they follow Paul's exhortation to the church in Ephesus to perfect the saints "for the work of the ministry, for the edifying [building up] of the body of Christ (Eph. 4:12 KJV). A great number of pastors have found help in this by conducting a Lay Evangelism School or using Continuing Witness Training in their churches.

Others have used existing structures effectively as avenues for edification and growth. Some of the largest churches in the Southern Baptist Convention have grown, and continue to grow, through their Sunday school, the Bible teaching ministry of the church. Further, more and more Baptist churches are seeking to knock on every door, cross over every threshold in their community, and share a personal witness for Jesus Christ with each person present.

Someone once asked D. L. Moody, the great evangelist, "Why do you use so many different methods in reaching people for Christ and in building a great congregation?" Moody indicated he was not always happy with his methods and that he would be glad to hear what methods the inquirer used. The inquirer replied, "I don't have any methods, and I am not reaching many people." Then Moody said, "I like my methods better than your methods." Methods must never become an end in themselves. We must let the Holy Spirit of God lead us in developing activities that will help us lead as many people to Jesus Christ as Lord and Savior in as short a time as possible.

Second, Jesus used the meeting with the woman at the well to teach us that there should be no place for prejudice in the Christian's life. In biblical times some people believed that a cow was worth more than a woman. A woman was considered more a thing than a person. However, Jesus treated the Samaritan woman with dignity and respect. Here is a respected man speaking to a disrespected woman, a Jew speaking and ministering to a Samaritan. Jesus should be our example as we seek to reach people of other races, cultures, and backgrounds. We must remember that God so loved the world—all of mankind—that he sent Jesus to die for our sins, redeem us, and make us heirs of God, joint heirs with Jesus Christ.

How we think ultimately determines how we act. Sometimes we are not aware of our prejudices and are shocked when we become aware of them. Some people are uncomfortable around people of other races and cultures, the very rich or very poor persons, the highly educated or illiterate, or even persons with physical limitations or deformities. We must follow the example of Jesus and minister to the needs of those we meet, regardless of their conditions.

Third, Jesus shows us that he can make the most unlikely person, who receives him as Lord and Savior, an excited and effective witness. The woman at the well had many things against her—her race, sex, and lifestyle. However, in spite of all of this, her brief encounter with Jesus Christ so changed and empowered her that she was able to go back to the people who knew her best and tell them of Jesus, the Christ. They "believed on him" because of her witness (John 4:39 KJV).

Jesus said, "Ye have not chosen me, but I have chosen you, and ordained you, that ye should go and bring forth fruit, and that your fruit should remain" (John 15:16 KJV). In Matthew 12:30 Jesus declares, "He that is not with me is against me; and he that gathereth not with me scattereth abroad" (KJV).

We cannot be neutral about Jesus. We are for him or against him. We are gathering with him or scattering abroad. We can join Jesus in reaching the world with the gospel or we can—through indifference, carelessness, or even open disobedience—refuse to share the gospel and face the judgement of God upon our sin.

Jesus Spoke to Her Interests and Her Needs

Jesus started with this woman where she was, her immediate needs, and quickly led her to think of her greater eternal needs. He captured her attention by requesting something from her. "Jesus saith unto her, Give me to drink" (John 4:7 KJV). She replied, "How is it that thou, being a Jew, asketh drink of me, which am a woman of Samaria? for the Jews have no dealings [literally, no friendly dealings] with the Samaritans" (John 4:9 KJV). Many non-Christians feel that Christians do not understand them or care about them. Jesus knew that a good way to make a friend was to ask that person to do something for himself. Sometimes we make a cripple out of a person by doing more and more for the individual without asking something in return.

As true believers and followers of Jesus Christ, we must follow his example by demonstrating genuine love to unbelievers by relating to them on a personal level. We can do this by building bridges of understanding and communication with them through ministry and witness and by asking for a response.

Jesus also offered this woman something. He offered her the gift of God—living water—eternal life: "Jesus answered and said unto her, If thou knewest the gift of God, and who it is that saith to thee, Give me to drink; thou wouldest have asked of him, and he would have given thee living water. The woman saith unto him, Sir, thou hast nothing to draw with, and the well is deep: from whence then hast thou that living water?" (John 4:10–11 KJV). The woman was still thinking in terms of the physical, so Jesus gently lifted her thoughts to the spiritual.

Vincent, in *Greek Word Studies,* reminds us that the word translated "gift" contains the sense of bountiful, free, and honorable. Here was a woman who, throughout her life, had been hedged in by limitations, and Jesus offered her a life that was bountiful. She had found a high price tag on all her relationships in life, even with her husbands, and now Jesus offered the gift of a new life that was free. She was a disillusioned, disgraced woman, but Jesus offered her the gift of a new life that was honorable. Jesus spoke to her interests and her needs, offering her a whole new life through the gift of eternal life.

Jesus Stirred Her Conscience

Jesus said, "Go, call thy husband, and come hither" (John 4:16 KJV). Jesus was helping this woman understand that all of us have sinned, and that the wages of sin is death—eternal separation from God, who is the God of life. He wanted her to realize that the greatest sin—the sin from which all other sins flow—is the unwillingness of a person to let Jesus—God's gift—become her Lord and Savior.

The responses given by the woman are so typical that as you witness to non-Christians you will hear them given to you over and over again. Her first reply was a denial of guilt. "The woman answered and said, I have no husband" (John 4:17 KJV).

One night as I shared with a man and his wife about how a person becomes a Christian, the man suddenly blurted out, "you talk to me like I'm a sinner. I want you to know that my business is honest and respectable. I love my wife and I am faithful to her. I would die for my children. I try to be a decent man and help others."

I said to the man, "I believe all that you told me. In fact, on the way over to your house the pastor told me many fine things about you. May I ask you a question or two? If Jesus suddenly appeared in our midst could you say, 'I am as good as Jesus'?"

He replied, "No, I could not and neither could you!"

"That's right," I said. "Romans 3:23 declares, 'For all have sinned, and come short of the glory of God.' And in Romans 6:23 we read, 'For the wages of sin is death [separation from the life of God]; but the gift of God is eternal life [God's kind of life] through Jesus Christ our Lord'" (KJV).

"Do you have any goals for your life that you have not reached?" I asked.

The man replied, "Of course I have."

Then I explained to him that God's goal for his life was that he be like Jesus. To become a Christian and be like Jesus, you must acknowledge that you are a sinner and cannot save yourself. Repent—change your mind about sin and change the direction of your life (toward God and away from sin)—and ask Jesus Christ to forgive your sin and take control of your life: "That if thou shalt confess with thy mouth the Lord Jesus [Jesus as Lord], and shalt believe in thine heart that God hath raised him from the dead, thou shalt be saved. For with the heart man believeth unto righteousness; and with the mouth confession is made unto salvation" (Rom. 10:9–10 KJV).

Suddenly the man dropped to his knees and asked God to forgive him, cleanse him, and fill him with the Holy Spirit, that he might be the man God wanted him to be. Praise God, the gospel is still the power of God unto salvation!

The woman at the well also attempted to ridicule Jesus: "The woman saith unto him, Sir, I perceive that thou art a prophet" (John 4:19 KJV). I remember a semi-

nary professor who translated this verse in this way,
"Oh! You are a preacher!" He went on to say that when
people are becoming convicted they sometimes try to
make the person witnessing to them feel ridiculous and
embarrassed. If this happens we must never become frustrated, but quietly and earnestly we must explain to them
our love and concern for them and how, through Jesus
Christ, they can experience forgiveness, freedom, and the
abundant life, now and forever.

The woman at the well also wanted to argue. She said,
"Our fathers worshipped in this mountain; and ye say, that
in Jerusalem is the place where men ought to worship"
(John 4:20 KJV). Sometimes, as you witness, someone may
say, "there are so many religions and denominations, how
can I know who is right?" Don't get involved in an argument. Simply say, "I am sure you will agree with me that
Jesus is right." To know what Jesus said we need to read
the Bible, which tells us about Jesus. Then, read some
simple, brief passages from the Bible about who Jesus is,
what he has done, and how the person can experience and
benefit from Christ's life, death, and resurrection. If we can
help people to come to know Jesus as their Lord and
Savior, they will find Jesus can, and will, help them find
answers to questions that bother them.

Jesus Showed Her the Way of Life By Revealing Himself

"The woman saith unto him, I know that Messias
cometh, which is called Christ: when he is come, he will
tell us all things. Jesus saith unto her, I that speak unto
thee am he" (John 4:25–26 KJV).

I grew up in a home broken by sin and by divorce.
My mother was a loving, caring person. She helped me
feel that I was loved and that I was important. She
taught me that I could do anything I was asked to do. I

felt sccurc and safe in my home, although we were very poor and faced a number of crises as I grew up. We tried to be a decent family, but did not attend church except on rare occasions, usually during some difficult period in our lives. The only person who read the Bible in our home was my grandmother. We had no family worship, nor did we say grace at mealtimes. So, I grew up as a young man without much knowledge of God, the church, the Bible, or the Christian life.

During all of my growing-up years, only two people ever made any attempt to talk to me about how I could become a Christian. During a revival, which someone insisted I attend, a man came up to me on a number of nights, grabbed me by my shoulders, shook me, and said, "I used to be a criminal and now I'm a Christian. Why don't you get saved and be like I am?" To tell the truth, I deeply resented him and his rough tactics, and certainly did not want to be like him. As far as I can remember, he said nothing to me about Christ, nor did he tell me how to become a Christian.

As we witness to others we must brag about Jesus, not about ourselves. We must help the lost person understand who Jesus is, what he has done for us, how we can receive him as our Lord and Savior, how to live a full and meaningful life on earth, and how to go to be with Jesus when we die.

A few years later, when I was just a few days short of my twentieth birthday, I was working with a construction crew in St. Louis County. After work I decided to go to East St. Louis to see my grandmother and get a good home-cooked meal. When I entered my grandmother's home she clapped her hands together and said, "Praise God! We are in a revival at our church and I want you to go with me to church tonight."

I was so startled and agitated at her request that I shouted out, "Every time I come to your house lately you keep asking me to go to church, to get saved, and to give my heart to Jesus. Can't I get a meal without a sermon?" She reached out and put her hand on mine until I stopped shouting and said, "I'm going to keep asking you until you go, and keep praying for you until you become a Christian." As mean as I was, I didn't want to hurt my grandmother, so I said, "Alright, I'll go with you tonight."

When we arrived at the church and started down one side of the auditorium, she kept trying to get me down in the front, but I finally said, "This is as far as I go." She slipped into the pew first, and I had to sit next to the aisle.

I endured the singing and finally the evangelist began his message. It seemed to me that each time he named a sin he pointed right at me. I was sure someone had told him I was there and where I was seated so he could point at me. I know now that wasn't true, but I sure believed it then.

As the evangelist closed his message he asked us to stand and close our eyes. I stood, but I wasn't about to close my eyes. I wanted to see what was happening and, besides, I wasn't about to let a preacher tell me what to do. The choir began singing the invitation hymn. They sang it over and over until I thought they were going to sing until someone responded or dropped dead.

I stood looking around the auditorium doing everything I could to keep my mind off the invitation. Suddenly I felt a slight touch on my arm, and I turned to look into the face of a well-built, handsome young man who said to me, "Are you a Christian?" I was so startled and confused by this question that I yelled, "No!" The young man looked at me for a moment and then stepped away.

I wondered why he had singled me out, and felt sure he would never do that again; but even as these thoughts flashed through my mind the man came back to me and said, "Would you like to become a Christian tonight?" My reply was, "Not tonight, buddy, not tonight." He smiled and said, "Why not tonight?" I said, "I don't know why not tonight. Are you a preacher or something?"

He looked at me for a few moments and said, "Oh no, I'm not a preacher. I've just been saved three days. If I'm not doing this right, would you forgive me?" I didn't know what he was doing, much less whether he was doing it right.

Finally he said, "Will you go with me down to the front and let me pray with you?" I said, "Yes, if you don't get the preachers in on it." I didn't know much about preachers, and I didn't want to get too close to them. The man agreed and we went to the front of the auditorium. I thought we would stop at the end of the aisle. I would let him pray, and then I would leave quickly through an exit door at the front.

However, he took my arm and we walked to the front, then turned and walked clear across the front to the other side of the auditorium. When the preacher came to us, the young man said, "He doesn't want to talk to you; he wants to pray with me." This impressed me. He said he wouldn't let the preacher interfere—and he didn't.

The next thing I knew, this young man was on his knees, and he asked me to kneel with him. I had never seen a grown man on his knees unless someone knocked him on his knees, but I did what he asked and knelt by him. I asked this man why he came directly to me twice when there must have been five hundred people present.

"Three nights ago I walked past this church on the way to a park three blocks from here, to kill myself," he said. "I had no hope and wanted to end it all, but as I passed the church I heard people singing about hope and forgiveness and strength and joy. I slipped into the back of the church and listened. Soon the preacher began talking about Jesus, how he loved everyone, how he could forgive our sins and give us a new start in life. I went forward to this very spot where we are now and asked God to forgive me, save me, and use me to help others. Something happened to me three nights ago that changed my life.

"During the invitation tonight I prayed and asked God if there was someone in the building who needed him like I needed him three nights ago. I also asked him to show me the person and give me the courage to tell that person how Jesus can help him. I opened my eyes and looked directly at you. That is why I came to you." Then he put his hand near his heart and said, "If I could just take Jesus out of my life and put him in your life," and he placed his hand near my heart, "you would never give him up." Although, when I went forward I never expected to become a Christian, I suddenly wanted Jesus to become my Lord and Savior.

When I asked my new friend how I could become a Christian, he told me to pray to God and ask for forgiveness. I said, "How can I talk to God?" He said, "Just talk to God like you talk to me." To this day I remember what I said. I said, "God," and then I stopped. I suddenly realized that I had to go to work the next morning with some of the toughest and most ungodly men I knew. I continued my prayer, saying, "If you will forgive my sin and help me be a witness where I work—the best I know how—I give you my life right now."

My new friend said, "Did you mean that?" and I replied, "Yes, I did," and I did. He asked, "Are you going to live for God?" and I said, "Yes, I am. I am going to buy me a Bible and read it and do whatever God tells me to do." That experience happened fifty-eight years ago, but it is as real today as it was the night I gave my life to Christ.

The first man who talked to me about God talked more about himself than Jesus and I went away lost. The second man who talked to me about God introduced me to Jesus, who forgave my sin and empowered me with his Holy Spirit so that my life, through Jesus, is full, meaningful and eternal.

True witnesses for Jesus Christ reveal Jesus to their lost friends and share with them Jesus' words from John 14:6: "I am the way, the truth, and the life: no man cometh unto the Father, but by me" (KJV). Another great passage to use with lost friends is John 1:11–12: "He came unto his own, and his own received him not. But as many as received him, to them gave he power to become the sons of GOD, even to them that believe on his name" (KJV).

Conclusion

Jesus, speaking to those who believe on him, said, "Ye have not chosen me, but I have chosen you, and ordained you, that ye should go and bring forth fruit, and that your fruit should remain" (John 15:16 KJV). And, again, Jesus said, "All power is given unto me in heaven and in earth. Go ye therefore, and teach [disciple] all nations, baptizing them in the name of the Father, and of the Son, and of the Holy Ghost: Teaching them to observe all things whatsoever I have commanded you: and, lo, I am with you alway, even unto the end of the world. Amen" (Matt. 28:18–20 KJV).

May God help us master the Master's method of sharing the gospel with a lost world that desperately needs to hear the Good News of God's love, redemption, forgiveness, and freedom; and may they experience, through Jesus Christ, new life that lasts through this life and forever.

Select Bibliography
of Works by Delos Miles

Dissertation

"A Manual For Dialogical Laboratories on Evangelism." (S.T.D.: San Francisco Theological Seminary, 1973.)

Books

Seminar on Urban Studies. Wake Forest: SEBTS, 1968–92.

Church Growth: A Mighty River. Nashville: Broadman, 1981.

How Jesus Won Persons. Nashville: Broadman, 1982.

Master Principles of Evangelism. Nashville: Broadman, 1982.

Sent Forth to Grow. Atlanta: SBC Home Mission Board, 1982.

Introduction to Evangelism. Nashville: Broadman, 1983.

L. R. Scarborough: Shaper of Evangelism. Nashville: Broadman, 1983.

Overcoming Barriers to Witnessing. Nashville: Broadman, 1984.

Church Growth: CD 0291. Nashville: The Seminary External Education Division of the Southern Baptist Seminaries, 1986.

Evangelism and Social Involvement. Nashville: Broadman, 1986.

Miles, Delos and Robert Dale. *Evangelizing the Hard-to-Reach.* Nashville: Broadman, 1986.

God Is for You: Meeting Life-Needs Through Personal Bible Study. Nashville: Broadman, 1989.

Articles and Parts of Books

"Becoming Bold Witnesses." Biblical content. *Adult Teacher* 15 (October–December 1984): 6–176.

"A Wholesome and Intelligent Evangelism." *Faith and Mission*, 2 (spring 1985): 23–24.

"Deacons Communicating the Gospel." *The Deacon* 17 (October–December 1986): 9–11.

"The Theology of Youth Evangelism." *Church Training* 17 (March 1987): 46.

"Unique Contributions of Southern Baptists to Evangelism." *Baptist History and Heritage* 22 (January 1987): 38–46.

"Witnessing, a Biblical Perspective." In *Witnessing, Giving, Life.* Nashville: SBC Stewardship Commission, 1988.

"Church Social Work and Evangelism: Partners in Ministry." *Review and Expositor* 85 (spring 1988): 273–83.

"Church Social Work and Evangelism as Partners." In *Evangelism in the Twenty-first Century,* ed. by Thom Rainer and Lewis Drummond. Nashville: Broadman, 1989.

"The Lordship of Christ: Implications for Evangelism." *Southwestern Journal of Theology* 33 (spring 1991): 43–44.

Notes

"A Tribute to Delos Miles," J. Chris Schofield

1. The biographical data on Delos Miles found in this section is drawn from three sources: personal conversations I have had with Delos Miles, a biographical data sheet on Delos Miles, and his chapter titled "The Spiritual Autobiography," in Delos Miles, *Introduction to Evangelism* (Nashville: Broadman Press, 1983), 161–75.

2. This portion is reproduced from Dr. Miles's spiritual autobiography, *Introduction to Evangelism*, 166–75.

3. Notice that in most of his writings each chapter begins with a Scripture lesson. Also note that in all of his books, Scripture references and examples abound. Truly, the Bible and its teachings form the foundation for all his writings.

Chapter 1, "Jesus Christ: Our Model for Being the Gospel," Ken Hemphill

1. Delos Miles, *Master Principles of Evangelism* (Nashville: Broadman Press, 1982), 20.

2. Delos Miles, *Introduction to Evangelism* (Nashville: Broadman Press, 1983), 80.

3. Miles, *Introduction*, 83f.

4. Ibid., 85.

5. Ibid., 86.

6. Miles, *Master Principles*, 94.

7. Raymond Calkins, *How Jesus Dealt With Men* (New York: Abingdon-Cokesbury Press), 14.

8. Miles, *Master Principles*, 40.

9. Gaines S. Dobbins, *Evangelism According to Christ* (Nashville: Broadman Press, 1949), 201.

10. Robert Coleman, *The Master Plan of Evangelism* (Westwood, N.J.: Fleming H. Revell Co., 1963), 38.

11. Dobbins, *Evangelism*, 197.

12. Delos Miles, *How Jesus Won Persons* (Nashville: Broadman Press, 1982), 14, 38.

13. Miles, *Master Principles*, 27f. Miles refers to the exposure of our true selves as the principle of vulnerability.

14. Ibid., 29.

15. Ibid., 33.

16. Kenneth Hemphill, *The Antioch Effect* (Nashville: Broadman & Holman, 1994), 177.

17. Miles, *Master Principles*, 60.

18. Ibid., 62.

19. Delos Miles, *Overcoming Barriers to Witnessing* (Nashville: Broadman Press, 1984), 81.

Chapter 2, "A Theology of Evangelism," Paige Patterson

1. Elton Trueblood, *The Company of the Committed* (New York: Harper & Row, 1961), 52.

2. Ibid., 49.

3. Bertrand Russell, *Mysticism and Logic* (New York: W. W. Norton and Company, Inc., 1929), 48.

4. Mark McCloskey, *Tell It Often—Tell It Well* (San Bernardino, Calif.: Here's Life Publishers, 1985), 139. This monograph, by the way, is, in my view, the finest ever written on personal evangelism.

5. Elton Trueblood, *The Incendiary Fellowship* (New York: Harper & Row, 1967), 24–25.

6. Ibid.

7. Paige Patterson, "When the Devil Aimed at Baptists," *SBC Life* (September 1997): 11.

8. Trueblood, *Company,* 23.

9. Please see notes in *The Criswell Study Bible,* 1609–11. In these pages, I discuss more extensively the doctrine of election as found in Romans 8.

10. Cited in Thom S. Rainer, ed., *Evangelism in the Twenty-First Century* (Wheaton, Ill.: Harold Shaw Publishers, 1989), 48.

11. Trueblood, *Fellowship,* 31.

12. Trueblood, *Company,* 53.

Chapter 3, "Prayer and Presence Evangelism," Lewis A. Drummond

1. Charles L. Culpepper, *The Shantung Revival* (Dallas: Crescendo Publications, 1971), 13–14.

2 Bertha Smith, *Go Home and Tell* (Nashville: Broadman Press, 1965), 15–17.

Chapter 4, "Evangelism and Personal Holiness," Henry T. Blackaby

1. This section, "Highway to Holiness," is an excerpt from Henry Blackaby, "Highway to Holiness," in *Revival,* eds. John Avant, Malcolm McDow and Alvin Reid (Nashville: Broadman & Holman, 1996) 159–73.

Chapter 5, "Revival/Spiritual Awakening and Incarnational Evangelism," Alvin L. Reid

1. W. T. Stead, ed., *The Story of the Welsh Revival* (London: Fleming H. Revell, 1905), 6.

2. Quoted in J. Edwin Orr, *The Flaming Tongue* (Chicago: Moody Press, 1973), 5. Italics added.

3. I will use the terms as synonyms.

4. For specific examples of this historical reality, see Alvin L. Reid and Malcolm McDow, *Firefall: How God Has Shaped History Through Revivals* (Nashville: Broadman & Holman, 1997).

5. To read more about this revival, see John Avant, Malcolm McDow, and Alvin Reid, eds., *Revival: Brownwood, Fort Worth, Wheaton and Beyond* (Nashville: Broadman & Holman, 1996).

6. Occasionally there are studies which focus on the evangelism of special men, e.g., Arthur S. Wood, *John Wesley: The Burning Heart* (Grand Rapids: Eerdmans, 1967). A rare study which examines in a general way various revival leaders with attention to their evangelistic commitment is Mendell Taylor, *Exploring Evangelism* (Kansas City: Beacon Hill, 1964). Still, much more study could be done.

7. Delos Miles, *Introduction to Evangelism* (Nashville: Broadman Press, 1983), 49. The author is indebted to Dr. Miles for his consistent model of an evangelism professor who utilizes the power of the pen for the glory of God.

8. Martin E. Lodge, "Great Awakening of the Middle Colonies" (Ph.D. diss., University of California), 111.

9. Peter Cartwright, *The Autobiography of Peter Cartwright* (New York: Abingdon Press, 1956), 37.

10. Ibid., 38.

11. Brian Edwards, *Revival: A People Saturated with God* (Durham, England: Evangelical Press, 1990), 60.

12. Wood, *John Wesley,* 74.

13. Cited in Edwards, *Revival,* 102.

14. Edwards, *Revival,* 65–66.

15. See John Avant, "The Biblical Foundation for Evangelism," in *Evangelism for a Changing World,* eds., Timothy Beougher and Alvin Reid (Wheaton: Harold Shaw, 1995), 95–110.

16. George Whitefield, *George Whitefield's Journals* (Edinburgh: Banner of Truth, 1985), 60.

17. Wesley Duewel, *Revival Fire* (Grand Rapids: Zondervan, 1995), 95.

18. Whitefield, *Journals*, 216.

19. "The Quotable Whitefield," *Christian History* Issue 38, vol. XII, no. 2, 28.

20. Garth M. Rosell and Richard A. G. Dupuis, eds., *The Memoirs of Charles G. Finney* (Grand Rapids: Academic Books, 1989), 158. Italics added.

Chapter 6, "The Urban Challenge: Developing Ethnic Churches in the United States," David F. D'Amico

1. This article is a revised edition of David F. D'Amico, "Ethnic Ministry in the Urban Setting," *Review and Expositor* 92 no. 1 (winter 1995): 39–56. Used with permission.

2. Two examples of outstanding African-American churches in urban settings that have been featured in full length books are the Allen Temple Baptist Church in Oakland in G. Willis Bennett, *Guidelines for Effective Urban Ministry* (Nashville: Broadman Press, 1983), and the Saint Paul Community Baptist Church in Brooklyn in Samuel G. Freedman, *Upon This Rock: The Miracles of a Black Church* (New York: Harper Collins, 1993). William Pannell, in *Evangelism from the Bottom Up* (Grand Rapids: Zondervan, 1992), discusses the challenges of urban evangelism from an African-American perspective. Delos Miles in *Evangelism and Social Involvement* (Nashville: Broadman Press, 1986), deals with a controversial issue and provides a balanced perspective. He presents several cases of congregations and ministries that have combined evangelism and social action effectively, including the Bronx Baptist Church.

3. Oscar Romo, *American Mosaic: Church Planting in Ethnic America* (Nashville: Broadman Press, 1993), 43.

4. Cited in Romo, *American Mosaic*, 166, 168. This SBC agency is presently called the North American Mission Board.

5. Cited in Romo, *American Mosaic*, 169. For an analysis of ethnic church growth, pastoral leadership characteristics of selected groups, and ecclesiastical implications for the future, see David F. D'Amico, "Evangelization Across Cultures in the United States: What to Do with the World Come to US?" *Review and Expositor* 90 no. 1 (winter 1993): 83–99.

6. Charles Chaney, former vice president of church extension, Home Mission Board, SBC, declared in 1988: "Between 1980 and 1984 Southern Baptists began 1,400 new ethnic congregations. The total Southern Baptist Convention increase in churches was only 700. . . . Except for our ethnic churches, our decline in baptisms would have been 18 percent greater." Cited in David F. D'Amico, *Selected Issues of Cross Cultural Evangelism* (Louisville: The Southern Baptist Theological Seminary, 1994), 16–17.

7. Douglas Hall, Rudy Mitchell, and Jeffrey Bass, eds., *Christianity in Boston* (Boston: Emmanuel Gospel Center, 1993), B-1, B-5.

8. For a succinct treatment, see D'Amico, "Ethnic Ministry," 42–46.

9. Due to the limitation of space, few case studies can be presented here. There are numerous monocultural ethnic congregations, mainly Asian and Hispanic, in Southern California, Houston, New York, Chicago, and Miami. For a description of multicultural congregations agglutinated in one central location, see William Travis, "His Word to His World: First Baptist Church, Flushing, New York," *Urban Mission* 6 no. 3 (January 1989):

37–41; Joe Westbury, "Golden West: Six Congregations in One," *Missions USA* 61 no. 4 (July–August 1990): 47–59; Douglas Hall, "An Urban Ministry in Context: Boston's Emmanuel Gospel Center," *Urban Mission* 11 no. 2 (December 1993): 15–24; and Jason Fitzgerald, "The Multi-congregational Church," *Urban Mission* 11 no. 2 (December 1993): 44–49.

10. Patricia Guile, "The Best Ten Weeks," *Missions USA* 53 no. 1 (January–February, 1982): 39.

11. Lindsay Cobb, director of language missions, Metro Chicago Baptist Association, telephone interview, 31 July 1996.

12. See Francis DuBose, *How Churches Grow in an Urban World* (Nashville: Broadman Press 1978); C. Kirk Hadaway, Francis DuBose, and Stuart A. Wright, *Home Cell Groups and House Churches* (Nashville: Broadman Press, 1987); "Francis DuBose: Modeling Missions," *The Commission* 56 no. 2 (February–March, 1993): 20–27.

13. "The Church of the Nations," *Thirty-six Anniversary Brochure,* 1994.

14. Professor DuBose discusses the complexities of dealing with tensions of shared facilities in "Sharing Spaces," Hinsdale, Ill.: Del Rey Communications, 1992, videotape.

15. Jean Baptiste Thomas, interview, 11 June 1994, 14 July 1996.

16. David K. Chan, "A Documentation and Diagnostic Study of the Houston Chinese Church, Houston, Texas," unpublished paper, 1990, 13.

17. David K. Chan, interview, 11 June 1993.

18. Chan, interview.

19. Ibid.

20. Chan, "A Documentation," 4.

21. Chan, interview.

22. For a study of different patterns of church life among Korean-Americans in California, see Bong E. Choi, "Cultural Identity, Leadership, and Evangelistic Strategies for Korean-American Churches" (Th.M. thesis, The Southern Baptist Theological Seminary, 1995.)

Chapter 7, "Community Ministries and Evangelism," Thom S. Rainer

1. This chapter is revised and taken from Thom Rainer's work titled *Effective Evangelistic Churches* (Nashville: Broadman & Holman, 1996). In the original chapter, charts and graphs were used that are not present in this chapter. Most of the research data used in *Effective Evangelistic Churches* was compiled from information gathered from a survey of 576 Southern Baptist churches in America with attendance ranging from sixty to six thousand. Throughout this chapter, the author will move from first person singular to first person plural when he is referring to the survey team which aided him in compiling the information. Also, when the author mentions a follow-up interview, he is referring to one hundred follow-up interviews held with selected pastors and churches following the primary survey. For more on the methodology employed by Rainer, see *Effective Evangelistic Churches*, 4–9.

2. C. Kirk Hadaway, *Church Growth Principles: Separating Fact from Fiction* (Nashville: Broadman Press, 1991), 169.

3. Ibid.

4. Ibid.

5. Ibid.

6. Lausanne Covenant, article 5, "Christian Social Responsibility."

Chapter 8, "Pastoral Models for Doing the Gospel," Danny Forshee

1. Rick Warren, *The Purpose Driven Church* (Grand Rapids: Zondervan, 1995), 103–107.

2. The first imperative is in the present tense; the remaining three are in the aorist. Paul strongly advised Timothy to start doing the great work of evangelizing. For more information on this text, see Thomas Lea and Hayne Griffin, Jr., *1 and 2 Timothy, Titus,* vol. 34, in *The New American Commentary,* ed. David S. Dockery (Nashville: Broadman Press, 1992), 245–46.

3. C. Peter Wagner, *Your Church Can Grow,* 2nd ed. (Ventura, Calif.: Regal Books, 1984), 61, says that the pastor is the "primary catalytic factor for growth in a local church."

4. For more information about Baxter's life, see Richard Baxter, *The Life of Richard Baxter: Chiefly Compiled from His Own Writings* (New York: American Tract Society, 1835). A more detailed biography on Baxter's life is much needed. The information regarding Baxter's pastoral evangelism is taken from his classic work, *The Reformed Pastor; or The Duty of Personal Labors for the Souls of Men* (New York: American Tract Society, 1850).

5. Baxter, *The Reformed Pastor,* 89.

6. Ibid., 103.

7. Ibid., 117.

8. Ibid., 147.

9. Ibid., 252–53.

10. Ola Winslow, *Jonathan Edwards 1703–1758* (New York: Macmillan, 1941), 134.

11. Jonathan Edwards, *A Faithful Narrative of the Surprising Work of God,* in *The Great Awakening,* ed. C. C. Goen (New Haven and London: Yale University, 1972), 151.

12. Jonathan Edwards, "Sinners in the Hands of an Angry God," in *Select Works of Jonathan Edwards,* vol. 2 (London: Birling and Sons Limited, 1959), 191.

13. See Patricia Tracy, *Jonathan Edwards, Pastor* (New York: Hillard Wary, 1979), 78. Tracy also points out, on page 112, that Edwards insisted on personally catechizing young children. Edwards was "always ready to receive a child or adult in his study and to give private counsel."

14. Keith Hardman, "God's Wonderful Working: The First Great Awakening," in *Christian History* 8, no. 3, issue no. 23 (1989): 12-15.

15. John Armstrong, "The Prince of Preachers," in *Christian History* 10, no. 1, issue 29 (1991): 26–27.

16. Timothy Albert McCoy, "The Evangelistic Ministry of C. H. Spurgeon: Implications for a Contemporary Model for Pastoral Evangelism" (Ph.D. diss., The Southern Baptist Theological Seminary, 1989), 203. Spurgeon was also a proponent of church planting. McCoy, on pages 203–4, points out, "Over the next ten years (1871–1880), the number of total additions to church membership was sustained at an impressive rate. On average, 446 persons per year were added. Yet, largely due to the substantial number of people who were sent out to form other churches, the average net increase for this period dropped to only 111 persons per year."

17. McCoy, "Evangelistic Ministry," 215–16. Charles G. Finney engaged in this exercise when he served as pastor of the Chatham Street Chapel in New York City from 1832 until 1836. For more information on Finney's pastoral evangelism, see Daniel B. Forshee, "The Pastoral Evangelism of Charles Grandison Finney with Applications for Contemporary Pastoral Evangelism" (Ph.D. diss., Southwestern Baptist Theological Seminary, 1995).

18. For more information on Spurgeon's preaching, see his classic work, *Lectures to My Students* (Grand Rapids: Zondervan, 1977).

19. Lewis Drummond, "The Secrets of Spurgeon's Preaching," in *Christian History* 10, no. 1, issue 29 (1991): 15.

20. Charles Spurgeon, "Compel Them to Come In," in *Christian History* 10, no. 1, issue 29 (1991): 19. McCoy, on page 212, "C. H. Spurgeon," aptly states, "Spurgeon's undeniable intention was to win people to Christ, and every facet of his ministry, including his preaching, was subordinated and directed toward that end."

21. Johnny M. Hunt, First Baptist Church, Woodstock, Ga., to Daniel B. Forshee, 11 July 1997. The total number of baptisms at First Baptist Woodstock from 1986 until March 1997 was 4,191.

22. Johnny Hunt, *Out of the Poolroom* (Woodstock, Ga.: Johnny Hunt, 1995), 19.

23. Johnny Hunt to Daniel B. Forshee, 12 June 1997.

24. Ibid.

25. Ibid.

26. Ibid.

27. "Biographical: Dr. John Ed Mathison," Frazer Memorial United Methodist Church, Montgomery, Ala., to Daniel B. Forshee, 11 July 1997.

28. "Biographical."

29. John Ed Mathison to Daniel B. Forshee, 30 May 1997.

30. "Biographical: Dr. John Ed Mathison." See also John Ed Mathison, *Every Member in Ministry* (Nashville: Discipleship Resources, 1988).

31. Mathison, to Daniel B. Forshee.

32. Ibid.

33. Ibid.

34. This information was sent to me from Indian Hills Community Church with no title on 16 July 1997.

35. "Pastoral Evangelism: Pastor Gil Rugh," from Bill Mize, to Daniel B. Forshee, 2 June 1997. Mize is an associate pastor at Indian Hills who works in the area of outreach and evangelism.

36. "Pastoral Evangelism."

37. Ibid.

38. Robert Anderson, *The Effective Pastor* (Chicago: Moody Press, 1985), 237.

39. Phyllis Thompson, "Touching Eternity," *Missions USA* 61 (November–December 1990): 18.

40. Bryan McAnally, "Rocky Mountain High," *SBC Life* 5, no. 8 (June–July 1997): 1–2.

41. Ibid.

42. Martin Thielen, "Worship in the Fastest Growing Churches in Middle Tennessee," *Proclaim* 24, no. 4 (July–September 1994): 27. Four of the five churches are not associated with a denomination; one is part of the Southern Baptist Convention.

43. John Bisagno, *How to Build an Evangelistic Church* (Nashville: Broadman Press, 1971), 54.

44. Steve Palioti, "Devil of a Class," *Raleigh (N.C.) News and Observer,* 19 January 1997, 4(C).

Chapter 9, "Understanding Strategic Evaluation," Harry L. Poe

1. Lyle Schaller, *Activating the Passive Church* (Nashville: Abingdon Press, 1981), 89.

Chapter 10, "Creating a Culture for World Evangelism: How Are We Doing?" Phil Roberts

1. Official Watchtower statistics indicate there are 5,599,931 publishers worldwide, with a U.S. membership of 984,548. Worldwide baptisms for 1997 were

375,923, with 52,686 of those recorded in the U.S. Notably, little attention has been given to the study of new religious movements as forces in world missions. Walter Martin included a chapter in his book *The Kingdom of the Cults* (1965) entitled "The Cults on the World Mission Field." This chapter has been updated for the latest edition of the book (Minneapolis, Minn.: Bethany House Publishers, 1997). It remains as one of the few significant contributions to the study of the cults as a world missions force.

2. The official 1997 church almanac of the Church of Jesus Christ of Latter-day Saints calculates membership at 10.07 million members. There were 317,798 worldwide convert baptisms in 1997.

3. *Doctrines of the Gospel Student Manual: Religion 231 and 232* (Salt Lake City: Church Educational System, Church of Jesus Christ of Latter-day Saints, 1986), 60. This quote is from Spencer W. Kimball, *The Teachings of Spencer W. Kimball*, 423.

4. Joseph Smith, "Religous History of Joseph Smith," in *Pearl of Great Price*, 1:19.

5. The question is often asked which church provides the most converts for Mormonism? With over 2,000,000 members in South America and over 800,000 in Mexico, it appears that probably more Roman Catholics than any other church movement are won to Mormonism.

6. President Boyd K. Packer, "The Peaceable Followers of Christ," *LDS Church News*, 12 March, 1998, 4.

7. For more information on this issue, see R. Philip Roberts with Sandra Tanner and Tal Davis, *Mormonism Unmasked* (Nashville: Broadman & Holman, 1998), 24.

8. The merits of deploying career missionaries versus two-year student workers are many. They will not be dis-

cussed here. But note should be made that generally all of Southern Baptist missionary appointments are career assignments.

Chapter 11, "Telling the Gospel One on One," G. William Schweer

1. For this definition, see Delos Miles, *Introduction to Evangelism* (Nashville: Broadman Press, 1983), 47–56.

2. Leighton Ford, *The Christian Persuader* (Philadelphia: Westminster Press, 1966), 67.

3. Kenneth S. Wuest, *First Peter in the Greek New Testament* (Grand Rapids: William B. Eerdmans, 1952), 57.

4. Charles H. Kraft, *Communication Theory for Witnesses* (Nashville: Abingdon Press, 1983), 45.

5. James F. Engel, *Contemporary Christian Communications* (Nashville: Thomas Nelson Publishers, 1979), 83.

6. John W. Drakeford, *The Awesome Power of the Listening Ear* (Fort Worth: Latimer House, 1976), sound recording.

7. Engel, *Contemporary Christian Communications*, 161.

8. Ibid., citing Everett M. Rogers, *Diffusion of Innovations*, (New York: Free Press, 1962), 161.

9. Engel, *Contemporary Christian Communications*, 161.

10. Ibid., 163.

Chapter 12, "Proclaiming Christ to American Religious Groups," George W. Braswell, Jr.

1. See George W. Braswell, Jr., *Understanding Sectarian Groups in America, Revised* (Nashville:

Broadman & Holman, 1994), for an overview of religious pluralism in the United States.

2. See George W. Braswell Jr. *Understanding World Religions, Revised* (Nashville: Broadman & Holman, 1994), especially pages 21–44 on Hinduism.

3. See Braswell, *Understanding Sectarian Groups in America, Revised,* 197–239.

4. See Braswell, *Understanding World Religions, Revised,* 111–130.

5. See Braswell, *Understanding Sectarian Groups in America, Revised,* 273–308.

6. See George W. Braswell Jr. "The Twenty-First Century Church and the Islamic World," in *Faith & Mission* 2 (spring 1994): 64–80.

7. See Braswell, *Understanding Sectarian Groups in America, Revised,* 7–53.

8. See *Doctrine and Covenants* (Salt Lake City: The Church of Jesus Christ of Latter-day Saints, 1985), for an overview of the beliefs of Mormons through revelations to Joseph Smith.

9. See Braswell, *Understanding Sectarian Groups in America, Revised,* 55–95.

10. *New World Translation of the Holy Scriptures* (Brooklyn: Watchtower Bible and Tract Society of Pennsylvania, 1984), 1327.

Chapter 13, "Inductive Versus Deductive Methods of Telling the Gospel," Bill Mackey

1. Delos Miles, "A Wholesome and Intelligent Evangelism," *Faith and Mission,* 2 (spring 1985): 29.

2. Ibid.

3. Ibid.

4. Ibid., 28.

5. Ibid., 30.

6. This analysis of the four soils is further explained in Bill Mackey and Bobby Jackson, *Friendship Witnessing Guide* (Columbia, S.C.: South Carolina Baptist Convention, 1994).

7. Steve Sjogren, *Conspiracy of Kindness* (Ann Arbor, Mich.: Vine Books, 1993).

8. Donald Atkinson and Charles Roesel, *Meeting Needs—Sharing Christ: Ministry Evangelism in Today's New Testament Church* (Nashville: LifeWay Press, 1995).

9. Larry Gilbert, *How to Reach Your Loved Ones for Christ When You Don't Have the Gift of Evangelism* (Lynchburg, Va.: Church Growth Institute, 1986). A supplemental book to Gilbert's is Douglas Porter, *How to Develop and Use the Gift of Evangelism* (Lynchburg, Va.: Church Growth Institute, 1992).

10. *Network* (Grand Rapids, Mich.: Zondervan, 1993).

11. Bill Hybels and Mark Mittelberg, *Becoming a Contagious Christian* (Grand Rapids, Mich.: Zondervan, 1994).

12. Lee Strobel, *Inside the Mind of the Unchurched Harry and Mary* (Grand Rapids, Mich.: Zondervan, 1993).

13. George Barna, *Evangelism that Works* (Ventura, Calif.: Regal Books, 1995).

14. William Fay and Ralph Hodge, *Share Jesus Without Fear* (Nashville: LifeWay Books, 1997). The socratic approach is also developed in Fay's "Witnessing without Argument."

15. D. James Kennedy, *Evangelism Explosion, IV* (Wheaton, Ill.: Tyndale House Publishers, 1996).

16. Jack Smith, *Building Witnessing Relationships* (Alpharetta, Ga.: North American Mission Board).

17. Sally Morgenthaler, *Worship Evangelism: Inviting Unbelievers into the Presence of God* (Grand Rapids, Mich.: Zondervan, 1995), 79.

18. George Hunter III, *Church for the Unchurched* (Nashville: Abingdon Press, 1996).

19. Harvest Evangelism, 6155 Almandan Expressway (400), San Jose, CA 95160–0310; telephone: 408–927–9052.

20. Ted DeMoss and Robert Tamasy, *The Gospel and the Briefcase* (Wheaton, Ill.: Tyndale House Publishers, 1985).

21. Mapping Center for Evangelism, Chris Cooper, director, 8615 Rosehill Road, Suite 101, Lenexa, KS 66215; telephone: 913-438–7301.

22. The street address for Love Lines, not to be confused with the MTV "Love Lines," is Love Lines—Crisis Center, 2535 Central Avenue N.E., Minneapolis, MN 55418.

23. The street address for the Billy Graham Evangelistic Association is P.O. Box 779, Minneapolis, MN 55440–0779.

24. Two official websites, among others, are www.billygraham.org and www.graham-assn.org.

25. David Pierce, *Rock Priest* (Eastbourne, Great Britain: Kingsway Publications, 1993).

26. David Pierce is founder of Steiger International, Amsterdam, The Netherlands. The International base is in New Zealand: Steiger, International, P.O. Box 13550, Wellington, 6032, New Zealand. The U.S. base: Steiger U.S.A., P.O. Box 7263, Minneapolis, MN 55407.

27. The mailing address of Reign Ministries is: Royal Servants Int'l—Reign Ministries, Inc., 5517 Warwick Place, Minneapolis, MN 55436.

Chapter 14, "Christian Apologetics and Intentional Evangelism," L. Russ Bush

1. For New Testament usage of the term, see Hans-Georg Link, "Apology," in *The New International Dictionary of the New Testament Theology,* ed. Colin Brown (Grand Rapids: Zondervan, 1975), 1:51.

2. See L. Russ Bush, ed., *Classical Readings in Christian Apologetics: A.D. 100–1800* (Grand Rapids: Academie Books, Zondervan, 1983), ix, xiii–xviii.

3. Johannes Quasten and Joseph C. Plumpe, eds., *Ancient Christian Writers,* vol. 23: *Athenagoras.* Translated and annotated by Joseph Hugh Creehan (Westminster, Maryland: Newman, 1956).

4. Irenaus, *Against Heresies,* book II, chap. 1.

5. Athanasius, *Incarnation of the Word,* chaps. xxxiii–xl.

6. Thomas Aquinas, *The Summa Contra Gentiles.*

7. Thomas Aquinas, *The Summa Theologica,* question II.

8. See Bush, *Classical Readings,* 375–86.

9. See Colin Brown, *Philosophy & the Christian Faith* (Downers Grove: InterVarsity Press, 1968).

10. A valuable source that elaborates on this point is B. H. Carroll, Jr., *The Genesis of American Anti-Missionism* (Louisville: The Baptist Book Concern, 1902).

Chapter 15, "Evangelistic Preaching in the Twenty-First Century," Wayne McDill

1. Alvin Toffler, *Future Shock* (New York: Random House, 1970), 16.

2. Marshall McLuhan and Quenton Fiore, *The Medium Is the Message* (New York: Random House, 1967), 63.

3. John R. W. Stott, *Between Two Worlds* (Grand Rapids: William B. Eerdmans, 1982).

4. Stanley J. Grenz, *A Primer on Postmodernism* (Grand Rapids: William B. Eerdmans, 1996).

5. Ibid.

6. Michael Sack, "The Multiplex Congregation," *Leadership Journal* 17(fall 1995): 50.

7. George Barna, "The Pulpit-meister: Preaching to a New Majority," *Preaching* 12 (January–February 1997): 11–13.

8. Ibid., 11.

9. Ibid.

10. Ibid., 12.

Contributors

Henry T. Blackaby, President
Henry Blackaby Ministries
Kennessaw, GA 30144

George W. Braswell, Jr.
Missions and World Religions
Southeastern Baptist Theological Seminary
Wake Forest, NC 27587

L. Russ Bush
Academic Vice President
Southeastern Baptist Theological Seminary
Wake Forest, NC 27587

David D'Amico
World Associates
New York, NY 10016

Lewis A. Drummond
Billy Graham Professor of Evangelism
Samford University: Beeson Divinity School
Birmingham, AL 35229

Roy J. Fish
Professor of Evangelism
Southwestern Baptist Theological Seminary
Fort Worth, TX 76122

Daniel B. Forshee, Asst. Professor
Evangelism & Church Growth
Southeastern Baptist Theological Seminary
Wake Forest, NC 27587

Ken Hemphill, President
Southwestern Baptist Theological Seminary
Forth Worth, TX 76122

Bill F. Mackey, Director
Leadership Development & Evangelism
South Carolina Baptist Convention
Columbia, SC 29210–8239

Wayne V. McDill
Professor of Preaching
Southeastern Baptist Theological Seminary
Wake Forest, NC 27587

Paige Patterson, President
Southeastern Baptist Theological Seminary
Wake Forest, NC 27587

Harry L. Poe, Dean
Academic Resources & Information Services
Union University
Jackson, TN 38305–3697

Thom S. Rainer, Dean
Billy Graham School of Missions, Evangelism
  and Church Growth
Southern Baptist Theological Seminary
Louisville, KY 40280

Alvin L. Reid
Evangelism & Church Growth
Southeastern Baptist Theological Seminary
Wake Forest, NC 27587

Phil Roberts, President
Midwestern Baptist Theological Seminary
Kansas City, MO 64118

J. Chris Schofield, Manager
Prayer Evangelism and Church Renewal
North American Mission Board
Alpharetta, GA 30022-4176

G. William Schweer
Professor of Evangelism
Golden Gate Baptist Theological Seminary
Fairfield, CA 94533

Jack Stanton, Director
International Institute of Evangelism
Southwest Baptist University
Bolivar, MO 65613